SERIES VII   CYCLE C

LECTIONARY PREACHING WORKBOOK

For All Users
Of The Revised Common,
The Roman Catholic, And
The Episcopal Lectionaries

Jerry L. Schmalenberger

CSS Publishing Company, Inc.
Lima, Ohio

Dedicated to the memory of Amos John Traver and Russell Auman, Hamma Divinity School homiletics professors who shaped my preaching. And in honor of Richard W. Powell, who profoundly shaped my style of ministry.

Acknowledgments
Special thanks to Sarah Lau and Cindy Carroll for their help in typing the rough copy of this manuscript. And as always, to my beloved wife, Carol A. Schmalenberger, for doing the final edits and formatting.

Copyright © 2003 by
CSS Publishing Company, Inc.
Lima, Ohio

Some scripture quotations are from the *New Revised Standard Version of the Bible*, copyright 1989 by the Division of Christian Education of the National Council of the Churches of Christ in the USA. Used by permission.

Library of Congress Cataloging-in-Publication Data

Schmalenberger, Jerry L.   .
   Lectionary preaching workbook : Series VII. Cycle A / Jerry L. Schmalenberger.
       p.   cm.
   "For all users of the revised common, the Roman Catholic, and the Episcopal lectionaries."
   ISBN 0-7880-1812-4 (alk. paper)
   1. Lectionary preaching. 2. Common lectionary (1992). 3. Bible—Homiletical use. I. Title.
BV4235.L43 S35 2001
251'.6—dc21   2001025080
                                                                                                        CIP

For more information about CSS Publishing Company resources, visit our website at www.csspub.com or e-mail us at custserv@csspub.com or call (800) 241-4056.

ISBN 0-7880-1960-0 Binder
ISBN 0-7880-1977-5 Paperback   PRINTED IN U.S.A.

Table Of Contents

Sermon Planner/Builder

Date: _____ Cycle/Season: _____ Sunday: _____

Cycle/Season/Sunday theological clue _____

_____

Psalm/central thought: _____

_____

Collect/prayer concern/focus: _____

_____

Sermon text(s): _____

Summary of sermon text(s): _____

_____

_____

_____

_____

_____

_____

_____

_____

Pastoral perspective: _____

_____

_____

_____

_____

Stories/illustrations: _____

_____

_____

_____

_____

Type of sermon: _____

Sermon plan/sketch: _____

_____

_____

_____

_____

_____

The Church Year Calendar

The Christmas Cycle

Advent

	Color
First Sunday Of Advent	purple or blue
Second Sunday Of Advent	purple or blue
Third Sunday Of Advent	purple or blue
Fourth Sunday Of Advent	purple or blue

Christmas

Christmas Eve	white
The Nativity Of Our Lord	white
First Sunday After Christmas	white
Second Sunday After Christmas	white

Epiphany

The Epiphany Of Our Lord	white
The Baptism Of Our Lord (First Sunday After The Epiphany)	white
Second Sunday After The Epiphany	green
Third Sunday After The Epiphany	green
Fourth Sunday After The Epiphany	green
Fifth Sunday After The Epiphany	green
Sixth Sunday After The Epiphany	green
Seventh Sunday After The Epiphany	green
The Transfiguration Of Our Lord (Last Sunday After The Epiphany)	white

The Easter Cycle

Lent

Ash Wednesday	black or purple
First Sunday In Lent	purple
Second Sunday In Lent	purple
Third Sunday In Lent	purple
Fourth Sunday In Lent	purple
Fifth Sunday In Lent	purple
Sunday Of The Passion (Palm Sunday)	scarlet or purple
Maundy Thursday/Holy Thursday	scarlet or white
Good Friday	black or no paraments
Holy Saturday	white

Easter

Vigil Of Easter	white or gold
The Resurrection Of Our Lord (Easter Day)	white or gold
Second Sunday Of Easter	white
Third Sunday Of Easter	white
Fourth Sunday Of Easter	white
Fifth Sunday Of Easter	white

Sixth Sunday Of Easter			white
The Ascension Of Our Lord			white
Seventh Sunday Of Easter			white
The Day Of Pentecost			red

The Pentecost Cycle

The Season After Pentecost

Revised Common/ Episcopal	Lutheran (Other than ELCA)	Roman Catholic	Color
Trinity Sunday	Trinity Sunday	Trinity Sunday	white
		Corpus Christi	green
Proper 4	Pentecost 2	Ordinary Time 9	green
Proper 5	Pentecost 3	Ordinary Time 10	green
Proper 6	Pentecost 4	Ordinary Time 11	green
Proper 7	Pentecost 5	Ordinary Time 12	green
Proper 8	Pentecost 6	Ordinary Time 13	green
Proper 9	Pentecost 7	Ordinary Time 14	green
Proper 10	Pentecost 8	Ordinary Time 15	green
Proper 11	Pentecost 9	Ordinary Time 16	green
Proper 12	Pentecost 10	Ordinary Time 17	green
Proper 13	Pentecost 11	Ordinary Time 18	green
Proper 14	Pentecost 12	Ordinary Time 19	green
Proper 15	Pentecost 13	Ordinary Time 20	green
Proper 16	Pentecost 14	Ordinary Time 21	green
Proper 17	Pentecost 15	Ordinary Time 22	green
Proper 18	Pentecost 16	Ordinary Time 23	green
Proper 19	Pentecost 17	Ordinary Time 24	green
Proper 20	Pentecost 18	Ordinary Time 25	green
Proper 21	Pentecost 19	Ordinary Time 26	green
Proper 22	Pentecost 20	Ordinary Time 27	green
Proper 23	Pentecost 21	Ordinary Time 28	green
Proper 24	Pentecost 22	Ordinary Time 29	green
Proper 25	Pentecost 23	Ordinary Time 30	green
Proper 26	Pentecost 24	Ordinary Time 31	green
Proper 27	Pentecost 25	Ordinary Time 32	green
Proper 28	Pentecost 26	Ordinary Time 33	green
	Pentecost 27		green
	Reformation Sunday		red
All Saints' Sunday	All Saints' Sunday		white
Thanksgiving Day, USA			white
Christ The King	Christ The King	Christ The King	white

Introduction

I wrote this Cycle C of *The Lectionary Preaching Workbook* while serving as an Evangelical Lutheran Church in America Global Mission Volunteer. While preparing the manuscript, I was teaching homiletics and practical theology at the Lutheran Theological Seminary in Hong Kong and The Augustana Hochschule in the little town of Neuendettelsau, Germany.

The comments on the scripture readings are not intended to be scholarly exegesis but rather close to the ground homiletical insights and practical creative "takes" on the passages which are intended to plumb the many possibilities for proclamation.

I have made a valiant effort to use inclusive language throughout even at the risk of sacrificing the facility of language and smooth flow of words.

This is the third in a three-volume set based on A, B, and C cycles of the liturgical lectionary. When the lessons varied among Revised Common, Roman Catholic, and Episcopal, I usually went with the Revised Common or the one which all three groups listed as the same. Most often it was the Gospel for the day on which I based the Possible Outline Of Sermon Moves.

There will be found a variety of homiletical plots used: the extended metaphor, narrative, dialogue, my own based on audience reaction, letter sermon, Lowry's homiletical plot, and even the traditional three points and a poem are employed as examples of how one might construct an interesting and persuasive message.

When it seemed the time would be right, I have included suggested sermon series throughout the year by inserting a "heads up" note and suggested themes over the Old Testament or Second Readings for the season.

Many of the metaphors and sories have come from my collection of these over 45 years of preaching and from keeping homiletical journals. These have been published by CSS in the 1999 work titled: *These Will Preach: Stories And Metaphors For The Pulpit*. Others have come from my recent service as an ELCA Global Mission Volunteer teaching in Sumatra, Indonesia; Hong Kong and Mainland China; Liberia, West Africa; Jamaica; Argentina, Uruguay, and Suriname, South America; and Bavaria, Germany. Thus, you will find an international flavor to many of them.

In considering the homiletical possibilities and needed background for the narrative, I used the following Bible Commentaries and reference books:

The International Commentary, Zondervan, 1986

The Anchor Bible Commentaries, Doubleday and Company, Inc., 1965

The New Bible Commentary, 21st Century Edition, InterVarsity Press, 1954

The New Interpreter's Bible, Abingdon, 1995

The Interpreter's Bible, Abingdon Press, 1956

The Daily Study Bible, The Westminster Press, 1965

The International Bible Commentary, Marshall Pickering/Zondervan, 1986

The New Jerome Biblical Commentary, Prentice Hall, 1990

The Interpreter's Dictionary of the Bible, Abingdon Press, 1962

Word Biblical Commentary, Thomas Nelson, Inc., 1998

The New International Commentary on the New Testament, William B. Eerdmans Publishing Company

The Interpreter's One Volume Commentary on the Bible, Abingdon Press — Nashville & New York, 1971

The Gospel According to Luke, E. J. Tinsley, Cambridge University Press, 1969

The Epistle to the Hebrews, Thomas Hewitt, William B. Eerdmans Publishing Company, Grand Rapids, Michigan, 1970

A Letter to Hebrews by J. H. Davies, Cambridge at the University Press, 1967

The Bible Knowledge Commentary, Walvoord and Zuck, Chariot Victor Publishing, 1985

Vines Expository Commentary on Isaiah, W. E. Vine, Thomas Nelson Publishers, Nashville, 1997

Getting Started: Some Suggested Homiletical Formulas

A. The miracles and parables of Jesus
   1. Tell the story in your own words
   2. Tell what it teaches us about God
   3. Explain what it reveals about us
   4. Prayerfully discover why the author wanted this preserved
   5. Look for a fresh flip side focus
   6. Answer the "so what?" (What we do about it?)
   7. Frame by returning to the first few sentences

B. An audience reaction sermon

listener's response	sermon moves
Ho hum!	Build a fire
Why bring that up?	Transition (bridge)
What's the point?	Give the focus
For instance?	Give an example
What about you, preacher?	Give your witness
So what?	Action challenge
Finish up!	Frame the sermon

C. The homiletical plot[1]
   1. Upsetting the equilibrium   Oops!
   2. Analyzing the discrepancy   Ugh!
   3. Disclosing the clue and resolution   Aha!
   4. Experiencing the Gospel   Whee!
   5. Anticipating the consequences   Yea!

D. Thomas Long's sermon forms[2]
   1. If this ... then this ... and thus this
   2. This is true ... in this way ... and also in this way ... and in this other way
   3. This is the problem ... this is the response of the Gospel ... these are the implications
   4. This is the promise of the Gospel — here is how we might live out that Gospel
   5. This is the historical situation in the text ... these are the meanings for us now
   6. Not this ... or this ... or this or this ... but this
   7. Here is a prevailing view ... but here is the claim of the Gospel
   8. This ... but what about this? Well, then this. Yes, but what about this? And so on
   9. Here is a story: simple story; story reflection. Part of a story: reflection; rest of the story: issue; story
   10. This? Or that?

E. A letter sermon
   1. Read the salutation
   2. Explain to whom you are writing
   3. Describe the setting in which you are writing
   4. Tell of your struggle with an important issue
   5. Refer to the scripture's advice on the issue
   6. Ask for their opinion and why you would ask them
   7. Close with a request for prayer for you that your action will be right
   8. Read your final good-bye and signature
   9. Put a PS on for fun and humor

F. Questions to ask in order to get started
    1. What is the traditional theme?
    2. Why did the writer want this told and what did it illustrate in early preaching?
    3. What does the story tell us about God and us humans?
    4. Can I find a fresh approach which may be a secondary focus?
    5. So what must we do this week in response to this account?

G. Some tests for your completed sermon
    1. Have I been inclusive in my language?
    2. Is my vocabulary understandable to fifth graders?
    3. Have I left room for inspiration in the pulpit?
    4. Have I included implications for our congregations?
    5. Have I acknowledged vital concerns of people this week?
    6. Is there more of God's grace than God's law?
    7. Have I made my own witness?
    8. Is there some humor for relief throughout the sermon?
    9. Does the sermon acknowledge the season of the church year?
    10. Is "so what?" answered with specific, clear steps to take?
    11. Does the sermon start where people are?
    12. Are there places where it would be more interesting if I used figures of speech?
    13. What one thing do I believe God wants them to remember?
    14. Have I been faithful to the scripture text?

----

1. Eugene L. Lowry, *The Homiletical Plot* (Atlanta: John Knox Press, 1980).

2. Thomas G. Long, *The Witness of Preaching* (Louisville: Westminster/John Knox Press, 1989).

An Introduction To The Advent Season

Happy New Year!

We begin the new church year with the first Sunday of Advent. Two years ago we read the Gospel from the book of Matthew. Last year we read from Mark and John. We now begin a year of reading from Luke. The first half of the year will be the life of Christ and the second will be his ministry and teachings. The Gospel of Luke is a lively book written by a well-educated medical doctor to the Gentiles and so explains Jewish customs and traces the lineage of Jesus back to Adam. He wrote this book and the book of Acts to give a government official by the name of Theophilus the complete story of Jesus' life and teachings. He tells of the role of women in Jesus' ministry, about the poor and oppressed, and that Jesus loved all sorts of people. Joy is very much a part of this writing as it tells of the hope of salvation to a sinful world.

We also begin a new season of the church year called Advent. Its emphasis is the preparation and anticipation of "the event" of the birth of Jesus. There will be a threefold emphasis in this season:
1. The Advent of our Lord born in Bethlehem at Christmas.
2. The Advent of our Lord in God's word and God's spirit.
3. The Advent of our Lord in glory at the end of time.

As we sense it in our secular world and also in our church, we will also sense it in the scripture readings: Joyful anticipation in this season.

The liturgical color for these four weeks is blue or purple, representing the hope of heaven. These four Sundays we'll hear:
1. Be alert, the Kingdom of God is near.   Luke 21:25-36
2. John the Baptist prepares the way.   Luke 3:1-6
3. John again. This time proclaiming the Good News.   Luke 3:7-18
4. Elizabeth receives a visit from Mary.   Luke 1:30-45

There are some Saints' days during this month of December which are worth considering for proclamation*:

December 3	Francis Xavier, missionary to Asia, 1552
December 6	Nicholas, Bishop of Myra, c. 342
December 13	St. Lucia, Virgin and Martyr
December 21	St. Thomas, Apostle
December 26	St. Stephen, Deacon and Martyr
December 27	St. John, Apostle and Evangelist

---

*For sermons based on the lives of these well-known Saints, see my *Advent And Christmas Saints*, CSS Publishing Company, 1984.

First Sunday Of Advent

Revised Common	Jeremiah 33:14-16	1 Thessalonians 3:9-13	Luke 21:25-36
Roman Catholic	Jeremiah 33:14-16	1 Thessalonians 3:12—4:2	Luke 21:25-28, 34-36
Episcopal	Zechariah 14:4-9	1 Thessalonians 3:9-13	Luke 21:25-31

Seasonal Theme   The joyful anticipation and preparation for the birth of Jesus in Bethlehem and into our hearts as well.

Theme For The Day   The anticipation of Jeremiah, Paul, and Jesus in the coming of the kingdom in our midst.

Old Testament Lesson   Jeremiah 33:14-16   *A Righteous Branch*

This is Jeremiah as messianic prophecy — he is anticipating the chosen descendant of David to come and gain back the Judean Kingdom. When he does restore it, there will be justice again (see Isaiah 11:3-44). "Righteous branch" simply says it will be out of the lineage of David. The promise will be kept. You can look forward to it.

New Testament Lesson   1 Thessalonians 3:9-13   *Paul's Prayers For The Thessalonians*

Paul is writing to a congregation he started in Thessalonica. The city was built in 315 B.C. by Cassander and named for his wife. It became a great free city and is now named Salonika and has a population of 70,000. When Paul brought Christianity there it was a key day for its becoming a world-wide religion. From there Christianity spread east. You can read about Paul's time there in Acts 17:1-10.

Paul writes to the Thessalonians that he is praying for the following:
1. That they may increase in their love for each other.
2. That they (and Paul) might be blameless before God when Jesus returns.
3. That he might somehow return to see them again. Verse 13 can be used as a benediction or perhaps a prayer at the conclusion of the sermon.

The Gospel   Luke 21:25-36   *Be Alert And Watch*

The main emphasis of Advent comes through in this passage as Jesus admonishes the people to be "on the alert" and be "on guard." We must not live our Christian lives half asleep — we must always be ready to appear in God's presence.

We also have the Second Coming of Jesus, the Christ. We know not when, what, or where. And, I would hold out, it could be our individual deaths. Or even more thrilling — it may have already taken place in the resurrection and the coming of the Holy Spirit. In that case our alertness is to spot it now in our midst as it breaks out on occasion.

The fig tree is not so hard to explain. Just like there are signs that summer is coming when it begins to sprout, so we can observe certain signs that Jesus is coming (compare 12:56).

Verses 32 and 33 are not as easy. Jesus must have seen Israel of the Old Testament being fashioned anew in his ministry. A new law of Israel was being announced by him.

Preaching Possibilities

It does seem appropriate this Sunday to print in the worship bulletin or use the first part of the sermon to teach about this being the first Sunday in the church year and the significance of Advent. A little preview of the next four Sundays could be meaningful.

A. All three readings can be used this first Sunday of Advent and of the new church year under a theme of anticipation. I will develop that further in the Possible Outline Of Sermon Moves.

B. The New Testament Reading can stand alone with an approach of what Paul prayed for then and what Paul would pray for now in our congregation: love for each other and being ready anytime for the coming again of Jesus the Christ.

C. If you do not wish to stress the Advent season, you could simply preach on "the lesson of the fig tree," verses 29-33 in Luke. Just like a tree's future and the coming of summer can be predicted by its behavior, so our lifestyle can be predicted by little signs we give off in our daily living and even in our participation (or lack of it) in the life of our congregation.

, What are the daily indications that God's kingdom is near? People are able to love their enemies and turn the other cheek? The unlovely are loved anyhow? Selfish people begin to share? The timid start to witness? The lonely find companionship? And so on.

Possible Outline Of Sermon Moves

A. Begin with a brief introduction to Advent and the new church year (see An Introduction To The Advent Season).

B. Announce that the major theme of these four weeks is anticipation for the big advent of Jesus' birth in Bethlehem and into our hearts again.

C. Move to the three readings today and how they all anticipate.
  1. Old Testament (Jeremiah) — One in the lineage of the great King David to re-establish the Judean Kingdom in Jerusalem when there will be justice again.
  2. New Testament — Paul writes how he is anticipating visiting them again and seeing their love for each other. And how they might look forward to the coming of the Christ again and that they will be ready for such an event.
  3. The Gospel — Jesus tells the people to read the signs which point to his returning. They are to anticipate it and be alert and ready anytime.

D. Move to the parable of the fig tree in Luke 21:29-33 and explain what Jesus was teaching. We can read the signs now that the kingdom is near (here) and give some examples of them.

E. Move to witnessing what all this means to you and what you are anticipating this Advent season.
  1. Signs of the presence of Christ with your congregation, like loving the unlovely.
  2. A renewal of the awareness of God's presence in your daily life, which will be hectic and busy.
  3. A new awareness of the joy that is ours as we prepare for the birth like a couple prepares for the birth of their child.

F. Move to a metaphor or story from below.

G. Frame your sermon by giving in reverse order the truths you have proclaimed today. Wish your people a happy new church year and Advent season.

Prayer For The Day

These four weeks of Advent, dear Holy Parent, help us to prepare for your coming again in Bethlehem and in our own congregation and hearts. Give to us a joyful anticipation which rises above the busyness of the season. And help us to live on the alert that we might recognize your kingdom and presence in our midst anytime. In Christ Jesus' name. Amen.

Possible Metaphors And Stories

The Dow Chemical Company in Pittsburg, California, had a leak of chlorine gas when a gasket broke in a one-inch pipe. About 75 to 80 pounds of chlorine went into the air — not enough for a serious health risk. Yet the company and county took no chances and set off the emergency alert system. Sirens blew and a computer called all of us residents who live nearby with instructions to "shelter in place." It means to stay indoors, tape cracks, close windows and doors. In about three hours the "all clear" was sounded.

Hasn't the time come to sound the alert in our spiritual lives? Perhaps we ought "shelter in place" in our churches and then go out into the world to serve.

David Brenner on the *Tonight Show* told about signs he never quite understood:

1. The International House of Pancakes on their door: "We have menus in Braille."
2. A New York restaurant was even better: "For bathrooms, use the stairs."

What signs with mixed messages do we give out to people who see us practice our discipleship?

Another sign — this one at Broadlawns Hospital in Des Moines: "If you are pregnant, inform the technologist." What are the signs of the near kingdom?

At all the professional football games, behind the goalpost is a fan holding a banner which says, "John 3:16." I would someday like to sit next to that banner bearer with a sign saying, "and 17," for it is the wonderful news that Jesus is our savior, not our judge.

There is a beautiful scene in the television movie *The Scarlet and the Black*, when Monsignor O'Flaherty of the Holy See in Rome finally baptized General Kaplan of the German SS after World War II. After visiting the general every week for a long time, O'Flaherty baptized his former bitter enemy in 1959. Kaplan hated the monsignor because he had helped prisoners of war escape. Only our Christian faith can turn enemies into friends like this.

Second Sunday Of Advent

Revised Common	Malachi 3:1-4	Philippians 1:3-11	Luke 3:1-6
Roman Catholic	Baruch 5:1-9	Philippians 1:3-6, 8-11	Luke 3:1-6
Episcopal	Baruch 5:1-9	Philippians 1:1-11	Luke 3:1-6

Seasonal Theme   The joyful anticipation and preparation for the birth of Jesus in Bethlehem and into our hearts as well.

Theme For The Day   Preparing the way for the coming of our savior into our congregation and into our community and home.

Old Testament Lesson   Malachi 3:1-4   *A Messenger To Prepare The Way*

In verse 4:5 it seems the messenger who is to come to prepare the way is Elijah. However, we Christians have generally identified this messenger as John the Baptist. Whoever paired this reading with the Gospel for today must have had that in mind as well.

Perhaps the covenant referred to here is that with Levi (2:48), as the job of this messenger was to prepare for God's return to the temple in a time of judgment. The right offerings needed to be given so that God might again bless the people. Malachi probably had in mind a priest who would bring much needed reform (see 2:7, Job 33:23, and Ecclesiastes 5:6). In verse 3 there is a fire which may be a hyperbole of the results from real justice wherever God rules.

New Testament Lesson   Philippians 1:3-11   *Paul's Prayer For Philippians*

In this letter of joy, Paul lays out for us the symptoms of the Christian life.
1. *Christian joy.* Christianity is the religion of a joyous heart and a radiant lifestyle.
2. *Christian offering.* The Greek word used in verse 6 is the beginning and ending of an offering to God. So our lives are an offering to God (see Romans 12:1).
3. *Christian togetherness.* We share the grace of God, the work of the gospel and in suffering for the gospel, and fellowship with the Christ.
4. *Christian maturity.* He prayed that their love would grow (vv. 9 and 10).
5. *Christian goal.* We are to set as our goal to live such a life that the praise is given to God. Some of us can be close to perfect in our practice of the faith, but we are so demanding, astringent, and austere that we actually turn people off to Christianity.

The Gospel   Luke 3:1-6   *Here Comes John*

It's a great passage to preach on using the personality of this prophet of the wilderness. As time went on, the relationship between John the Baptist and Jesus became more clear. All four Gospels associate him with the beginning of Jesus' ministry.
1. In Mark, he is addressed like a new Elijah who summons Israel to repent.
2. In Matthew, he has the same apparel, but he knows Jesus.
3. In this Luke passage, his coming is an historic moment and a renewal of prophecy. He is presented as the last of the prophets before the Messiah.
4. In John's Gospel, the Baptist is more aware of the importance of Jesus.

We do know that Jesus took the arrival of John as a sign that God's kingdom was on its way. The scripture quoted (Isaiah 40:4ff) was scripture which was usually connected with the coming of the Messianic Age. John's message was that the king is coming. Fix not just the roads, but your hearts.

Preaching Possibilities

A. For a suggested sermon plot on John the Baptist as a character sermon, see my Second Sunday Of Advent (pp. 14-16) in Cycle A of *The Lectionary Preaching Workbook, Series VII*. Of course this Luke account can stand alone or be linked to the Second Reading in how we are to be as Christians for the coming of this Messiah.

B. The Old Testament will also preach by itself as we consider what does it mean to be a messenger and how does one prepare the way today? And what needs to be changed in our temple to make it ready for the birth of the Savior this year's Christmas?

C. I'll go with all the readings, first reviewing last week's message, proceeding to this week's and then anticipating the weeks ahead until Christmas.

Possible Outline Of Sermon Moves

A. Begin with a review of last Sunday's message of the Advent season and the beginning of the Church's New Year. There are certain signs which point to Jesus' coming again and soon.

B. Run through last week's three readings' emphasis.

C. Move to today and tell how we continue the theme of joyful anticipation of Jesus' coming again.
  1. Malachi says a messenger is sent to us to prepare the way. Reforms are needed in the temple.
  2. Paul writes to the Philippians the symptoms of the Christian life which we ought to be able to see.
  3. Bold prophet John the Baptist is the man with the message to get ourselves ready.

D. Move to your own preparation for this year's Christmas and list how you think your congregation ought to prepare, too.
  1. Perhaps increased time for prayer and decreased shopping binges.
  2. Perhaps more on self-examination and less on self-aggrandizement in greetings and social customs.
  3. Perhaps more attention to the needs of the poor and less on the wants of us who have so much.
  4. Perhaps less emphasis on matching gifts given to you and more on giving away with no thought of return on the investment.

E. Move to a story from Possible Metaphors And Stories.

F. Frame your sermon, imagining how John the Baptist celebrated Jesus' birth over the years making the points above.

Prayer For The Day

Prepare our hearts today, O God, for your rebirth in them again. Give us a calmness and a sanity as we enter into this time which can be so stressful and hectic. Show us the symptoms of the Christian life, which will point others to Jesus as well. In his name. Amen.

Possible Metaphors And Stories

On CBS news a man by the name of Al Copeland in New Orleans had millions of lights in his front yard for Christmas. One thinks first, how beautiful! Then it's reported the neighbors are suing him for disturbing the peace! I think the light of Christ is like that. When we really let it shine, those who prefer the darkness will always complain and try to extinguish the light.

It was explained to me that the louvers in our parking garage ramps will automatically open up when the carbon monoxide level reaches a certain concentration. The airing clears the ramp of the dangerous gases. Perhaps the church ought to have something similar to ventilate the stale and dank air of a museum and bring in the fresh air of the Spirit. Advent promises that new ventilation.

In a church newsletter authored by friend/pastor Dan Johns was the story of Chippy the parakeet. Cleaning the cage one day, the owner was disturbed by the telephone and got the hose of the vacuum cleaner too close and sucked the bird right into the sweeper bag. Quickly she took the bag off, pulled out the bewildered bird, and stuck it under the water faucet. The bird survived, but now its owner describes it this way: "Chippy doesn't sing much any more; he just sits and stares."

Our church has many who don't sing much any more, but just sit and stare. How shall we minister God's loving grace and profound joy to them?

William Barclay tells how, at the coronation service in Westminster Abbey after all the congregation was seated, a squad of cleaners unexpectedly emerged with brushes and vacuum cleaners and proceeded to sweep the carpets so that they would be absolutely clean for the coming of the Queen. So here John is the courier for the King. He says to get things cleaned up. Soon he comes.

Third Sunday Of Advent

Revised Common	Zephaniah 3:14-20	Philippians 4:4-7	Luke 3:7-18
Roman Catholic	Zephaniah 3:14-18	Philippians 4:4-7	Luke 3:10-18
Episcopal	Zephaniah 3:14-20	Philippians 4:4-7 (8-9)	Luke 3:7-18

Seasonal Theme   The joyful anticipation and preparation for the birth of Jesus in Bethlehem and into our hearts as well.

Theme For The Day   John the Baptist calls for repentance and thus prepares the way for the Messiah who brings a new baptism of Spirit and water.

Old Testament Lesson   Zephaniah 3:14-20   *A Celebration Hymn*

This is Zephaniah's hymn of celebration for a worship of deliverance. Yahweh has removed the enemy. He is the true king who has heard the prayer of the humble. Verses 16-18 are Yahweh rejoicing in his victory. God has removed disaster from the people. Verses 19-20 tell the people God will gather the dispersed. "At that time" is reflecting the work of a disciple.

New Testament Lesson   Philippians 4:4-7   *Joy, Gentleness, And Peace*

Here is the joy, gentleness, and peace of the Christian life. This reading will also be used in the readings for Thanksgiving, extending on through verse 9. Consistent with this "Epistle of Joy" we have more urging to know the quality of Christian joy and of gentleness. These are two great elements of the Christian life: joy and gentleness.

The Greek word for gentleness is *epieikes*. It has been translated many ways: forbearance, softness, the patient mind, modesty, forbearing spirit. The Greeks said it was "justice and something better than justice." Others have claimed it meant "to meet a person half way." I like Barclay's comment concerning *epieikeia*, "A man has the quality of *epieikeia* if he knows when not to apply the strict letter of the law, if he knows when to relax justice and to introduce mercy." He will deal with people in love as we hope God will deal with us. Again Barclay, "Justice is human, but *epieikeia* is divine."

In verses 6 and 7 we see that Paul advises the Philippians to take everything to God in prayer as an antidote for worry. The result of faithful prayer is that it will bring peace to our hearts. This is because we are praying to a powerful, all wise, and loving God.

The Gospel   Luke 3:7-18   *The Baptist's Message*

The crowds which John was preaching to seemed to think of themselves as chosen by God for special status. John confronts them and they ask what they should do. Typical of Luke's Gospel is repentance and then the stress on social justice. So he advised:

1. Give one of your coats to those who have none.
2. Give some of your food to those who are hungry.
3. Tax collectors collect no more than you are supposed to.
4. Be satisfied with your wages and don't extort money.

Then in verses 16-17 John's baptism is contrasted with the Messiah's baptism of Holy Spirit and fire. See Malachi, chapter 4 for an Old Testament example of the judgment. In Luke's tradition, the fire will soon be associated with the Holy Spirit (Acts 1:5).

The figure of the slave who is not worthy to untie his master's sandals is from Mark 1:7. The fire and spirit connection has special significance for Luke — it anticipates the events of Pentecost (Acts 2:3-4) and the tongues of fire.

As a homilitician it is clear to me that John preached for specific results and he got them. His message was not in theological niceties but in life itself.

The "good news" in verse 18 is hard for me to see. One commentator says that by Luke's time this word translated "good news" meant preaching on the mission of the church.

Preaching Possibilities

A. The hymn of celebration from the Old Testament, the joy and gentleness of the New Testament, and the promise of one coming by John will all go together this week. If it were not Advent and that time of year our congregation considers Christmas season no matter what the liturgical calendar reads, I would focus on that word of gentleness in Paul's Philippians passage. Notice there is plenty of gentleness in the comments on the scripture readings.

One could begin with John's character and message and then talk of his promise of who is to come, and then back into Philippians as examples of Christian joy and gentleness this promised Messiah will bring. A finish could be to use Zephaniah's hymn of joy as is and without further comment. Why not try chanting it in plainsong fashion?

B. Still another possibility would be to explain the background of the Zephaniah passage, read it as a hymn of joy, and then move to Paul's advice for the Christian life and a way to prepare for Christmas this year:
1. Rejoice in the Lord (v. 4).
2. Let your gentleness be known (v. 5).
3. Don't worry (v. 6). (Bobby McFerrin reggae metaphor?)
4. Pray prayers of thanksgiving and supplication (v. 6).
5. Know the peace of God (v. 7).
6. Be in Christ Jesus (v. 7b).

Possible Outline Of Sermon Moves

Today is the day I preach a biographical sermon about that fascinating character of the Bible, John the Baptist.

A. Introduction: tell of John's birth as a cousin of Jesus.*
B. Review some history and present him as a desert man and the first prophet to speak in many years.
C. Present his message: repent, be baptized, live the life of social concern for others.
D. Now tell how his message is for us as we prepare for Jesus' coming also.
E. Contrast his baptism for repentance and our baptism with the sealing of the Holy Spirit, his good news with our good news.
F. Continue telling of his life: the arrest, the decapitation, and the sending of his disciples to question Jesus about Messiahship. Use as a closing Paul's blessing from the New Testament reading: Philippians 3:7.

Prayer For The Day

We thank you, O God, for giants of the faith down through the ages like John the Baptist. Help us to hear his warning and invitation to repent and thus be better prepared for the Messiah to come into our lives again this year. We pray thankfully knowing your peace will guard our hearts. And please, teach us to be gentle people. In the name of Jesus, John's cousin. Amen.

Possible Metaphors And Stories

Signs on three exactly same-looking doors at Augustana College, Sioux Falls, South Dakota: *Men-Women-Mechanical.* Perhaps mechanical is close to being a third form of the human race. We must never lose our God-given humanness.

A little sign on my desk says, "Joy is not the absence of trouble, but the presence of God." The great preacher George A. Buttrick used to say, "Joy is what we are chosen for and joy is what we have to offer to all who will come. It is a deep sense of joy not dependent on the number of things we get done in a day — for this is not the opposite of unhappiness but the opposite of unbelief."

After riding a public bus for four hours, then walking about three miles back into the Sumatran jungle, we arrived at the *Bona ni Pinesa* (village of origin) of one of my Batak Christian Seminary students. After catechizing approximately 150 on Saturday evening, we drank coffee they had picked and roasted, and then we sang. A beautiful *Kebaya*-clad girl named Omega stood and lined out hymn after hymn to familiar tunes. The next morning I preached a naked, simple gospel: of Jesus born in Bethlehem with a ministry in Galilee, died on the cross for our forgiveness but Easter resurrection that we too might come out of the grave, and returned in spirit to be with us here and now. And then while the old women chewed *napuran*, we sang and sang and celebrated the presence of that same spirit with us still. A pig was killed and a *hula hula* (celebration) was held. We ate *sac sang* and they presented me an *ulas* (cloth of deep friendship). That simple, without-frills Christianity touched me deeply as we sang hymns of joy in God's presence. It was "the basics" at Tapiannauli bush village and it was full of joy.

At a church meal after a funeral, a man told me they were expecting a baby any time now, so each night in cold, cold Iowa, he removed the battery from his car and kept it in the house where it would be warm and ready to start the car. Might we anticipate the coming of the Christ-child with such eager and careful anticipation.

---

*A Bible dictionary like Harpers will prove helpful in learning more about the life of John the Baptist.

Fourth Sunday Of Advent

Revised Common	Micah 5:2-5a	Hebrews 10:5-10	Luke 1:39-45
Roman Catholic	Micah 5:1-4	Hebrews 10:5-10	Luke 1:39-44
Episcopal	Micah 5:2-4	Hebrews 10:5-10	Luke 1:39-49 (50-56)

Seasonal Theme   The joyful anticipation and preparation for the birth of Jesus in Bethlehem and in our hearts as well.

Theme For The Day   Our God makes arrangements to be with us as a human and elects Mary to be the mother of Jesus the Incarnate.

Old Testament Lesson   Micah 5:2-5a   *The Anticipated Messiah Of Peace*

On this Fourth Sunday of Advent, shortly before Christmas, we first read from the Old Testament prophet Micah several things about the coming of the promised Messiah. He will come from Bethlehem (see 1 Samuel 16:1, 17:12, and Matthew 2:6). He will come from ancient lineage and rule in Israel, he will care for his "flock" which will be secure, and he shall be a person of peace. This reference to peace is probably an indictment by Micah of false prophets who shouted, "Peace" (see 3:5).

I think the beauty of the passage is in verse 4 in the description of the anticipated Messiah.

New Testament Lesson   Hebrews 10:5-10   *The Obedient Sacrifice*

First we have a quotation from Psalm 40:6-9 to say that animal sacrifices are not what God wants. God wants obedience. Before Micah the practice of sacrifice had degenerated into mechanical acts in the temple. Because God wants obedience, Jesus is the perfect sacrifice perfectly doing God's will. See 1 Samuel 15:22; Psalm 50:14; Hosea 6:6; Isaiah 1:10-20; and today's Micah 6:6-8. So all the other prescriptions for mechanical temple sacrifice are abolished (v. 9b) and Jesus opens up the way to God for us through the once and for all sacrifice of his body. Good theology for this so near sentimental nativity of our Lord.

The Gospel   Luke 1:39-45   *Mary Visits Elizabeth*

In this narrative, even before birth, cousin John the Baptist acknowledges the Christ. John's mother at Ein Kerem shows prophetic insight recognizing Mary as the mother of her Lord. I have no idea why "Mary's song of praise" or the "Magnificat," as it is often called, is not part of the reading for this Fourth Sunday of Advent. I will include it anyway.

For Mary to be chosen by God to be Jesus' mother was at once a great joy, and it would be a great sorrow. Someone has preached that Jesus came not to make life easy but to make people great. So, too, for Mary. There would be sad, bewildering, single motherhood ahead for her.

Preaching Possibilities

A. The three readings will work together under the theme of "Three things to remember this Christmas."
    1. Micah: Jesus out of Bethlehem is our peace.
    2. Hebrews: Jesus came as our once and for all perfect sacrifice.
    3. Luke: Mary was chosen by God to be the mother of the incarnate Christ — a special baby with a special mission on God's behalf for all the world.
B. The Second Lesson will stand alone if you want to do the near impossible and hold off until Christmas Eve for your "Christmas message." This Jesus — whose birth we soon celebrate — what did he do? He got rid of the need for a sacrifice for our sins. He will do it once and for all. You can forget those ritual offerings for forgiveness. This is the start of something big! Forgiveness and atonement with

our creator, a new way to treat each other, a spiritual presence with us now. We will be sanctified by him (Hebrews 10:10). Never again will any human need say God wouldn't understand. God has "been there, done that."

C. You might consider a two-part sermon based on the Luke Gospel Reading. Today can be, "This Baby And Mother Will Be Special" with Part Two on Christmas Eve or Day as, "The Baby Is For Everyone."

Possible Outline Of Sermon Moves

A. Begin by remembering your own first child and when you felt life for the first time (or use below metaphor).

B. Move to Luke's account of Mary's visit to Elizabeth's home in Ein Kerem a few miles from Jerusalem. Tell it in your own words.

C. Move to explain how Roman Catholics use verse 42 as part of their devotional, "Hail Mary, full of grace…." Now move to explain why you think Luke included this narrative in his presenting of the gospel to Theophilus.
   1. This was no average pregnancy.
   2. This birth had been promised for a long time (v. 45).
   3. This cousin John would prepare the way for Jesus as we have seen earlier in the Advent season.
   4. Mary's life as a single parent and mother of one who threatened the religious establishment would not be easy.

D. Move to explain what you believe this says to us in the weeks when we observe the birth of our savior again.
   1. God loves us so much as to make these kinds of arrangements — so we ought to love God and one another.
   2. God keeps promises so we can be at peace.
   3. God knows what it's like to be human. God has "been there, done that."
   4. This is news we ought to share with others.

E. Frame your sermon after using one of the stories below giving these points in reverse order and then finishing the story of how you first felt new life in your pregnancy or your wife's pregnancy.

Prayer For The Day

We rejoice with Elizabeth and Zechariah at the coming birth of our Savior Jesus again this year. Give to us a quiet joy and peace as we celebrate how much we are loved by you and how well you now know our human situation. Move us to share all this good news with others. In Jesus' name. Amen.

Possible Metaphors And Stories

I took my son, his wife, and our grandson to the airport today. It's the day after Christmas and the place was jammed. The birth of the Christ child still has the power to move people in great numbers all over the world!

At Pacific Lutheran Theological Seminary, an East German organist named Sietzman said he lives in a socialist country and their people live alone. "Here people talk to each other and they even touch me. I feel good then and warm and together." After the PLTS community sang, "A Mighty Fortress," he sat down and improvised "The Magnificat." Wow! Together our souls can magnify the Lord.

The church sexton got the paper roll which plays the carillon bells in the church tower in the player upside down. It played continuously and a very strange melody indeed! I think we often play a melody very strange to the rest of the world and one which goes backwards to shepherds, angels, and camels, rather than forward to missiles, genetics, and nuclear challenges of the future.

I remember an advertisement on television for Diehard batteries. In the middle of a very cold night the ready-to-deliver wife and husband waded through the snow to their car. He tried to start it, but no success. She raised the hood, flipped a booster switch, and the engine started. No matter life's conditions, let us be ready for this birth.

An Introduction To The Christmas Season

We begin on December 24 the Christmas season, which continues until Epiphany, which is always January 6. While the secular practices of our Western culture provide strong competition against it, we Christians try our best to emphasize during all these days the coming of God in human form and the birth of Jesus in Bethlehem. The word *Christmas* comes from "The Christ Mass" which was observed in the early Roman Catholic mass.

The liturgical color is white representing nativity and birth.

The Nativity Of Our Lord

Revised Common	Isaiah 9:2-7	Titus 2:11-14	Luke 2:1-20
Roman Catholic	Isaiah 9:2-7	Titus 2:11-14	Luke 2:1-14
Episcopal	Isaiah 9:2-4, 6-7	Titus 2:11-14	Luke 2:1-14 (15-20)

Seasonal Theme   The Savior is born into the human world and circumstances.

Theme For The Day   The Savior is born in Bethlehem in order to bring light to a dark world and provide for us forgiveness for our sins.

Old Testament Lesson   Isaiah 9:2-7   *Light To Those Still In Darkness*

The hope for the future reign of justice is always a part of the Old Testament kingship ideas (see 11:2-5 and 2 Samuel 23:3-7). Here we have the promise of the restoration of the Davidic Kingdom. In their dark days there is hope for a new David who will bring light to them. Verse 3 assures us there will be great joy when their oppressors are overthrown. This new transcendent king will be a wonderful counselor, etc. (v. 6b). And from now on this reign will be about justice and righteousness. Compressed, we can say about this marvelous passage:

1.   Light came to those still living in the dark.
2.   There will be great joy, a very special child is born who will be a Prince of Peace.
3.   And he will rule with justice and righteousness.

For a Christmas Eve candlelight worship service you just can't beat verse 2b using the rest to describe the light which has come.

New Testament Lesson   Titus 2:11-14   *Grace Appears*

The Old Testament tells us of a promised one to come and bring peace and justice. This reading tells us what the grown-up Jesus' mission was. The coming Gospel tells us of the beginning of the whole operation.

The work of Christ, according to Paul, has a twofold meaning: 1) redeems us from iniquity (v. 14a), and 2) separates from the world those people who belong to Christ (v. 14b and 1 Peter 2:9-10). So Titus says God's grace has appeared (a nice way to announce the birth of Jesus) and that grace is teaching us to live differently — self-controlled, upright, and godly — while we wait (vv. 12, 13). Characteristic of this letter to Titus from Paul is the importance of good works. Perhaps this is a wise choice for Christmas Eve or Day when we so stress the gifts of God.

The Gospel   Luke 2:1-20   *The Birth Of Jesus*

Luke views Jesus' birth affecting all of the world so we can begin with a decree from the Emperor. The shepherds, who understand what they heard and saw, stand in contrast with the "religious" of the day who didn't seem to understand.

There is an interesting theme of Luke which already comes out. As people do their ordinary work, they find themselves in God's presence. Recognizing the "signs" which God gives and acts on means they find a peace which is much more than the absence of trouble. The meaning of the song of the angels does not signify we can bring about peace on our own. Peace comes to those whom God favors (v. 14). Notice that upon the return of the shepherds after seeing the baby Jesus, the shepherds glorified and praised God for all they had heard and seen.

The shepherds were simple men to whom came the first announcement of Jesus' birth.

Some other ideas to remember for the biblical accounts of our Savior's birth which can add background and color to your sermon:

1. The stable was a limestone cave. Today, they'll show you one under the altar in the Church of the Nativity in Bethlehem. This is the church under siege in 2002.
2. The shepherds and "Wise Men" did not arrive at the manger at the same time. The Wise Men probably arrived six months to two years after the birth.
3. The shepherds were out at night because it was lambing time and these were temple flocks eventually used for temple sacrifice.
4. Usually at a new birth the local musicians gathered and played in celebration. No chance here, but the angels sang!
5. Bethlehem is seventy miles south of Nazareth — it's a long trip, especially for an almost-due pregnant woman.
6. Micah 5:2 predicts the birth of the Messiah will be in Bethlehem.
7. Light is the typical symbol of divine revelation.
8. The sign that all this is true is the simple surroundings (see Isaiah 7:14-15).

Preaching Possibilities

It's the Nativity of Our Lord and we must retell the story all have come to hear.

A. One possibility is to use all three readings:
    1. Isaiah tells us it's light to those still living in darkness.
    2. Titus tells us the birth of Jesus is the arrival of God's grace for us.
    3. Luke tells us it's a Savior who is born.
B. Another way to organize would be to use personalities:
    1. What Christmas meant to Mary and Joseph.
    2. What Christmas meant to the shepherds.
    3. What Christmas meant to the angels.
    4. What Christmas means for us tonight.
C. Because most of us preach this sermon on Christmas Eve, the Old Testament Isaiah account really works well, especially if it is a candlelight service: Isaiah 9:2b, light for those in darkness. The light is for everyone:
    1. It is to eliminate the darkness of sin and fear.
    2. It shows us a new way in a dark world.
    3. It illuminates the way to peace.

Possible Outline Of Sermon Moves

A. Begin by retelling the birth story in your own words.
B. Move to your own memories in hearing this story in your home church as a child.
C. Announce what you most like in the story.
    1. Jesus comes to common people in common circumstances. He knows what it is like.
    2. Jesus' birth is first announced to shepherds, not kings or princes. We are included.
    3. The angels' anthem: be not afraid and God's people will have peace. We need not be afraid and can also have peace for our troubled lives.
D. Tell your hearers what this says to us now:
    1. God loves us this much to go to all this trouble.
    2. We, like the angels, have peace to proclaim.
    3. We, like the shepherds, must return home and share the news that we have a God who came in person so understands, modeled the godly life for us, went to the cross for our forgiveness, came out of the grave so that we might also, and is with us now in spirit. (This summary is important as we very well might have those listening who have not heard this Gospel before, or at least for a long time.)
E. Relate a story or metaphor from below.
F. Frame your sermon by summarizing in reverse order and then going back to your memory of hearing this story of Christmas as a child.

Prayer For The Day

On this special night of your light coming into our dark world, we celebrate with Mary, Joseph, the shepherds, and angels your birth into our world in order to save us and know how it is it be human. Help us to share this light of the gospel out in our dark world where we live, work, and play. Make our voices angelic, too, full of good news of a savior and peace — glorious Christmas peace. Amen.

Possible Metaphors And Stories

"Mama Gannah" (Amanda Gardner), the Bible Woman of Liberia, West Africa, said of the missionary nurse, Marie Jensen, who raised and taught her, that when she taught, she "... wore Ma Jensen's skin." Since then many letters have arrived from my students there which have said, "Today I wore your skin ... I taught them about Jesus." Jesus put on our skin in the incarnation and asks us to wear his skin in the world in our ministry.

Julie Walters, 34, an actress making the film, *She'll Be Wearing Pink Pajamas*, announced during a nude scene that a new ruling by the Screen Actors Guild was that all technicians must also get nude during the filming. The naked truth was that it was a bluff; she told them after they had done it.

Jesus came to earth to strip just like us and share what it's like to be fully human — it's called the incarnation.

In the movie *Sacrifice*, the African woman says, "I just want peace. I want to come home to kindness again. I'll fight with you, but don't ask me to kill." We Christians have the great gift of peace and the great task of peacemaking.

I heard the story of a new captain of a battleship. On his first cruise out of New York Harbor he spotted a light ahead. He radioed ahead and said for the light to identify itself and take a 90 degree turn right. No response. He radioed again, "Look, I'm a battleship and I can blow you out of the water. Take a 90 degree turn to the right." The response came back, "I'm the lighthouse and you take the 90 degree turn."

We have a light in the darkness to give us direction. We often try to move the lighthouse rather than alter our course. Now this will really preach.

Note: I have found the Christmas cards sent to me as their pastor often make good illustrations for my preaching. It is effective to hold them up, tell who they are from, and read the message which best illustrates what you are trying to say. However, be prepared for an avalanche of religious cards next year!

First Sunday After Christmas/Holy Family

Revised Common	1 Samuel 2:18-20, 26	Colossians 3:12-17	Luke 2:41-52
Roman Catholic	1 Samuel 1:20-22, 24-28	Colossians 3:12-21	Luke 2:41-52
Episcopal	Isaiah 61:10—62:3	Galatians 3:23-25; 4:4-7	John 1:1-18

Seasonal Theme   The Savior is born into the human world and circumstances.

Theme For The Day   The maturing of Jesus from a sentimental infant in a Bethlehem manger to a savior here in the midst of our congregation.

Old Testament Lesson   1 Samuel 2:18-20, 26   *Hannah Is Blessed*

Each year Hannah and Elkanah would visit their son Samuel, who served in the temple at Shilo, modern Sielam, wearing a linen *ephod*. This was the traditional dress for one serving in the worship. Mother Hannah would bring new clothing to her son and thus receive a blessing from Eli for her generosity. Evidently the blessing of more children worked, as Hannah had five more! And that is what this story is about. A favored wife who remained childless and was derided by the other wife who was fertile. Not to be able to produce children, especially sons, was a very difficult situation for a woman in those days.

While not a part of the reading "The Song of Hannah" (1 Samuel 2:1-1) is a beautiful one and may be the basis of the "Song of Mary" (Luke 1:46-55). And, of course, verse 2:26 sounds very much like our Gospel passage today (Luke 2:40). In verse 26 Samuel is pictured in contrast to the evil sons, as he is favored by God.

New Testament Lesson   Colossians 3:12-17   *Clothed In Grace*

Paul begins by using three precious words used by the Jews: chosen of God, holy, and beloved. The Jews themselves are God's chosen people, a holy (*hagios*) nation, and loved by God. The words which follow are easy to understand. Barclay defines them further.

1. *Compassion*: a heart of pity.
2. *Kindness*: wine which has grown mellow with age. The virtue of the person whose neighbor's good is as dear to them as their own.
3. *Meekness*: (*praotes*) self-controlled because he is God controlled. This is my favorite New Testament word. It seems to mean strength and sweetness combined for gentleness.
4. *Patience*: (*makrothumia*) Never losing heart with one's fellow person.
5. To these garments with which we Christians are to clothe ourselves, Paul adds *Love* (v. 14). Here is the glue which holds us together in an unbreakable fellowship.
6. *Peace*: (v. 15) The word here for "rule in your heart" is the same word for "umpire." It's an athletic word. So Paul is recommending that we let peace be the unique content of our hearts. It will preach!

Notice in verse 16 the very early church was a singing church. Our Christian thankfulness has always been offered in praise to God.

Verse 17 gives us a worthwhile test for Christian behavior: Would we do it in the presence of the Christ?

The Gospel   Luke 2:41-52   *The Boy Jesus In The Temple*

Right on the heels of the birth narrative we have Jesus going to his first Passover and becoming a man at the age of twelve. It was similar to our rite of confirmation. Probably Joseph thought him with Mary and Mary thought him with Joseph. The men and women usually traveled separately with the women starting out earlier and traveling more slowly.

Jesus' answer to his parents is interesting. It sounds as if this may be when he began to realize who he really was. Still, he did not "lord it over" his parents. At his baptism, Jesus later became fully aware of his unique son-ship — but that awareness surely began to dawn on him here.

Notice again the similarity of verse 52 and the Old Testament verse in 1 Samuel 2:26.

Preaching Possibilities

Because this is the Christmas season and the First Sunday after Christmas we'll need to continue the story of Jesus' birth by growing him, using the Gospel of Luke for today.

A. However, the New Testament Lesson is rich for proclamation and would easily stand alone under the theme: "The Perfect Christian Wardrobe." You might begin by mentioning that on Christmas Eve we heard that Jesus was born and then wrapped in swaddling cloths. After we are "reborn" into the faith, what ought we, according to Saint Paul, be clothed in?

B. Or we could connect the Samuel story and the Jesus story by using the two very similar verses: Luke 2:52 and 1 Samuel 2:26. They both loved God and other humans as they matured physically and spiritually.

C. There are also three liturgical days right after Christmas which make for interesting biographical preaching:

December 26	Saint Stephen, Deacon and Martyr
December 27	Saint John, Apostle and Evangelist
December 28	The Holy Innocents, Martyrs

D. If you wanted to do a completely topical sermon you might use the title: "After Christmas Hangover," which might relate well in our culture. One could talk about how some may have the effects of their Christmas celebration still with them, like bills coming due and perhaps a headache from too much to drink. Then move to what we ought still to have a hangover from: the birth of Jesus. Mary and Joseph saw the obligation to grow Jesus in their faith. We might use Paul's advice to the Colossians to put on a Christian wardrobe. It all has to do with maturing the tiny baby Jesus like Samuel had to mature also.

Possible Outline Of Sermon Moves

A. Move to reviewing the celebration of Jesus' birth last week.

B. Now move to the story in the Gospel and tell it in your own words if it has already been read from the Bible.

C. Move to the task before us to grow Jesus up, just like Mary and Joseph's task. We also must get him out of the manger as a baby and into our hearts as a savior. Eli had to do it for Hannah and Elkanah's son Samuel, and Paul described in the New Testament Lesson the kind of clothing we ought to put on if we "grow up" our Christian faith.

D. Move to the fact of the similarity of 1 Samuel 2:26 and Luke 2:52. Call attention that Samuel's and Jesus' maturity both called for not only loving God but also loving other people. The Christmas infant is growing!

E. Tell one of the metaphors or stories below.

F. Move to what you believe this all means for your congregation and ministry: in youth ministry and Christian education, in social ministry, in stewardship and evangelism.

G. Frame your sermon by returning to the celebration last week of the birth of Jesus and move to Mary and Joseph finding him in the Temple — we join them also in maturing the baby to an adult savior.

Prayer For The Day

Help us, dear Holy Parent, to move the Christmas infant Jesus out of the manger, and into our hearts as a savior. Just like Samuel and Jesus grew up, help us to love you and love all sorts of people as they did. Bless all parents here today that they might have guidance from you in their holy responsibilities of parenting. And show us the way as your congregation to become a people of mature faith confident of Jesus in our midst. In Christ's name. Amen.

Possible Metaphors And Stories

I never could put my heart into preaching about the time Mary and Joseph left Jesus in Jerusalem after Passover. Why didn't they keep a closer watch on their twelve-year-old son? Then, when pastor of First Lutheran Church, Tiffin, Ohio, my wife and I did the same thing! Our little daughter, Bethany, was left at the church as I drove home thinking my wife had taken her. Somehow after that, this story in the Gospel of Luke took on a new relevancy!

A favorite story at St. John's, Des Moines, is about the Christmas Eve that Pastor Louis Valbracht wanted to let a doll down from the chancel ceiling and into a manger in front of the altar. He was preaching and gave the signal to Pastor Louis Piehl, who stood to the side with a fishing rod and reel, to let the baby Jesus down. All went well until Piehl ran out of line about one foot short of the baby being at rest in the manger. Finally Valbracht came out of the pulpit and pushed the doll into the manger, which pulled Piehl out into the chancel. He ran back to the wings, which pulled the baby back in the air, and so on! How many secular forces try to keep the baby from coming again this year!

Letty Cottin Pogrebia in *Growing Up*: "Don't be the man you think you should be; be the father you wish you had."
Parenthood is an awesome responsibility and a godly act.

In 1522 the great reformer Martin Luther preached on married life and said, "God lays souls into the lap of married people, souls begotten from their own bodies on which they may practice all Christian works. For when they teach their children the Gospel, parents are certainly their apostles, bishops, and ministers."

Second Sunday After Christmas

Revised Common	Jeremiah 31:7-14	Ephesians 1:3-14	John 1:(1-9) 10-18
Roman Catholic	Sirach 24:1-2, 8-12	Ephesians 1:3-6, 15-19a	John 1:1-18
Episcopal	Jeremiah 31:7-14	Ephesians 1:3-6, 15-19a	Luke 2:41-52 or Matthew 2:1-12

Seasonal Theme   The Savior is born into the human world and circumstances.

Theme For The Day   Jesus as the incarnate God and the one who makes us his children and has grace upon grace for us here and even today.

Old Testament Lesson   Jeremiah 31:7-14   *Joy And Restoration Coming Soon*
Jeremiah writes an oracle which promises great joy as all the people scattered in exile return to their land. See Isaiah 49:8-13. Then he pictures the gathered people now as a new restored nation just like a lush, well cared for, irrigated garden, or a shepherd gathering all the sheep back in the secure fold. There will be many expressions of joy: singing, dancing, mourning into joy, sorrow into gladness, even the priests will share in the prosperity!

New Testament Lesson   Ephesians 1:3-14   *Blessings In Christ*
This is one long sentence in the original Greek language. Let's list the main points:
1. God chose us.
2. We were chosen for heavenly things like holy, blameless, love.
3. God adopted us into God's family. We have moved from the family of the world to the family of God.
4. We are redeemed and forgiven.
5. God has revealed God's will for us, and God's inheritance.

Then in verses 11-14 we have Paul's example of a unity possible in Christ. "Us" and "we" mean the Jews and "you" means the Gentiles. The Gentiles received God's word (v. 13). It was good news (v. 13b) and they were sealed with the Holy Spirit. And Paul claims the Holy Spirit is the "pledge" of our inheritance. The Greek word is *arrabon*, which means the down payment which guarantees the rest of it would be forth coming. So, when we have the experience of the Holy Spirit, it is to have a preview of the blessings of heaven, which is still coming. Perhaps a metaphor could also be an appetizer of the main meal being prepared for us. Phew! Better take only a couple ideas out of this long winded one sentence course in Pauline theology.

The Gospel   John 1:(1-9) 10-18   *Word Became Flesh*
In the Christmas season we have had the beautiful story of Jesus, the incarnate, God's birth. Now the writer of the Gospel of John gives us the theology. It's meat on the bones, folks. Perhaps we are now far enough away from the sentimentality of Christmas so as to have ears willing to learn about what all this beautiful story teaches us about our God and about us, too. Some comments which might enrich your preaching:
Verses 10 and 11 tell us what happened at the incarnation. This literally means he came to his own home and folks refused to welcome him.
Still, in verse 12 we are told that some received him and to them would be given the privilege of becoming members of God's own family.
Verse 14 gives us the heart of it. God completed the long process of revelation by becoming a human being. Not only that, God came to live among us. This is the theme of John's book. The Greek literally means "pitched his tent." The "we" means the disciples who saw his glory. Then comes "grace and

truth." Grace means the extravagant goodness of God and truth is eternal reality as revealed to humans. Verse 16 no doubt wants us to know the pre-existence of Christ.

"Grace upon grace" in verse 16 indicates "pitied on abundantly," or "wave upon wave" of it. Then comes for the first time in this prologue — the name of Jesus Christ.

In verse 18 we learn that Jesus was (is) a window into God at work (A. M. Hunter). "Close to the father's heart" comes from the Greek "in the bosom of the father" meaning the close fellowship of a meal. Because Jesus has this intimate fellowship, he is able to reveal and disclose his nature and interpret God to us.

So the Gospel about to be unfolded is the truth about God put in human terms and acted out in words and ministry.

For preaching, here is one other interpretation from Tyndale's *New Testament Commentary*: The grace in verse 16 means grace to meet every need that arises (see 2 Corinthians 12:9). And perhaps before grace should be the word "even."

Preaching Possibilities

One could use all three of these readings by working with the theme of Christmas one more time. Explain it is still the Christmas season and today we have three ideas about God's presence with us because:

A. Jeremiah says there ought be great joy and dancing because God's people are gathered again, like a shepherd gathers his lost sheep, or they have a lush garden.

B. Paul writes to the Colossians about being chosen by God for membership into God's own family.

C. John most celebrates that God's word took on human love and skin and lived here with us. All this (B and C) began with the coming of Jesus in Bethlehem.

Of course the New Testament Reading will stand alone, but it won't follow the birth and temple narrative very well. Paul's long sentence has lots of sound theology which could get too heavy or be considered not right for this season of the year. Nevertheless, if you want, this could serve as an outline:

A. We have been chosen by God for great things.

B. We are now children of God, part of God's intimate family.

C. God wants very much to forgive and save us.

D. All this is ours as we are sealed with the Holy Spirit and marked with the cross of Christ.

So let's all join Jeremiah's people and celebrate by singing and dancing. Move back the pews; here we come!

Possible Outline Of Sermon Moves

A. Introduction: Remind your hearers that we have heard Luke's account of the birth of Jesus and of his visit in the Temple at age twelve.

B. Today we hear of another early Christian who wrote his description of what and how God did these things. John is beginning his Gospel as a theologian and not so much a historian. In his prologue he tells us great truths about Jesus coming in the world.

   1. Those who welcome his coming into the world can be God's own children.

   2. That which many had spoken now God puts into flesh and bones.

   3. The main element of this God incarnate is grace. Lots of grace, waves of it.

   4. Jesus also brought the truth about God. He is a window to God's heart. He is the only one who has revealed God like this because he and God have an intimate fellowship, like a baby at its mother's breast.

   Another or secondary way of stating the above is:

   1. It's one thing to say you love children; it's another to adopt them as your own family member.

   2. It's one thing to speak words of caring for us; it's another to put those words into action and do them.

   3. It's one thing to love those who deserve it; it's another to have grace for those who don't (and over and over).

4. It's one thing to know about God; it's another to reveal God through our intimate relationship with the divine.
C. Move to "So What?" Because all this is true, what do we do about it here in our congregation?
1. We can be God's presence for others on Jesus' behalf, especially when they have need of that presence in their lives.
2. This is very good news that God doesn't give up on us and continues to offer grace. It must be shared.
3. As God's own children we then are sisters and brothers here and must learn to treat each other that way in our congregational life.
D. Frame your sermon by returning to your reminder of Luke's account and now John's account of the incarnation, closing with a verse or two of the great hymn, "O Word Of God Incarnate."

Prayer For The Day

Christmas has come again today to us, dear God, as John reminds us that you came to live in our midst and you love us even when humans would give up. We thank you for your grace upon grace and ask that we might know the best way to celebrate it. Oh, how thankful we are that you became flesh and this worked forgiveness and grace for us in Bethlehem's grown up savior. Amen.

Possible Metaphors And Stories

I was seated on a plane headed home, wearing a black suit and clerical collar. Ron Zalenski came to me and wanted to sit in the empty seat next to me. He had driven out from his home in Wisconsin to go hunting. His wife called to tell him their twenty-year-old son, Stephen, was in a car wreck, and was barely alive in the hospital. They were Roman Catholics. Seeing me on the flight, he asked, "Please, let me sit next to you. I'm afraid."

There is often a ministry of presence called for when words are of little use. Just be there and stay close.

In an Indian language in Mexico where the only living gift they know is a chicken, they translate John 1:14: "The Word was full of chicken and truth."

When an orchestra plays, there is a "sideman" who is not the lead musician but "sides" the lead musician. The "sideman" usually stands nearby the leader and supports the star by the way he or she plays the second part of the music.

Jesus is our "sideman." We are called to "side" each other. May the melody be great!

Because Dwaine Pittman was ill on the day we seven were examined before the Rite of Confirmation, the questions Reverend Wessel had promised us were out of order. I gave the answers I had memorized anyway for each seventh question. Reverend Wessel never let on they were the wrong answers. What an example of grace he demonstrated to us that day!

On a bus ride in Egypt out to the pyramids I kept asking the driver to stop so I could take a picture. It seemed now was the best shot. Then as we got closer, it seemed much better. Grace is like that. It first opens up better and better with grace upon grace like those huge stones piled one upon another.

An Introduction To The Epiphany Season

This is the oldest liturgical season of our church year, dating back to the second century. The word *epiphany* means manifestation and the dawning. So we have scripture, which describes it as dawning on people who Jesus really is. It is the "showing forth" of the Messiah to us Gentiles. Thus we have many stories of the beginnings (manifestations) of Jesus' ministry, his first miracles, and so forth, which was an epiphany (a dawning) on him and others who he was and what his ministry would be.

Depending on the date of Easter, the season can be from one to six weeks. It always begins with the arrival of the Wise Men and ends with the Transfiguration of our Lord. In these events it dawns on the Wise Men, as well as on Jesus and the disciples.

The liturgical color for the season is green for growth, as Jesus grows, with the exception of Epiphany Sunday, the Transfiguration of our Lord, and the Baptism of our Lord, when it is white.

The Epiphany Of Our Lord

Revised Common	Isaiah 60:1-6	Ephesians 3:1-12	Matthew 2:1-12
Roman Catholic	Isaiah 60:1-6	Ephesians 3:2-3, 5-6	Matthew 2:1-12
Episcopal	Isaiah 60:1-6, 9	Ephesians 3:1-12	Matthew 2:1-12

Seasonal Theme   Jesus calling his disciples and it dawning on them who this person is they are following. Light into a dark world.

Theme For The Day   The visit of the Wise Men to see the baby Jesus and how people reacted to the coming of the Savior into the world.

Old Testament Lesson   Isaiah 60:1-6   *Radiance Of God's Presence*

What marvelous poetry! It's all about light and glory. Into a world of despair and darkness (ch. 59) comes the radiance of God's presence. The light is a spiritual word for being in God's presence and the dark is life apart from God. So you have a new day of light and its dawning over Jerusalem. Verse 1 says, "Your new day is dawning." The brightness of the New Jerusalem attracts many to come into this dawning light, which is reflected in the faces of those who come to it. And their hearts beat with the excitement of the dawning.

New Testament Lesson   Ephesians 3:1-12   *Gospel To Be Shared*

Paul claims to be one of those to whom the mystery about Christ had been revealed. Because of Christ, the gospel is also to be shared with us Gentiles. This gift of grace involved a certain stewardship which he fulfilled in his proclamation to the Gentile people. Since Paul is the apostle to the Gentiles, we have a share in the promise God made to the Jews. We too are a part of the body.

Then in humility, Paul said that he was the least of those chosen — nevertheless *he was chosen* — to share the gospel. No wonder Paul is often considered one of the greatest humans ever to live. Here he revealed how convinced he was of being God-chosen for a divine task — and he lived out of that conviction. The confidence of calling gave him a courage and confidence that we can have as well.

The Gospel   Matthew 2:1-12   *Arrival Of The Wise Men*

To question whether there were actual Wise Men is to miss the point. It is a marvelously valuable story which Matthew presents as a gift to the Christ Child. It tells us that people have come from far and near to worship Jesus. It tells us there was a sense of awe about this thing God was beginning that would eventually lead to our salvation. So tell it with all its majesty and amazement and reverence. It is a lovely and inspirational tale.

There are interesting characters in the passage: the cunning, powerful, and cruel king Herod; the chief priest and teachers of the law who were completely indifferent; and the Wise Men who knelt down and worshiped him. The gifts were symbolic:
1. Gold was a gift given to kings.
2. Frankincense was a gift for a priest.
3. Myrrh was a gift of embalming fluid for someone dying.

The gifts were foretelling that this Bethlehem baby would be our king and perfect priest who would go to the cross and die for us.

Preaching Possibilities
A. The familiarity and attractiveness of the visit of the Wise Men on this day will almost compel us to preach on the Gospel.

B. The Old Testament Isaiah passage, however, can be used first to introduce the theme for this new season of the liturgical year — light into darkness and the dawning of that light into our own lives. It's an opportunity for transition from the Christmas theme of light coming to those who lived in darkness to the dawning of that light into the individual lives of people in the Gospel readings for the entire Epiphany season. It culminates in the Transfiguration of Jesus when the disciples saw Jesus in a whole new light.

C. There is the possibility of a series of Epiphany sermons based on verse 1 of Isaiah 60: "your new day is dawning," speaking in turn of the new day dawning for each person each week of Epiphany and always bringing it close to the ground with what our new day filled with God's light might look like.

Epiphany	— Wise Men
Baptism of our Lord	— Jesus
Epiphany 2	— John the Baptist
Epiphany 3	— Peter and Andrew
Epiphany 4	— The Disciples

But for this day the hearers will want to experience again the visit of the Wise Men to Bethlehem and revel in its beauty. The challenge will be to make the quaint message close to the ground and relevant for this new millennium and for those who would romanticize it.

Possible Outline Of Sermon Moves

A. Introduction: One of the most familiar stories connected with Jesus' birth is the arrival of these Wise Men Matthew writes about.

B. Move to sharing your early memories of the Wise Men when you were a child growing up.

C. Show your people Christmas cards you received this year which have the Wise Men on them.

D. Move to retelling the story of the arrival of the Wise Men in your own words.

E. Move to stating that certain signs like a new star in the sky indicated the Messiah had arrived. Now what signs might indicate the Messiah's arrival in our day and community?
1. The unlovely are loved intentionally.
2. Justice is practiced with grace and mercy.
3. The Gospel is shared with enthusiasm.
4. Our practice of discipleship is taken seriously.

F. Move to these Wise Men and tell of their response to coming into Jesus' presence. Read verse 11 then explain the symbolism of the gifts:
1. Gold was a gift for a king.
2. Frankincense was a gift for a priest.
3. Myrrh was a gift of embalming fluid for someone who will die.

G. Ask the question what gifts would (should) wise people offer to Jesus born into our congregation and community?
1. Perhaps a regular tithe in the offering. Or a tithe of the amount spent on celebrating Jesus' birthday this year.
2. Perhaps a son or daughter encouraged to go into the ordained ministry.
3. Perhaps something you can do well in service to the church and the Christ.
4. Perhaps attendance at his birthday party of bread and wine in communion.

H. Move to one more question: Where do you think the star might stop in your community "... over the place where the child is" now?
1. Our own home where Christ's presence is acknowledged.
2. Our own church where Christ is actually present in the sacrament and preaching and ministry to others.
3. An institution of mercy run by the church like a hospital, treatment center, mission station, etc.

I. Frame your sermon by returning to your memory of Christmas and Wise Men when you were young.

J. Finish by reading verse 12.

Prayer For The Day

Dear God, we rejoice with those wise people of old that you have come in flesh to understand and be with us. May your star shine brightly over this church, community, and the homes represented here in your sanctuary. And show us the proper way to respond with offerings to that Christ here. In Jesus' name. Amen.

Possible Metaphors And Stories

In the Batak language of Sumatra, Indonesia, there is a word which means professional jealousy or even worse — *elat*. It reflects an attitude of not really wanting some plan or program to go well so they don't try very hard. *Elat* describes King Herod in today's Gospel.

At the O'Hare airport in Chicago, Illinois, there are two neon tubes which help the pilot know where to park the plane so the jetway will work well. They are about two feet apart and one is orange and the other red. When they come together, the pilot stops. She is where she is supposed to be. These Wise Men had a signal as to where they should be also. It was a long way from home and in a little house where the infant Jesus was (John 2:11).

Have you ever wondered what happened to the gifts given to Jesus by the Wise Men? I have. There is never an indication that Jesus ever accumulated any wealth. My guess is that he gave them away to those who needed them! He has done that with thousands of gifts offered to him since then by faithful Christians. The Wise Men had guarded them, but Jesus found a way for them to be used for others.

In Shakespeare's *Richard III* we read the words: "When our brief light has set, there's the kingdom of perpetual night" (*Carmina I*).

In Shakespeare's *Much Ado About Nothing*, Act 2, Beatrice is speaking of her gift of happiness and says, "There was a star danced, and under that was I born."

The Baptism Of Our Lord
First Sunday After The Epiphany
First Sunday In Ordinary Time

Revised Common	Isaiah 43:1-7	Acts 8:14-17	Luke 3:15-17, 21-22
Roman Catholic	Isaiah 42:1-4, 6-7	Acts 10:34-38	Luke 3:15-16, 21-22
Episcopal	Isaiah 42:1-9	Acts 10:34-38	Luke 3:15-16, 21-22

Seasonal Theme   Jesus calling his disciples and it dawning on them who this person is they are following. Light for a dark world.

Theme For The Day   A celebration of our baptism and its significance for our lives here and now.

Old Testament Lesson   Isaiah 43:1-7   *Promises Of Restoration And Protection*
This is beautiful poetry in which the writer describes God's work of restoring and protecting people. There is some remembering of the events of the Exodus and a strong confidence in God's near presence. Israel is restored and then protected. God will call on even these remote lands to give up their scattered people to their homeland. They were created by God (v. 7) and thus they belong to God. Isaiah realizes the present reality of the people, but also he can smell victory in the days ahead.

New Testament Lesson   Acts 8:14-17   *Receiving The Holy Spirit*
Philip's taking "The Way" into Samaria was of great significance to the beginning church. It was important to the church's leaders that it was done correctly and that the dimension of the Holy Spirit was included. So Apostles Peter and John, who had done well in taking Pentecost out into the world, were sent to Samaria to check on Philip's evangelism methods. The rumor was that Samaritans had been received into the faith but without any proof of their having the Holy Spirit. The result recorded in 6:6 proved that "Phil" was okay, so they added the laying on of hands and, sure enough, the Holy Spirit was added. How's that for what we used to call Confirmation and now call "Affirmation of Baptism"?
This Philip's ministry is exciting. E. M. Blacklock of the *Tyndale New Testament Commentary* says of him, "He is like Stephen in doctrine and outlook, like Paul in his evangelism, a clearly marked character with something of the Old Testament prophet about him."

The Gospel   Luke 3:15-17, 21-22   *The Baptism Of Jesus*
John lived in the desert. His message was one of terror and judgment. His message called for people to share with each other and to serve God where God had placed them, and he was only the forerunner. He was a great preacher dealing in real, close to the ground life.
For Jesus, his cousin's emergence was a call to action. It had been eighteen years since he had begun to realize his was a unique life to be lived. He went to his cousin to join the people who were looking for their God.
This was an intimate experience with God. The words of God in verse 22 come from two places: Psalm 2:7 as a description of the promised Messianic king. Then comes the second part which is from Isaiah 42:1, which is a description of the servant of the Lord.
I wonder how this description of Jesus' baptism came to Luke. Perhaps Jesus often told it to his disciples including Peter. And perhaps John Mark heard Peter preach about it. And perhaps Luke possessed Mark's writings about it. Perhaps.
Of course we could raise the question why Jesus needed this baptism for forgiveness. He was without sin. Perhaps an example. Perhaps to give his cousin some support for the cause. Perhaps joining others seeking God. However, I'll not worry my people with the question at all.

Preaching Possibilities

A. Many preachers use this Sunday to teach about Baptism. The New Testament Reading for this day is much better material for Christian Baptism than the Gospel account of cousin John baptizing Jesus in the Jordan. We must remember this was not Christian Baptism as Jesus had not yet died on the cross and made possible forgiveness by grace and atonement with God. If we keep this in mind, we can use both New Testament texts with Jesus' own baptism seen as an example for us and the Acts account as instruction on the Holy Spirit as part of Christian baptism.

B. At the beginning of the Epiphany season, the baptism of Jesus in the Jordan can also be developed as one of the beginning examples, after last week's Wise Men, of it dawning on folks who Jesus was. In the story it "dawned" on cousin John, and on Jesus himself, as Luke relates the experience.

C. The Old Testament Isaiah account is an opportunity to speak about Isaiah as we will have several of his readings in a row. *Harper's Bible Dictionary* or *All the Men of the Bible* will provide background material on Isaiah as a personality. Then there are two main elements in his message: *God restores* and *God will protect*. Verse 1b also connects to the theme of Baptism where God gives us, and calls us, by name. There is promise in that. So this Isaiah lesson can be used in support of Baptism or it can stand alone as an example of what is promised on God's behalf for us, God's people. The title could be: "You can count on this."

Possible Outline Of Sermon Moves

A. Begin by telling of one of the most meaningful baptisms you have ever performed.

B. Move to introduce this Sunday as "The Baptism of our Lord" and why it comes at the beginning of the Epiphany season.

C. Explain that the three scripture readings were all chosen to teach us about Baptism.
1. In Baptism God calls us by name and promises to restore and protect us over and over. Read Isaiah 43:1b and 4.
2. In Baptism we join the family of God and make our own public witness like Jesus in Luke 3:16, 21, 22. It was like an ordination to begin Jesus' public ministry and mission, as it can be for each one of us also.
3. In Baptism we are given God's equipment and presence called the Holy Spirit, like in the Acts account. Be sure to read the words in your baptism liturgy which indicate the giving of the Holy Spirit. Then read also the words of Acts 8:17.

D. Use metaphors and stories between 1, 2, and 3 above, or if you have them, tell of a baptism meaningful to you between each one.

E. Turn to the liturgy "Affirmation of Baptism" and conduct it from the pulpit. It would also be meaningful if you did a baptism at the end of this sermon. If you just don't have that many, consider using a doll and doing a baptism so all can see.

Prayer For The Day

We celebrate our baptism today, dear God, because you have named us and promised to restore and protect us. Let your Holy Spirit's presence always be here, coming into our lives and hearts and affirming our membership in your family. For all the benefits of our precious baptism, we do give thanks. In Jesus' name. Amen.

Possible Metaphors And Stories

In Joe Wold's book *God's Impatience with Liberia* (p. 104), Louis Bowers went across the Saint Paul River to the village of Parakwele. There, fourteen men were ready to be baptized by the local evangelists.

The Zo stood up and said, "I forbid these men to be baptized. If they are, by this time tomorrow they will be dead."

The men went outside for a *palaver*. They came back and said, "We will be baptized; if we die we will be with Jesus."

When the service was over, the Zo came to Bowers secretly and said, "Tell me about this Jesus. His power is greater than mine."

How does one describe the power of Jesus?

The Dean of the Church Divinity School of the Pacific and I came out of the common room and waited and waited for the rain to stop, only to discover the lawn sprinklers above us were on, causing it to appear like rain.

Perception and reality are often very different. Let's throw the water of baptism so broadly it appears as though it is a downpour.

On *Real People*, two who had been prisoners in the German concentration camp at Dachau used the date of their release by the Rainbow Division of the U.S. Army as their birthday to celebrate each year.

At the date of our baptism we were set free as well.

I often watch in early morning as the doves perch on the upper rim of our fountain, waiting for the water to come on and the upper basin to fill so they can drink and bathe in it.

When it does finally begin, the upper basin must fill before any water flows to the larger lower one.

And so we do our ministries from the overflow of our baptismal waters and many wait for us.

Dr. Joseph Sittler, on April 24, 1983, was asked how he would define baptism. He said, "It is an enactment of the fact that you weren't consulted in the first place."

Second Sunday After The Epiphany
Second Sunday In Ordinary Time

Revised Common	Isaiah 62:1-5	1 Corinthians 12:1-11	John 2:1-11
Roman Catholic	Isaiah 62:1-5	1 Corinthians 12:4-11	John 2:1-11
Episcopal	Isaiah 62:1-5	1 Corinthians 12:1-11	John 2:1-11

Seasonal Theme   Jesus calling his disciples and it dawning on them who this person is they are following. Light for a dark world.

Theme For The Day   Jesus came to be with us in our good times as well as bad and to change our water into wine as well.

Old Testament Lesson   Isaiah 62:1-5   *The Vindication And Salvation Of Zion*

The writer prophet is pledging himself to prayer for God to save God's people.

Verse 1 indicates victory, for Zion is coming soon. Jerusalem will then be like a crown for God.

Verse 2's "new name" is a metaphor (cf. 60:14) and is used in connection with the concept of a marriage between God and the people, which is also in Hosea, Jeremiah, and Ezekiel.

Verse 5 extends the metaphor to say it's like a son marries a young woman, so God marries mother Jerusalem (cf. 3:25); "Builder" can be translated as God.

For more on the prophet as an intercessor for Jerusalem see Genesis 20:7; Jeremiah 14:11.

New Testament Lesson   1 Corinthians 12:1-11   *Spiritual Gifts*

It sounds like there were members of the Corinthian congregation who were putting heavy priority on speaking in tongues (*glossolalia*). See Mark 16:17, Acts 2:4, and 10:46 for additional references. *The Interpreter's One-Volume Commentary on the Bible* defines this as "... the ecstatic utterances of emotionally agitated religious persons, consisting of a jumble of disjointed and largely unintelligible sounds. Those who speak this way believe that they are moved directly by a divine spirit, and that their utterance is therefore quite spontaneous and unpremeditated."

Paul tells them that just because there is the ecstatic in their church services, it doesn't prove the presence of the Spirit of God. It is interesting that Paul acknowledges there are some who can "discern the spirits" (v. 10). And this is itself a grace gift (*charisma*).

So to all this Paul advises that there are many gifts which God gives for the common good: wisdom, knowledge, faith, healing, working of miracles, prophecy, discernment of spirits, kinds of tongues, and their interpretation.

For preaching we have about God's gifts: 1) many varieties, 2) all coming from the same origin even though they are outwardly quite different, and 3) their common intent.

Verse 7 is central for me as a summary. Each person possesses special gifts important for the life and vitality of the congregation.

The word *activates* in verses 6 and 11 is also loaded with possibilities. It literally can mean "energizes everything in everything." The "Energizer Bunny" will work in at least the children's sermon.

So what is Paul's conclusion? Anything and anyone which glorifies Jesus as Lord speaks by the Holy Spirit.

The Gospel   John 2:1-11   *The Wedding At Cana*

Because it is the Epiphany when we see Jesus' ministry beginning and it dawns on people who he is, we have this story of his first miracle which took place nine miles from his home town, Nazareth, in the village of Cana.

The six stone jars were at the entrance for water to be used in washing in the Jewish ritual of purification. Of course many explanations have been put forward how Jesus did this. C. S. Lewis takes it literally as a creative act of God incarnate. Jesus short circuits the natural process of making rain into wine. Maybe.

Then there is the rationalism that they already had drunk a lot, so water goes into vessels like into a mostly empty ketchup bottle. Maybe.

Perhaps the real message is that Jesus celebrated at a marriage feast and that he had compassion for a host who ran out of wine.

Then there is the symbolism which started in Mark 2:19-22 with new wine bursting the old wine skins of Judaism. Jewish legalism which is represented by the water of purification here becomes the good news which gladdens the marriage feast of the kingdom (Matthew 22:1-14). So in this story, Judaism is the water and the wine is Christianity — the Christ makes all the difference! And it all "dawns" on them in the joyous fellowship of a wedding reception.

And this is a big miracle, folks! Six jars each holding about twenty gallons.

I'll translate verse 4: "Mother, don't worry about it— it's okay."

Preaching Possibilities

A. Here is an interesting idea put forth by A. M. Hunter in the Cambridge *Gospel According to John* commentary. John's word for miracle is a *sign*. A wonder with a meaning in it. John always emphasizes the spiritual truth. In his first twenty chapters he lists seven signs.
   1. Water into wine (ch. 2): the difference Christ makes.
   2. Healing of the officer's son (ch. 4): Faith the one thing needful.
   3. Healing the cripple (ch. 5): Christ the restorer of lost power.
   4. Feeding the multitude (ch. 6): Christ the bread of life.
   5. Walking on water (ch. 6): Christ our guide.
   6. Healing of a man born blind (ch. 9): Christ our light.
   7. Raising of Lazarus (ch. 11): Christ our life.
   (Note: Numbers 2, 4, and 5 above are also in the Synoptic Gospels.)
      Consider it for an Epiphany sermon series or next summer during the Pentecost season. It will preach.
B. I don't see a strong connection between the readings for today. Perhaps Paul's spiritual gifts could help the new way of religion illustrated in the water into wine at Cana but it would strain the exegesis.
C. While not an easy passage, Isaiah's promise to pray for the people of Zion, a vindication and a salvation could stand alone as what we prophets ought to do and what God's people can expect.
D. Of course, the Second Reading is full of possibilities. The three numbered points in the comments on the readings will work as the main moves for a sermon.
E. Then, there is also the possibility of taking three or four of the spiritual gifts and talking about them. I would use knowledge, faith, healing, and working of miracles. The idea of the spirit "activating" these is a great idea which can be expanded upon with questions about how God "activates" in our congregation: through prayers, through inspiration of worship, through encouragement of others, and so on.

Possible Outline Of Sermon Moves

A. Begin by telling of a social event like a wedding reception where the food or drinks ran out or something similar what happened to embarrass the host and hostess at Cana.
B. Tell of the same embarrassment of the hostess at Cana.
C. Explore at least two theories of how Jesus worked the miracle (don't take too long on this).
D. Move on to what John wanted to teach by telling this story right at the beginning of Jesus' ministry.
   1. Jesus came to celebrate life with us. God is here also in our good times.

2. Jesus came with a new way — the water of Judaism and legalism is changed into the wine of a Christianity and salvation by grace and forgiveness. It's a new day.

3. When the "wine runs out" in our marriages, our faith can bring us renewal and revitalization and restoration of our love and covenant of fidelity.

E. Move* to what this means for your congregation's ministry and program like marriage enrichment classes. Perhaps you need to re-examine the example set for the young. Does the faith look like a celebration or still the old Jewish legalisms of "thou shalt nots"?

F. Give your own witness as to how this miracle will change your life this week.

G. Frame the sermon by returning to your opening story of host embarrassment and summarize what has been learned by this miracle at Cana.

Prayer For The Day

When the wine runs out in our marriages, we pray for your help, O God. Help us always to be aware of your presence with us in our good times of celebration as well as our difficult times of struggle and pain. We are glad to be your people not bound by legalism but held together in a fellowship of celebration. In Christ's name. Amen.

Possible Metaphors And Stories

An Episcopal bishop was about to consecrate the elements for communion so he sent the altar girl over to fetch the pitcher of water to wash his hands. As he poured it out, he discovered it was the wine. He said, "This isn't water; it's wine!" The altar girl replied, "It was water when I brought it over here!"

Del Monico told on radio: A man seated in a wheelchair at the Vatican suddenly got up and walked away. Everyone was amazed and shouted and praised God for the miracle. But the man hadn't been ill. He was just resting for a little while in a vacant chair.

God is accustomed to doing miracles every day and they appear quite commonplace. On the other hand, some things which seem miraculous just aren't explainable yet. God most often works within God's own natural law.

Corinne Chilstrom wrote to me to tell of using a story about Doris Bergman. The choir director at a rehearsal said to Doris, "Doris, I think there is a solo in there!" And there was! He convinced her to sing and it was lovely and many congregations have been blessed since by that fresh, young choir director's *gift identification*.

In Shakespeare's *The Tempest*, Juno blesses Ferdinand and Miranda:
"Honor, riches, marriage blessing, long continuance,
and increasing, hourly joys be still upon you!"

A different approach at this sermon move would be to ask yourself just what water ought to be turned into wine in our community and how we can help it to happen.

Third Sunday After The Epiphany
Third Sunday In Ordinary Time

Revised Common	Nehemiah 8:1-3, 5-6, 8-10	1 Corinthians 12:12-31a	Luke 4:14-21
Roman Catholic	Nehemiah 8:2-6, 8-10	1 Corinthians 12:12-30	Luke 1:1-4; 4:14-21
Episcopal	Nehemiah 8:2-10	1 Corinthians 12:12-27	Luke 4:14-21

Seasonal Theme   Jesus calling his disciples and it dawning on them who this person is they are following. Light for a dark world.

Theme For The Day   Jesus begins his good news ministry in Galilee, in his home town, where he claims to be the promised one to come caring about the poor.

Old Testament Lesson   Nehemiah 8:1-3, 5-6, 8-10   *The Public Reading Of The Law*
This is not a familiar book of the Bible and we don't read from it often. The introduction to the *New Revised Standard Version* of the Bible tells us that Nehemiah continues the history of the Jews after their return from exile where Ezra leaves off. He inspired the people to repair the city walls, and with Ezra he provided religious leadership. A theme over and over in the book is the importance to Nehemiah of prayer.
     The section we read today is probably a misplaced section of Ezra, the main character.
     The people gather at the water gate to have Ezra read the law to them just two months after his arrival back in Jerusalem. This was probably portions of the Pentateuch. The language is Hebrew with the Levites translating it aloud in Aramaic, which was the common language of Palestine after the return from exile.
     When they heard the law read, they cried because they knew the punishment which was coming. But they are told to not cry for this day is holy and they have God's joy for their strength (v. 10).

New Testament Lesson   1 Corinthians 12:12-31a   *One Body*
     We continue on in reading from Paul's first letter to his Corinthian congregation. See also Romans 12:4-5. The simile is clear. Just as our bodies depend on all the organs functioning properly — so too the church. It won't do well unless all are considered important parts to its well being. Evidently, scholars have found this same analogy used in other Greek and Jewish material. Paul also claims that those parts of the body we think of as less honorable — are just as significant in the church (v. 23). The inferior gets more honor!
     Verse 26 is a beautiful analogy. If one part suffers, all suffer. If one part is honored — all will rejoice. So the church is a unified, functioning body of Christ. It will really preach.
     With verse 28 begins a different list of gifts. We have apostles, prophets, and teachers (see Ephesians 4:11). Notice speaking in tongues appears last again. Better cool it there, folks. Because there wasn't any fixed order of organization yet, these lists vary.

The Gospel   Luke 4:14-21   *Beginning Of Galilean Ministry*
     Continuing with the Epiphany season we read today of Jesus beginning his Galilean ministry by returning to his hometown synagogue in Nazareth and already meeting opposition. This account and Jesus' sermon give us a condensed outline of Jesus' ministry in the days ahead. Try comparing it with Acts 6:10—7:20. Luke must have written this purposely as the basic pattern of discipleship.
     Luke writes his Gospel making the main events in Jesus' life and ministry the working of the Holy Spirit. The text for Jesus' message is Isaiah 61:1-2. Perhaps Jesus expected these hometown Jews to recognize that the prophet-servant promised by Isaiah had arrived; but it was impossible for them to see beyond the return of a local kid they had watched grow up.

What made them so angry at Jesus was the compliment Jesus paid the Gentiles. These who thought of themselves as God's people were told that the Gentiles were also loved by God. So, it began to dawn on them that this new message their son was bringing to them was very different from anything they had ever heard.

Note, also, that Jesus went to synagogue on the Sabbath day (v. 16). He went even though things there were not as they should have been.

Preaching Possibilities

A. With the reading in order of Corinthians (*lectur continuum*) this Epiphany season, seldom will the Gospel accounts and the Second Reading work together. However, with some imagination we could link all three of today's readings in this way:
   1. Nehemiah tells of Ezra reading publicly the law to the people.
   2. Luke tells of Jesus reading publicly a new gospel of good work.
   3. Paul tells us how this new religion will function as the alive body of Christ in the world.
B. One could also do a sermon comparing Ezra's public message of law and Jesus' public message of good news gospel.
C. Of course the Second Lesson is rich in imagery calling for unity and respect for all Christians, and it also reminds us of the Church as serving as the alive presence of the body of Christ in the world. This is an image which can really be expanded upon. The message could be organized around these moves:
   1. *Title:* Paul's image of the church.
   2. Like our physical bodies have many parts with various functions, so too the body of the church.
   3. It is an inclusive church where all are respected.
   4. If one suffers, all suffer; if one is honored, all are honored.
   5. A more excellent way is when we each recognize the other as a valuable part of the body.
   6. Ours is a large responsibility to be together the resurrected body of Christ in our world and community.
   7. Give your own implications to the above.
   8. Frame it.

Possible Outline Of Sermon Moves

Title: The ministry begins in Galilee

A. Introduction: Tell of your own beginning of ministry or your experience of returning to your home town congregation.
B. Move to the Gospel today and tell in your own words the story of Jesus returning to the hometown synagogue.
C. Move to contrasting verse 15 with verse 29. Tell them the difference is the new gospel he was preaching:
   1. It is good news.
   2. It is a social gospel.
   3. It is the fulfillment of the promise of this scripture.
D. Move to the difference in this new message Jesus starts out to model and preach and teach.
   1. Based on grace rather than law.
   2. Inclusive of all people, even Gentiles!
   3. It is concerned with the oppressed, poor, blind, in prison.
E. Use here a story or metaphor from below.
F. List what you think are the implications for your congregation's life together and ministry.
   1. Are we ministering to the oppressed, poor, in prison?
   2. Do we present the faith as good news?

3. How would Jesus be received if he preached here today?
4. Who are our hometown boys or girls who should be invited to return and preach?
G. Frame the sermon by returning to your own experience of beginning ministry or preaching in your home church.

Prayer For The Day

Dear God, help us with our ministry here at (*your congregation*) that we might follow Jesus' example to care about the poor, the oppressed, those in prison, and those who are in need of healing. And watch over our members who are preparing to be, or already are, in ordained ministry. Give us the ability to celebrate your gospel because it is obviously very good news. In Jesus' name. Amen.

Possible Metaphors And Stories

When I was a much younger man, and on rare occasions invited to preach in my home congregation, an old woman named Emma Stahl would say at the door, "Jerry, you would have made such a good farmer." Another would say, "I remember when you were summoned into juvenile court for working nights." It's never quite the same in one's hometown!

(For Second Lesson) Here is another funny sign. It is in a Midas Muffler shop in Des Moines: "Please, let us know if you would like your old parts returned. Thank you. The shop manager."

I attended an ecumenical service at Saint John's Catholic Church in Des Moines. After being seated I discovered that two pillars holding up the sanctuary roof completely blocked my view of the pulpit. I wonder what church pillars block the message from the pulpit? Traditions, heresies, wrong perceptions, our own pride...?

I followed a large cement truck being towed up Lower Beaver Road. I wondered what happens when a truck full of concrete stalls and the barrel no longer rotates. I drove on out to the concrete place to ask. They carry a certain chemical with them just in case, and they can put it in this mix to keep it from setting up in the barrel of the truck.

What might we use to keep our minds and prejudices from setting up like concrete?

Fourth Sunday After The Epiphany
Fourth Sunday In Ordinary Time

Revised Common	Jeremiah 1:4-10	1 Corinthians 13:1-13	Luke 4:21-30
Roman Catholic	Jeremiah 1:4-5, 17-19	1 Corinthians 12:31—13:13	Luke 4:21-30
Episcopal	Jeremiah 1:4-10	1 Corinthians 14:12b-20	Luke 4:21-32

Seasonal Theme   Jesus calling his disciples and it dawning on them who this person is they are following. Light for a dark world.

Theme For The Day   The agape love God has for us and which we are to have for others even when it is not deserved or appreciated.

Old Testament Lesson   Jeremiah 1:4-10   *The Call Of Jeremiah*
     Jeremiah was very aware of his call by God to be a prophet and so spoke with authority on God's behalf. This beginning passage tells of his call. He was probably fourteen or fifteen at the time and was aware of his youth. So this is the beginning of a powerful prophetic ministry. When this fellow announced doom on a nation, it came — and when he promised peace it also came! And he did not need a "frequent flyer" card. What he prophesied from Jerusalem would determine the fate of tribes and nations far and near.
     Verse 5 is interesting to me. There is predestination of Jeremiah even before birth and perhaps at conception.

New Testament Lesson   1 Corinthians 13:1-13   *The Gift Of Love*
     Who hasn't heard this, Paul's greatest passage, read at a wedding? The last verse of chapter 12 states Paul "... will show you a still more excellent way." The way is then explained in chapter 13 as the way of Christian love, agape. It is a word Christians appropriated for a new kind of love for the unworthy. It is lavished on the other without considering whether the one loved deserves it. It tries for nothing for oneself but, rather, the best good for the loved one.
     So Paul is saying in this part of his first letter to the Corinthians that spiritual gifts are good; however, there is something far better and that is love. The linking together of faith, hope, and love is often found in the New Testament: Romans 5:2-5; Galatians 5:5f; Colossians 1:4f; 1 Thessalonians 1:3, 8; Hebrews 6:10-12; and 1 Peter 1:21f. Hope among these three big short lists is interesting. Christianity reached out to the women, oppressed classes, slaves, and so on, giving to them perhaps their only source of hope.
     I must admit a feeling of deep inadequacy in even trying to comment on this passage of such a great theme.

The Gospel   Luke 4:21-30   *Rage In The Synagogue*
     This is a continuation of last week's account of Jesus beginning his ministry in his hometown synagogue. Last week Luke said about his teaching: "... and was praised by everyone" (v. 15). Now we read further that as the newness and radicalism of Jesus' message became clear, the Jews were angered by it and verse 29 says, "They got up, drove him out of the town ..." (v. 29). It dawned on these Jews that this hometown boy, Jesus, was claiming that Gentiles were also loved by God! They had always held that Gentiles were created "... to be fuel for the fires of hell."
     Notice the difference between Jesus and John the Baptist. Jesus reads this passage from Isaiah which was basically good news. John proclaimed a message of threat and condemnation.

The verses 24-27 refer to events in 1 Kings 17-18 and 2 Kings 5. The idea is that insiders by demanding some kind of proof may miss the Messiah while outsiders will be able to recognize him. I like the picture in verse 30 of the crowd ready to hurl Jesus off the cliff and he walks right through them!

Preaching Possibilities
A. If you have not done a sermon on "the call," this might be the time for it, using the Jeremiah reading. We can challenge our young people to consider if God might have been counting on them from early on, like God did count on Jeremiah. There would be a slim connection between Jeremiah and Jesus beginning their ministry and becoming aware of their call. Also, both brought an unpopular message to their listeners.
B. Of course the Gospel goes with the theme of Epiphany when it dawned on the Jews what Jesus' message was. They were angry and resisted. Also, in the season of beginnings, we have the beginning of hostility toward Jesus. Especially if you did not preach on the Luke passage last week, this will make a dramatic narrative sermon this week, ending with Jesus facing the hometown crowd and walking right through them!
C. See last week's Possible Outline Of Sermon Moves for a way to treat the Gospel.

Because I believe no matter what the season of the church year and no matter what the Epiphany is in the Gospel, the Second Reading is so precious to so many, I will preach on it.

Possible Outline Of Sermon Moves
A. Begin by describing the love you have for several things and people, like a pet, a football team, a grandchild or child, a spouse, and so on.
B. Move to an introduction of Paul's 1 Corinthians 13 where he has been talking about spiritual gifts and now makes the point that Christian love is much more important.
C. Move to defining God's unique undeserved love for others, and so on. (See the comments on the Gospel.)
D. Read verses 4-7 as a description of this different kind of love:

It is	It is not
Patient	Envious or boastful
Kind	Arrogant or rude
Rejoices in the truth	Insists on own way
Bears all things	Irritable or resentful
Believes all things	Rejoice in wrongdoing
Hopes and endures all things	
Never ends	

E. Move to what having this love means for us:
   1. We can have this love for our enemies.
   2. We can have this love for those who don't deserve it.
   3. Having this kind of love can mature us in the faith.
   4. Having this kind of love moves us away from self-seeking to caring much more about the other.
   5. Having this kind of love helps us to think the best of others.
F. Move to an example of this new kind of love.
G. Move to explaining that we can't have this love on our own because of our human nature. But we have a moving example of it on the cross and we also have the help of the Holy Spirit here and now.
H. Frame your sermon by returning to your opening illustrations of different things and people you love.

Prayer For The Day

Help us with your spirit presence, dear God, to have love for you and for others even when they don't deserve it. Keep us always mindful of the undeserved, gracious love you have for us and the unlovely you would have us love on your behalf. We pray in Jesus' name, who loved us from the cross. Amen.

Possible Metaphors And Stories

In Shakespeare's, *Troilus and Cressida* we hear, "To be wise and love exceeds man's might; that dwells with gods above." And in *Twelfth Night*, "O spirit of love, how quick and fresh art thou."

"The theological paradox of our troubled time is that from the same traditions, beliefs, and practices now arise both the most heinous and the most humane attitudes and actions toward other individuals and groups. The task of the religious community is to distinguish the one from the other and to serve as a source of freedom, hope, and inclusion — to nurture the forces of life" (Glenn R. Bucher of the Graduate Theological Union, Berkeley, California).

(For the Gospel) In the video *Beyond Rangoon,* a story about the horrible suffering of the people of Myanmar (Burma), there is a scene where Daw Aung San Suu Kyi, whose party won the election but never took over because the military prevented it, faces down the soldiers and walks right through them. It reminded me of Jesus with the angry Nazareth crowd cliffside.

While I was greeting people at the door as guest preacher for the day, a woman came up behind me, put her arms around my waist and hugged me, thinking I was her pastor, Ken Caudill. When she saw who I was, she simply recovered by stating that she always greeted her pastor with a hug, as it was often her only hug all week.

There are many lonely who come for companionship to God's house. They need to find a way to touch each other.

Fifth Sunday After The Epiphany
Fifth Sunday In Ordinary Time

Revised Common	**Isaiah 6:1-8 (9-13)**	**1 Corinthians 15:1-11**	**Luke 5:1-11**
Roman Catholic	**Isaiah 6:1-8**	**1 Corinthians 15:1-11**	**Luke 5:1-11**
Episcopal	**Judges 6:11-24a**	**1 Corinthians 15:1-11**	**Luke 5:1-11**

Seasonal Theme — Jesus calling his disciples and it dawning on them who this person is they are following. Light for a dark world.

Theme For The Day — If we ask and trust God, God will do it. We can also perform miracles on God's behalf. An eye to see the possible will help.

Old Testament Lesson   Isaiah 6:1-8 (9-13)   *A Vision Of God In The Temple*

Homiletically, verse 5 is key. When Isaiah realized his own natural state and identified with the sinful state of his nation, it made him feel totally inadequate before God's appearing to him in glory in the Temple.

It ought be so with us. The more we apprehend what the Christ did for us on the cross for atonement, the more we become aware of our total unworthiness. Notice that because of Isaiah's contrite heart there is God's mercy (see 57:15). A seraph began to minister to him. So his sins were forgiven (v. 7).

In this unhindered fellowship with God, Isaiah could answer, "Here am I; send me!" So when the barriers between us and God are removed, there is nothing that can stop us from carrying out God's call to serve.

By the way, Rome was founded shortly after this time in Israel's history and King Uzziah's death. This was the power which eventually brought the devastation of Jerusalem and its Temple and the scattering of the Jews. So Isaiah has this vision of the Lord's glory in contrast with his and the nation's shame.

New Testament Lesson   1 Corinthians 15:1-11   *Christ's Resurrection*

Paul is doing a summary of the Good News he had brought to the Corinthians. It was news:
1. Which they had received.
2. In which they stand.
3. Through which they are saved.
4. Something to which they had to hold firmly.
5. It was something of first importance.

Then comes a list of appearances of Jesus in this earliest account of the resurrection.

First, notice James, the brother of Jesus, is listed (v. 7). Perhaps he also had denied Jesus and thus Jesus first appeared to those who had hurt him. That's amazing grace and God's forgiving love. He right away brought the gift of peace to Peter and James, who most were in need of it.

Verses 9-11 give us insight into this Paul, who was first a persecutor and then the greatest missionary of the Christian faith.
1. He had humility (v. 9).
2. Still he was aware of his worth because of what God had empowered him to do on God's behalf.
3. And he had a great fellowship. He preached the same Gospel as the other apostles (v. 11).

The Gospel   Luke 5:1-11   *The Call Of Fisherman As Disciples*

Moving out of the synagogue, Jesus now went lakeside with a boat for a pulpit. Here we have all the right conditions for a miracle.
1. The ability to see. Jesus saw a school of fish not far off.

2. The person willing to try. Even though they had tried all night, Peter said they would try again.
3. The person who, in faith, will try what others call hopeless. After all, fishing there is done at night and the night was over!

If we need a miracle, we have to accept Jesus and what he commands and attempt the impossible.

This story is not found in the other Gospels. It serves as the call of Jesus to the disciples (Mark 1:16-20).

The symbolisms can't be missed: catching fish is a sign of the Christian mission — to "catch" people for Jesus. This miracle of Jesus opens up for us God's mission in our world and who and how it will be carried out.

Preaching Possibilities

A. We could use the Epiphany theme of "dawning" today and include all the readings:
  1. The dawning on Isaiah the great glory of God and his need for forgiveness and atonement. Then it dawning on him God's mission for him.
  2. The dawning on Saint Paul that he too was an apostle with a gospel to proclaim.
  3. The dawning upon the disciples, especially James, John, and Peter, that they were following the Christ and had a mission to do: catch people for Christ.
B. Also a sermon on the call to service could be based on Isaiah's response to go and the disciple's decision to leave their fishing and serve.
C. Of course, Paul's summary of the gospel in the Second Reading will stand alone and provide plenty of meat for a doctrinal sermon on what we hold and believe:
  1. Christ died for our sins.
  2. He was buried and raised on the third day.
  3. He appeared to Peter and James.
  4. He appeared to Paul on the Damascus road in a vision.
  5. It is this gospel by which people are being saved.

Possible Outline Of Sermon Moves

*Let's use my homiletical formula based on how people listen to sermons.
A. *Build a fire.* It's tough to keep fishing when you haven't caught anything for hours. Now tell a fishing story here. It can be your own experience or a joke or someone else's fish story.
B. *Build a bridge.* We all have times when the situation seems hopeless and just not worth trying any longer.
C. *The focus.* If we trust in the Christ, we can still do miracles and overcome.
D. *An example.* See Possible Metaphors And Stories below.
E. *Witness.* Tell of a time you were ready to give up, and God helped you go on, and it made a difference.
F. *So What?*
  1. We must be God's instruments of encouragement to each other.
  2. We must learn to ask God very bravely for help when it seems hopeless.
  3. We must be confident that God wants to help and will do the impossible if we are people of prayer and (like Peter) try again.
  4. We must respond to and see all the miraculous things Jesus still does for us by following him.
G. *Frame.* Return to your opening "fire" and finish the fish story you began with.

Prayer For The Day

Hear us today, dear God, when we get discouraged and are ready to give up. Increase our trust in you to do miracles in our lives like you did with those early disciples. Shape our congregation into a fellowship of strong believers with an eye for the possible, enabling you to do great things here, too. In Jesus' name. Amen.

Possible Metaphors And Stories

In a small discussion groups on miracles, some questioned whether there really were any. A wife of a recovering alcoholic responded: "I don't know why you find these miracles so hard to believe. I saw beer turned into furniture in my own home."

A Pan Am flight crashed in a severe thunderstorm just after takeoff from New Orleans Airport. Sheriff Lee found an eighteen-month-old baby in the debris who was still alive and everyone else was killed. She was called by the media "Melissa, the miracle baby."

We have a miracle baby in Mary's son, Jesus in Bethlehem.

Tom Brokaw on the NBC *Nightly News* told of a Terry May on Thanksgiving who was at his brother's home for the big meal and had forgotten to turn on his beeper. Meanwhile the Tucson hospital had lungs and heart for a transplant for him. They put the message on the televised Dallas Cowboys football game. A neighbor saw it and came over and told him the hospital was looking for him. A helicopter was dispatched which took him to the hospital for a successful transplant. God shows the same kind of individual attention to us. The call comes over and over, in many different ways.

Barbara Lundblad at an ELCA Assembly said: "The reason they tie mountain climbers together is to keep the sane ones from going home."

It is in family and the church we are together. We give one another courage.

---

*Jerry L. Schmalenberger, *The Preacher's Edge*, (CSS Publishing Company: Lima, Ohio, 1996), p. 45ff.

Sixth Sunday After The Epiphany
Sixth Sunday In Ordinary Time

Revised Common	Jeremiah 17:5-10	1 Corinthians 15:12-20	Luke 6:17-26
Roman Catholic	Jeremiah 17:5-8	1 Corinthians 15:12, 16-20	Luke 6:17, 20-26
Episcopal	Jeremiah 17:5-10	1 Corinthians 15:12-20	Luke 6:17-26

Seasonal Theme   Jesus calling his disciples and it dawning on them who this person is they are following. Light for a dark world.

Theme For The Day   The radical nature of following Jesus as his kingdom disciples.

Old Testament Lesson   Jeremiah 17:5-10   *Choose Evil Or Righteousness*

Jeremiah includes a short poem comparing the way of evil people (vv. 5-6) and the righteous way (vv. 7-8). The persons who trust in people instead of God will be as unproductive as the salt land near the Dead Sea — it just can't support life. The righteous person, on the other hand, is blessed because his or her trust is in God. He/she will flourish like a tree close to water.

And when tough times come, as they will, that person will prosper like trees which produce and stay green. It is the heart, says Jeremiah, which is so deceitful and causes a person to choose the way of evil and sin. God knows those thoughts we can hide from others. So God can judge us according to what our deeds are.

New Testament Lesson   1 Corinthians 15:12-20   *Resurrection Of The Dead*

Paul's argument begins with verse 19: our hope is more than Christ with us here. Pity us if that's all we have. He starts this passage by confronting those in the Corinthian congregation who claimed there was no resurrection from the dead. He says if they are right, Paul's whole ministry has been in vain and that he has been un-representing God. And, he argues, if the dead are not raised, then Christ was not either. And their faith is useless — and those who died in Christ have perished.

In understanding this complicated but important passage, we must remember that the Corinthians were not denying the Resurrection of Jesus; they were denying the resurrection of the body. In the Jewish world, those of Sadducee background denied that there was anything after death (Acts 23:8). These probably had their influence in Corinth. But there were also Greeks in the congregation, and they see things quite differently.

Paul presents his argument in difficult to understand logic and we could wish he had written it more simply. These words are often spoken grave side and are rarely, I think, understood.

The Gospel   Luke 6:17-26   *Jesus Teaches And Heals*

This is Luke's Sermon on the Plain, similar to Matthew's Sermon on the Mount (Matthew 5-6). It is a collection of radical sayings which certainly are revolutionary. They turn the world's values upside down! Verse 24 seems to be the key. The words "already received" actually mean the final payment on a debt. That's all the rich will receive — just what the world values. However those who put their energies on loyalty to God and the Christ will have much more, if not here — then at least in eternity.

F. R. Maltby said, "Jesus promised his disciples these things — that they would be completely fearless, absurdly happy, and in constant trouble." Jesus teaches here that the joy of heaven will amply compensate for all the heartache we experience here on earth.

So, I guess we can be happy in the world's way for a brief time or happy in Christ's way right on into eternity.

Preaching Possibilities

Each of the three readings have individual possibilities. The only way I know to use all three would be to preach on something like: "Life's lessons for this week."

A. Jeremiah
   1. We can choose for the world or for God.
   2. Our natural inclination is to choose for the world.
   3. We have a promised life beyond the grave, says Saint Paul.
      Jesus taught the disciples life here would not be easy and it would not at all mesh with the world's values. But there would be joy.

B. Another possibility would be to ask the question, "Can we trust our heart for our choices?" Then use the Old Testament Jeremiah passage verses 9 and 10. We could confront the sentimental ideas we find in our culture, especially in our music, just to follow one's heart.
   1. Our very nature is to trust the world instead of God.
   2. Our heart's desires are often not what we really need as Christian disciples.
   3. Only God knows all our secret thoughts, and on that our judgment is based.

C. Alone, the passage by Saint Paul is an opportunity to preach about life after death and what we Christians believe.
   1. Our hope is not immortality but rather it is resurrection of the body.
   2. Our rewards may not be here on earth, but rather, in eternal life.
   3. Our hope is bigger than a good life here on earth — we have rather, a hope for eternity.

Possible Outline Of Sermon Moves

Title: "Discipleship as Radical Revolution"

A. Begin by explaining how both Matthew and Luke include a revolutionary sermon of Jesus to his disciples right after he has enlisted them in his ministry.

B. List what is so radical that Jesus tells them on the plain in Luke's account.
   1. The poor, not the wealthy, are blessed with the kingdom.
   2. Those who are ridiculed for their faith in Jesus will be rewarded in heaven.
   3. Those sad will receive joy.
   4. Those hungry will have plenty to eat.
   5. And the rich, full and happy, will be poor, empty, and mourning in the kingdom.
      The kingdom Jesus came to usher in radically changes the fate of all. It's revolutionary and astounding.

C. Move to a story from those in Possible Metaphors And Stories below.

D. Move to your witness as to how these radical ideas about God's kingdom affect your own discipleship.

E. List what you believe your congregation ought be doing to help Jesus usher in the kingdom.
   1. Develop a ministry to the poor in our community.
   2. Develop concern for the hungry in our community.
   3. Do much more teaching in the congregation about how radical discipleship really is.
   4. Be sure we have a solid intentional ministry of comfort for people who hurt — in the congregation and also in the community.
   5. Talk much more often and frankly about our financial stewardship.

F. Frame your sermon by returning to your opening comments about sermons of Jesus right after recruiting his disciples.

Prayer For The Day

Help us too, O God, who have been called to be your disciples here in (*name community*) to understand and carry out the radical nature of our discipleship. And bless us with the desire and wisdom to carry out a compassionate ministry to the poor, the hungry, and those who are hurting. They seem to be so special to you. In Christ's name. Amen.

Possible Metaphors And Stories

Mother Teresa of India said, "Unless life is lived for others, it is not worthwhile." That is the call of Jesus to live as his disciples and give our lives away for others.

Seminary Chaplain Ben Borson said: "When you invite Jesus into your heart, he does not come in alone." Put that with Marriott Hotel's claim, "Service, the ultimate luxury," and you have the life of a disciple.

I saw an ad for a brake and muffler shop that read: "We stand behind our exhaust systems and in front of our brake systems." Just like that, people must read our lives of discipleship as having integrity. The Native American calls it "walking the walk and talking the talk."

Alan Alda, in an interview about making movies, said that those now ages thirteen to 21 want three things: "Defy authority, destroy property, and take off clothes." How can God's people reach such an audience and how might we change their orientation toward a constructive lifestyle?

Seventh Sunday After The Epiphany
Seventh Sunday In Ordinary Time

Revised Common	**Genesis 45:3-11, 15**	**1 Corinthians 15:35-38, 42-50**	**Luke 6:27-38**
Roman Catholic	**1 Samuel 26:2, 7-9, 12-13, 22-23**	**1 Corinthians 15:45-49**	**Luke 6:27-38**
Episcopal	**Genesis 45:3-11, 21-28**	**1 Corinthians 15:35-38, 42-50**	**Luke 6:27-38**

Seasonal Theme   Jesus calling his disciples and it dawning on them who this person is they are following. Light for a dark world.

Theme For The Day   Having a radical, undeserved, God's love for the unlovely and living out the golden rule.

Old Testament Lesson   Genesis 45:3-11, 15   *The Reconciliation Of Brothers With Joseph*

One of the main elements I see in this passage of Joseph reconciling with his brothers is the way Joseph could see God's hand in his brothers selling him into Egypt (vv. 8, 9). The truth here is that spiritual persons, who can see God at work in all that takes place, are able to forgive and reconcile with those who have mistreated them.

So Joseph, now steward of the king, instructs his brothers to go back and bring father Jacob and all their families and move into Goshen, which was a fertile portion of the Nile area where they could well survive the five more years of drought.

The brothers, after many tears and conversations were now reconciled, jealousy no longer present, because Joseph was able to see God at work for their good in all that had happened to them. (The remnant was kept intact.)

New Testament Lesson   1 Corinthians 15:35-38, 42-50   *More Resurrection*

This follows on the heels of last week's reading on the same subject: the resurrection of the dead. Paul is addressing a very difficult subject by using human metaphors, ideas, and words. These are matters of faith, so we must refrain from literal interpretation when he is trying to express the unexplainable. Paul must have had the question from his Corinthian congregation asking what the body in our resurrection of the body was like. He answers using several analogies:

1. It will be a spiritual body not like our physical body.
2. It means like a seed planted, the old must die before the new body is present. (Paul's biology is faulty here; but it's a good metaphor for new life at our Easter.)
3. Creation has many kinds of bodies (v. 39). So we will be given a glorified body fitting for us at that time.

Then come the two examples of physical and spiritual bodies:

1. Adam, created by God from the dust of the earth,
2. And Jesus, from heaven.

We are both: while on earth, Adam, then into heaven as spiritual body. Only in Jesus do we inherit eternal life (v. 50).

Perhaps Paul should have said more simply that we don't know what this resurrected body of ours will be like, but we do know Jesus promised to bring us there to a place prepared for us (John 14:3).

The Gospel Luke 6:27-38 *Love For Enemies*

Following last week's reading, we continue Luke's Sermon on the Plain. It is comparable to Matthew's Sermon on the Mount in Matthew 5 and 6. Each of the teachings in this collection of the themes Jesus taught his disciples is a bomb shell. They illustrate to us just how radical and different Christian discipleship is compared with the conventional wisdom of the world.

The love we are to have for our enemies is a love we determine we will have for them. It's not of the heart, but of our will. Only by God's grace can we have this agape love of God for an enemy.

And notice this, our Christian ethic is not made up of all the things we don't do, but rather it is made up of the things we do:

1. Love your enemies;
2. Do good to those who hate you;
3. Bless those who curse you;
4. Pray for those who abuse you;
5. Turn the other cheek;
6. Share with those who ask; and
7. Do to others what you would like them to do to you.

Then Jesus makes the point painful to me. He really is saying it's not a big deal to love the lovely and deserving, but we are to love those who don't deserve it and will never even appreciate it! The reward probably will not be ours here but on into eternity.

Verses 35 and 36 urge us to be merciful and love like this, just like God does. Wow! It's very wildly radical stuff in this Sermon on the Plain. And, I must add, this is only possible in our human circumstances with a large portion of help from God's Holy Spirit.

Preaching Possibilities

Both the New Testament and Gospel texts are continuations from last week's readings and would lend themselves to a part 2 sermon continuing from last week.

A. New Testament Reading — Life after our death, part 2.

B. The Gospel — Sermon on the Plain, ethics for Christians, part 2.

C. Also, the Old Testament Reading can stand alone. We can talk about Joseph seeing the horrible things which happened to him, even by his brothers, as God's will in caring for him and his family. Be sure to make the distinction between God causing something bad to happen to us and God taking something bad which happened to us and bringing some good out of it.

D. I think one could also begin with Jesus' radical teachings of ethics for disciples and illustrating that kind of love with the Old Testament Reading of Joseph reconciling with his brothers who had sold him into Egypt. I'll go there.

Possible Outline Of Sermon Moves

A. Begin with a story of someone you never liked and how hard it was (is) to love that one. Or if that's too personal for you to use today, use one of the possible metaphors below.

B. Move to the story of Joseph and how he was able to love his brothers who had sold him into slavery.

C. Move to what Jesus taught the disciples in the Sermon on the Plain about radical love. List some things about this kind of love.

1. It is a positive ethic of what we are to do rather than what we are not to do.
2. It is not the world's way of getting even, getting revenge, and getting what's yours and what's coming to you.
3. This is God's love we have for the other and only possible with help through God's spirit.

D. Move to Jesus' clincher on this idea in verse 32. Anyone can love the lovely — we are much more radical than that!

E. Point to two verses which sum up the teaching today: Verse 31 — the golden rule in positive form. Verse 36 — be merciful, with God as our example.

F. Frame your sermon by returning to your opening story and tell how you will, in light of this sermon, try harder to have love for this person obnoxious to you.

Prayer For The Day

Help us to have your love for those who are so unlovely to us, O God, and help us also to have the kind of mercy on others which God has for us. Being a faithful disciple in our culture isn't easy. We need your help because you have called us, too, like James and John, Mary Magdalene and Priscilla. Make of us a congregation of radical love for others. In Christ's name. Amen.

Possible Metaphors And Stories

In the movie *Dead Man Walking,* Sister Helen loved the condemned regardless of his crime of rape and murder. She walked with him down the aisle to the chamber for injection to kill him. Others just couldn't understand a love like that. Wow! A powerful testimony to God's unconditional love for all sinners and how we must represent that radical love in our world and ministry.

"He likes me," little Elizabeth said after I put my hands on her head and blessed her at the communion rail while giving her parents Holy Communion.
The meal acts that out — God likes us ... and more.

I was very moved to see on the news Reginald Denny hug the mothers of the two men who had beaten him nearly to death during the Los Angeles riots.
We rarely live out our conviction that, because God radically forgave and loved us, we are to do the same toward each other.

The news was very moving. It pictured the families of the boys who had beaten a baby nearly to death and the parents of the baby, brought together by a black pastor. They hugged, cried, and prayed together. One family was African-American, the other Mexican-American. There is a way for all to be one family in Christ and to give forgiveness even to those who most hurt you.

Eighth Sunday After The Epiphany
Eighth Sunday In Ordinary Time

Revised Common	Isaiah 55:10-13	1 Corinthians 15:51-58	Luke 6:39-49
Roman Catholic	Sirach 27:4-7	1 Corinthians 15:54-58	Luke 6:39-45
Episcopal	Jeremiah 7:1-7 (8-15)	1 Corinthians 15:50-58	Luke 6:39-49

Seasonal Theme Jesus calling his disciples and it dawning on them who this person is they are following. Light in a dark world.

Theme For The Day Building our lives on Jesus' teachings and keeping our heart pure so as to produce good words and deeds.

Old Testament Lesson Isaiah 55:10-13 *Glad Times Are Coming*

A beautiful bit of poetry, metaphor, and personifications! Isaiah claims that God's word is like the rain and snow which comes down from heaven and waters the earth. This brings forth vegetation which blesses the people with food. So God's word will not be fruitless. It will produce the spiritual life accomplishing God's purpose.

Then in verses 12 and 13 we are promised God's joy and peace because the effects of sin have been reversed. What a nice piece of personification: the mountains will sing and the trees applaud. And thorns representing the effects of evil will be replaced with cypress and the brier with myrtle.

And all this will be our sign. The fertility of the earth will remind us again God is in control. Some would claim 13a symbolizes what God can do in our hearts in salvation. I'll not go there.

New Testament Lesson 1 Corinthians 15:51-58 *Life After Death Continued*

Verse 56 is the focus of this reading which is a continuation of the last two week's readings from Paul's letter to the Corinthian congregation, teaching them about resurrection and life beyond the grave. Today's portion is a summary of what Paul has been telling them about the coming day!

Both the dead and living will be changed (1 Thessalonians 4:13-18). Concerning the secondary trumpet, see Isaiah 27:13. Let's not confuse the translation "immortality" in verse 53 with the Greek idea of the immortality of the soul. Paul's teaching opposed this idea and championed instead the concept of resurrection of the body.

Paul sees Christ's victory is over sin which seeks to destroy humans — the law increases its power rather than correcting it. See Romans 7:7-25.

Notice in verse 58 Paul does not subscribe to a quietist monastic lifestyle because we have the promise of life beyond the grave; but, rather a lifestyle excelling in the work of the Lord.

The Gospel Luke 6:39-49 *The Blind Leading The Blind And A Tree And Its Fruit*

We have in this reading a collection of wise sayings Luke put together for the disciple's instruction. Let's look at them separately.

Verses 39-40. It's claimed that we cannot teach what we do not know. A teacher can rarely take his students beyond what he/she knows. This is probably true, but I will challenge this one day when I see Jesus face to face. I have often had students who soon knew more than I did about a topic in which I was leading them. Never mind! The truth is, the best teachers try to equip their students the best they can in their subject.

Verses 41, 42. Some humor by Jesus here. The truth is we ought not to be critical of others unless we are absent of these faults. This means we really ought not to be judgmental of others because we are very imperfect.

Verses 43, 44. The only way we can be judged is by our own deeds. Preaching, after all, is the Gospel through our personality. The best witness for our faith is the way we live it out.

Verse 45 reminds us that what we say is influenced most by our heart. Our speech often reveals our heart.

Verses 47-49. This is another metaphor and parable by Jesus. It is in Matthew 7:24-27. It really tells me that often the easy way is not the best in the long run. But his parable basically is about constructing the best foundation for our lives. It would make much sense in Palestine where rivers dry up in the summer; but, in winter after the September rains come, what had looked like a dry place is now a torrent of rushing water.

Barclay in writing about this parable says: "Happy is the person who sees things, not in the light of the moment, but in the light of eternity." If we base our lives on the foundation of Jesus' teaching, we will make it through the most severe storms.

In my book on *The Parables Of Jesus And Their Flip Side* (CSS Publishing Company, 2001) I say that the flip side here is that we must teach (and learn) how to rebuild after the certain floods do come.

Preaching Possibilities

A. The Old Testament Reading will stand alone and begs for interpretation and preaching. There is an opportunity to address:
   1. Peace and joy as promised by Isaiah.
   2. Nature's witness to God's faithfulness.
   3. God's word is like the blessings of rain.
   4. The fertile earth is a sign of God's presence.
   5. A world where sin is defeated.

   Of course, the idea here of God's word producing fruit like the rain will connect with the Gospel parable of building a life on Jesus' teachings as the foundation.

B. The New Testament Reading from 1 Corinthians is a good summary of Paul's theology about life beyond the grave. If we have not yet addressed that subject, I'm sure Paul would want us to do so today. This is a summary of the last two Sundays' teachings and will be of great interest to our listeners. At best we must present these teachings as human's best guess and what we really don't know for certain.

   These things Paul says today. At our deaths we:
   1. Have the resurrection of our changed body.
   2. Have the defeat of sin and the victory of Jesus.
   3. So we ought to live differently here in the meantime busy in the Lord's work.

Possible Outline Of Sermon Moves

Title: These Things Jesus Teaches Us About Living Life

A. Begin by telling of someone in your life who gave you so much good advice for your life.
B. Move to Jesus teaching the disciples on the plain about the life of disciples. These things he said:
   1. We rarely can teach what we don't know (see illustration 1 below in Possible Metaphors And Stories).
   2. We really ought not to be critical of others.
   3. Our deeds are that on which we are judged.
   4. Our relaxed speech often reveals our heart.
   5. We should build our lives on the strong foundation of Jesus' teachings.
      Notice that these above moves correspond to the comments on the Gospel passage above.
C. Move to our responsibility to minister to each other when:
   1. We have built our lives on the "world's wisdom" and it brought disaster to us. How do we start over and rebuild?
   2. Our hearts have produced words which reveal evil in our hearts, like envy, revenge, greed, and racial hatred.

3. Our deeds are not what they should have been and now we are reaping that harvest.
4. We are critical of everyone else but not seeing our own faults and thus friendless.
5. We have remained "spiritual runts" refusing to grow in grace and God's presence in our lives.
D. Close with an illustration from below.

Prayer For The Day

Teach us how to rebuild after the floods in our lives, O God, and to make it on more sound foundations. Help us to have cleaner hearts which will produce better speech and deeds in our discipleship. And we pray for the motivation to match our beliefs with our actions, especially all week outside this church building. We pray in Jesus' name, who is the solid dependable foundation. Amen.

Possible Metaphors And Stories

On all airlines instructions at the beginning of a flight, the attendant says, "In case of a loss of oxygen in the cabin, masks will drop down in front of you. Put your mask on first before helping an infant who needs help next to you." So with our spiritual lives, we must get ours in shape first, then we can help others with theirs.

I saw a very heavy trailer of a tractor-trailer combination, without the tractor, parked on an asphalt parking lot. The front support wheels were sinking deeper and deeper into the asphalt and may have already gone all the way through. The driver of the trailer probably thought it a solid foundation on which to park the trailer — but not so. Check your foundation. "On Christ the solid rock I stand; all other ground is sinking sand."

While in Amsterdam, I noticed how crooked many of the houses (especially around canals) are. They are braced with large logs up the front of the building. God's presence can support us and we ought to support each other.

On a US Air flight from Johnstown to Pittsburgh on a small commuter plane, I noticed through the open door to the cockpit that both pilot and copilot put their hands on the throttle as they took off. God would put a hand on ours as we fly together through dangers and easy times.

In Shakespeare's *Measure for Measure* we read the words, "Ask your heart what it doth know." And in Hamlet, "Are you like the painting of a sorrow, a face without a heart?"

The Transfiguration Of Our Lord
Last Sunday After The Epiphany

Revised Common	**Exodus 34:29-35**	**2 Corinthians 3:12—4:2**	**Luke 9:28-36 (37-43)**
Roman Catholic	**Daniel 7:9-10**	**2 Peter 1:16-19**	**Luke 9:28-36**
Episcopal	**Exodus 34:29-35**	**1 Corinthians 12:27—13:13**	**Luke 9:28-36**

Seasonal Theme   Jesus calling his disciples and it dawning on them who this person is they are following. Light for a dark world.

Theme For The Day   The Transfiguration of Jesus and our response to the near presence of God in our own lives.

Old Testament Lesson   Exodus 34:29-35   *The Shining Face Of Moses*

In keeping with this day of Transfiguration, we have the Old Testament Lesson about Moses coming down from Mount Sinai after spending forty days there in God's presence receiving the Ten Commandments. His face shone with God's glory (2 Corinthians 3:7). Still, he doesn't seem to know it! The folks were justifiably afraid, so Moses put a veil over his face and told them the terms of the restored covenant. This shining face of Moses will connect with the transfigured face of Jesus in the Gospel and with Saint Paul's description of this event in the Second Reading.

New Testament Lesson   2 Corinthians 3:12—4:2   *Our Transfiguration*

Paul uses the veil Moses put over his face because he had been in the presence of God. The glow becomes a metaphor to make his point. He says Moses put on that veil when he had finished speaking to hide the fact the glory, which used to be there, was fading. This is the Old Covenant: the old relationship between God and God's people was fast fading. The truth that came to the people by Moses was just a small part — what came through Jesus to them was complete and final.

Then Paul returns to the veil again. He claims that when the Jews hear the Old Testament, they have a veil over their eyes (v. 15) and fail to see the full meaning of it. This is rich, because we can ask: What is it that veils our hearing of the scripture?

But all of us see the glory of Jesus with no veil upon our faces — so we too are changed, knowing God's glory (v. 18). It will preach; but we must present it much more simply than Paul does as he seems to get tangled up in his metaphors, which is not all that unusual for his writing or our translating.

The Gospel   Luke 9:28-36 (37-43)   *The Transfiguration*

Something great happened and we just can't explain it all. There is no doubt this was one of several great events in Jesus' earthly life and ministry. He received at least God's affirmation to go on and head toward the cross and Jerusalem.

Of course Moses was the one who gave the people of Israel God's law and Elijah was perhaps the greatest of all the prophets. So we have a symbolic telling of Jesus to go on by the two greatest Old Testament heroes.

Verse 32 is interesting in that they saw Jesus' glory because they stayed awake! Homiletically we could ask: What puts us to sleep and thus causes us to miss so much? And then, what in life awakens us to see these things we otherwise would miss? This would probably work better at a later morning worship service than the earlier one when many are not yet fully awake!

Of course Peter wanting to stay and build a shrine (v. 33) is pregnant with possibilities. There are various responses to God's very near presence here. Peter wants to build a shrine and stay; the disciples wanted to get some sleep; and Jesus wants to go down the mountain and heal a boy who needed his help.

(Optional verses 37-43) There is demonstrated something of the rhythm of the disciples' Christian life: upon the mountain in the near presence of God and then into the valley to serve those in need in the world. Both are necessary for our spiritual well-being: retreat to God and advance into the world of Christian service.

One other thing I often wonder about. How much did Jesus' (or even Moses') appearance change and how much was it these people seeing them in a whole new light? Perhaps, after all, it was the disciples who were most transfigured!

Preaching Possibilities

A. The Old Testament story of Moses having a shining face after being in the direct presence of God and the Gospel's account of Jesus' face shining have to go together. And Paul's recounting of the Old Testament Moses story is just right to include as well. So I'll use all three in my outline of possible sermon moves.

B. Remember this is the climax of the Epiphany season when it began to dawn on people who this Jesus was they were following. It began with Jesus' baptism by his cousin John in the Jordan and ended with this nearness of Elijah and Moses up on the mountain. You may want to do a brief review of the themes or events you have preached on this season of Epiphany as you begin your sermon today, reminding your people of the "Epiphany" or dawning on people who Jesus was.

C. The Gospel will stand alone especially including the optional verses 37-43 and contrasting the spiritual life of nearness of God on retreat and the nearness of God to others as we take it into the world of the struggling and suffering.

D. Another way to organize would be to start with Paul's comment about a veil and then go to the Old Testament story of Moses and his veil. Then one can address: 1) What do we do when the old glory begins to fade? 2) What veils hide God's presence from us?

E. If it all seems like too much to try to cover in one day and in one sermon, you might try preaching a two-part sermon. One part at each of the two worship services (if you have two!).

Possible Outline Of Sermon Moves

A. Begin by telling in your own words that wonderful story of Moses coming out of the presence of God and even needing a veil.

B. Move to explaining how Paul used this metaphor of the veil.

C. Move to another time one in God's presence began to glow with God's glory. Read it from Luke (vv. 28-32). Now tell how you have questions you will ask about this experience when you arrive in heaven.

1. What is the best thing to do when we sense, like Moses, we are losing the old glory?
2. What things serve as veils for us and thus prevent us from seeing or having God's glory?
3. Who really changed that day upon the mountain of transfiguration? Jesus' appearance or the disciples' perception of him?
4. And can we also change in our appearance if we go into the near presence of God?
5. What is the correct response to such a religious experience? Stay there with Peter or go down the mountain with Jesus?

D. Move to what you think this transfiguration says to our congregational ministry.

1. We need to program spiritual retreats for closeness to God.
2. We need often to see Jesus in a whole new light like Peter, James, and John.
3. We need an active social ministry always connected with our spiritual experiences.
4. We all must ask what most in us needs transfigured. Our lack of compassion? Our failure to love the unlovely? Our unwillingness to witness to our faith? Or our poor practice of stewardship as one of God's most blessed with abundance?

E. Frame your sermon by returning to your opening words about Jesus' transfiguration, then Paul's interpretation, and then finish with Moses coming off the mountain.

Prayer For The Day

Help us to see Jesus in all his glory today and respond to that spiritual experience by going down into our community to serve and bring God's glory there to those who rarely see it. Change us, O God, and make us glow with your love for others and our love for you. And please remove the veils, which prevent us from realizing your glory and sharing it with others still without it. In Christ's name. Amen.

Possible Metaphors And Stories

The dictionary defines *transfiguration* as "change the form or appearance of" and also the word, *glorify*.

There is a town in Iowa named Correctionville. The surveyor has to make an adjustment every so often, because the earth is round. It needs to be about the width of a lot and half. State Route 32 follows this jog. Correctionville, Iowa's motto is: "Come jog down our street."

We need to make corrections in our straight lines and allow for adjustments in other lines also.

I was getting gas at a busy intersection in Des Moines (Harding and Hickman) when a brand-new red fire engine came up the street, siren blaring. An older woman did not hear the siren and pulled out in front of the engine. Its driver put on its brakes, burned rubber, and stopped. The sudden braking killed the engine and now it would not start. Finally some of us from the filling station pushed it over to the side. The battery was worn down trying to restart the motor. Meanwhile the lady in the Chevy went on down the street unaware.

We can have the finest equipment, but to no avail if we don't keep the battery charged. So too our spiritual lives ... and what havoc we wreak in the lives of others without ever even knowing it.

I saw the movie *Awakenings*. The setting is a hospital in the Bronx. A Dr. Sayers used an experiment in drug therapy with these people who seemed alive inside but in a trance outside. These patients had awakenings which let them come back for a while.

Can we bring awakenings in our spiritual lives gone dead on the outside? Memories of first communion, confirmation, youth groups, and so forth, that awaken in us the near presence of God.

Introduction To The Lenten Season

The forty days of Lent, corresponding to the forty days Jesus was tempted in the wilderness, make up the church's major time of penance and focus on Jesus' life and passion. In some churches, flowers are omitted from the altar, no weddings are performed, the vestments go from white to black or purple, the Hallelujah is not sung, and midweek worship is scheduled. All this is to reflect the seriousness of the season as the Gospel Readings point Jesus toward Jerusalem and the cross. Some congregations put away the Hallelujah banner in front of the congregation, not to be rediscovered until the Easter vigil on Easter morning.

A few Christians still use these days of Lent for fasting or giving up something. More emphasize doing something extra for the church.

The Gospels are from Mark and John and relate the physical journey toward Jerusalem and Holy week.

Midweek services are a good opportunity to preach a series on the Old Testament Lessons or the New Testament Readings.

Heads Up Notice

During this season of Lent we may have the opportunity to preach a series of five sermons for midweek services. The following are suggested themes from the Old Testament Lessons and from the New Testament Readings in Cycle C.

Old Testament Lessons	*A Season Of Promises*
Lent 1 Deuteronomy 26:1-11	A promise of first fruits
Lent 2 Genesis 15:1-12, 17-18	A promise of land
Lent 3 Isaiah 55:1-9	A promise of abundance
Lent 4 Joshua 5:9-12	A promise of Passover
Lent 5 Isaiah 43:16-21	A promise of something new

New Testament Readings	*Paul's Lenten Promises*
Lent 1 Romans 10:8b-13	Salvation is for all
Lent 2 Philippians 3:17—4:1	We have citizenship in heaven
Lent 3 1 Corinthians 10:1-13	We have a way out in times of testing
Lent 4 2 Corinthians 5:16-21	We can become a new creation
Lent 5 Philippians 3:4b-14	We have a righteousness from God

Another possibility for this Lenten season is to use the Old Testament Lesson and New Testament Reading together under the general theme of "Lenten Promises." An example would be for the Second Sunday in Lent: "A Promise of Land and Citizenship."

An Invitation To The Season Of Lent (In your bulletin)

The forty days leading up to Easter are called Lent in the church year. The name comes from the fact that the season is when the days are getting longer, so to lengthen = Lent. Sundays are not counted in the forty days, as they are always considered "little Easter." Beginning with Ash Wednesday and corresponding to Jesus' forty days in the wilderness, Lent is a time of penance, solemnity, and loyalty to the Christ and his church.

I found some practices meaningful for the congregation to emphasize this season, such as:
1. wearing a black robe rather than the white;
2. omitting flowers from the altar;

3. hiding the Hallelujah banner before Ash Wednesday and not using the word *Hallelujah* in the liturgy and hymnody until Easter;
4. bringing out the Hallelujah banner on the first service of Easter;
5. asking for a special daily sacrificial offering for all the forty days;
6. covering the altar and processional cross with a black veil; and
7. placing in the chancel a cross made from the trunk of the Christmas tree.

Ash Wednesday

Revised Common	Joel 2:1-2, 12-17	2 Corinthians 5:20b—6:10	Matthew 6:1-6, 16-21
Roman Catholic	Joel 2:12-18	2 Corinthians 5:20—6:2	Matthew 6:1-6, 16-18
Episcopal	Joel 2:1-2, 12-17	2 Corinthians 5:20b—6:10	Matthew 6:1-6, 16-21

Seasonal Theme Jesus and his disciples move toward Jerusalem and the cross.

Theme For The Day A call for repentance and returning to God who gives us free, undeserved forgiveness, which should bring forth in us humility and servanthood.

Old Testament Lesson Joel 2:1-2, 12-17 *A Call For Repentance*

Pethuel's son, the prophet Joel, whose name means "The Lord is God," laments over the ruin of his country by a severe plague of locusts that destroyed the crops on which they were all dependent. Joel thought that the plague was God's punishment on Israel. He believes that judgment and their repentance had to happen before a new day of blessing could come upon the land. So Joel calls for repentance and prayer by the people. Thus he calls for a "... solemn assembly" (v. 14). According to the introduction in the *New Revised Standard Version*, "Joel sees in the massive locust plague and severe drought devastating Judah, a harbinger of 'the great and terrible day of the Lord' " (2:31).

As we know, "the day of the Lord" in the Old Testament may mean an eschatological battle or some historical event which brings in the new age. However, for Ash Wednesday it's probably wise not to get tangled up in "last things" but rather to talk about the need for repentance and a solemn assembly of prayer.

New Testament Lesson 2 Corinthians 5:20b—6:10 *God's Righteousness*

I do not like the way this passage begins with the second half of verse 20. That first part is so very preachable! Paul reminds the Corinthians that we are Christ's ambassadors and that God works through him *and us*. Wow!

These two thoughts about Paul and the Christian are rich: "Ambassadors for Christ" in verse 20 and "... servants of God" in verse 6:4. And then this description of us in verse 10, which says, "... as having nothing, and yet possessing everything." This "preaches" in many of the places I have preached in the third world, like Suriname, Sumatra, Brazil, Uruguay, Liberia, and mainland China.

I believe the basic theology in this reading is in verse 21, which gives us our doctrine: sinless Jesus took on our sins in order that we might have God's righteousness.

Then there is the teaching of verse 6:1, which admonishes us not to accept this gift of God, called grace, in vain. Many have called this idea, "cheap grace."

The Gospel Matthew 6:1-6, 16-21 *Humble Religious Practices*

The Old Testament Lesson and this Gospel seem to contradict each other. While Joel calls for a public show of repentance, Matthew quotes Jesus telling the disciples in the Sermon on the Mount that their religious practices should be private and not for show in any way.

Give your offerings secretly.

Pray in private.

Don't show off your fasting.

Then comes the seemingly unconnected advice concerning our treasures in verses 19-21. And, of course the stories of people trying to store up their treasure here are numerous. Verse 21 is so profound and, especially for us wealthy Americans, it cries out to be preached by itself and with Spirit power.

Preaching Possibilities

A. If it were not for Ash Wednesday, we could use any of the readings by themselves.

B. Or we could even use one verse from any of the three readings. For instance:
   1. Joel 1:14 — Our need for this service of repentance
   2. 2 Corinthians 5:21 — We have the righteousness of God
   3. Matthew 6:21 — Locating our treasure

C. If we went with just the New Testament Reading, we could outline this way:
   1. We are ambassadors for Christ (v. 20).
   2. We have God's righteousness (v. 21).
   3. We are servants of God (v. 4).
   4. Though sorrowful, we can rejoice (v. 10).

D. After saying the above three possibilities in more liturgical churches where the imposition of ashes is practiced at this service, I still like to use the general message from all three readings as outlined below.

Possible Outline Of Sermon Moves

A. Begin with a prayer for this service to be meaningful to all who have come, that true repentance might be expressed.

B. Tell how the prophet Joel called for a service when the people repented of their many sins.

C. Move to list some reasons why we as a people ought to call such an assembly also: as a congregation, we have not lived out our discipleship as Jesus taught, to love each other and the unlovely, to go the extra mile, to pray for our enemies, to witness to our faith, to tithe and practice giving first fruits.
   *Move to pray a prayer of confession asking for forgiveness for the above shortcomings.

D. Move to the reminder of the words used during the imposition of ashes: "Remember you are dust and to dust you shall return." Remind your hearers that the shortness of life ought to make life here and now more rich and meaningful.
   *Move to a prayer of asking God to keep us mindful of how uncertain life is and how temporary this existence on earth is. And that we might live life to the fullest now.

E. Move to verse 21 in the New Testament Reading. This is what the symbol of the cross of ashes on our forehead means. We have forgiveness because of what Christ did on the cross.
   *Move to a prayer of thankfulness for the undeserved forgiveness God gives us who are repentant this night.

F. Move to the advice of the Gospel not to make our religious practices a matter of showing off. So while we are signed with the cross of ashes, let us not depart with pride. Rather, let us humbly go to serve.
   *Move to a prayer asking God to show us the way of humility and servanthood in response to all the marvelous good news of forgiveness we have tonight. Frame the prayerful sermon by reading Matthew 6:1; 2 Corinthians 5:21; and then Joel 2:14.

Prayer For The Day

Accept our attempt to admit our many sins tonight to remind each other of the shortness and uncertainty of life here. Help us always to rejoice in your loving forgiveness from the cross through your Son, Jesus the Christ. And teach us, during this season of Lent, humility and servanthood. In Christ's name. Amen.

Possible Metaphors And Stories

The saintly old Andrew Hsiao, many years president of the Lutheran Theological Seminary in Hong Kong, where I teach, told of his return to mainland China in 1979 to the little town where he grew up. He secretly took private communion to the ninety-year-old widow of the former pastor. She had no Bible, hymnal, or chance to worship all those years; but long ago she had memorized the psalms and could still recite them. And, like many Chinese, she could still pray. She insisted on receiving the sacrament on her knees. As he was giving her the bread, they heard someone coming up the stairs. Terror struck their hearts for fear they had been discovered. Then a seventy-year-old woman appeared, who wanted communion also. She was the little girl Andrew's father had baptized sixty years before! Andrew said the widow prayed a prayer of thanksgiving like he had never heard before or since. They cried tears of joy and real presence.

The headline in the *Contra Costa Times*, November 16, 1997, read, "Family Of Slain Palestinian Boy Donates Organs." An Associated Press story out of Jerusalem said that a nine-year-old Palestinian boy had died four days after an Israeli soldier shot him with a rubber-coated bullet. In a gesture of reconciliation, his family donated their son's organs to needy people regardless of whether they were Israeli or Palestinian.

In a four-hour procedure, the child's heart, liver, kidneys, and lungs were removed and sent to a hospital outside Tel Aviv. "Authorities were preparing to quell unrest after today's funeral."

The shooting came after a group of boys threw stones at soldiers near the Jewish enclave of Rachel's Tomb on the outskirts of Bethlehem. Those parents taught many a lesson about reconciliation.

On this beautiful sun-shining spring morning a bird flew into the kitchen window with a dramatic thud. The bird dropped to the ground stunned. After a while it regained its composure and flew away. Sudden trauma comes in the middle of such nice times and God helps us recover and go on.

In *The Covenant Book of Worship* published by Covenant Press in 1981 (p. 11): "The rhythm which emerges in biblical worship moves between memory and anticipation. Its integrity lies in its backward look of faith, its forward gaze of hope, and its present response of love."

Now that's worship.

---

*These short prayers may be offered by someone else other than the preacher. This will bring more emphasis on prayer and also provide a variety in sound of voice.

First Sunday In Lent

Revised Common	Deuteronomy 26:1-11	Romans 10:8b-13	Luke 4:1-13
Roman Catholic	Deuteronomy 26:4-10	Romans 10:8-13	Luke 4:1-13
Episcopal	Deuteronomy 26:(1-4) 5-11	Romans 10:(5-8a) 8b-13	Luke 4:1-13

Seasonal Theme   Jesus and his disciples move toward Jerusalem and the cross.

Theme For The Day   This first Sunday in Lent we look at Jesus' temptations, and ours, and call for a devout observance of this special season of the year.

Old Testament Lesson   Deuteronomy 26:1-11   *First Fruits And Tithes*

These are two liturgical practices recommended in this passage for those who finally got to their promised land. The first was the "first fruits" when they were to bring the first produce of their harvest (Leviticus 23:9-14) to the priest in the temple. In this fashion each one in the nation could come before God and state their faith in God.

The second liturgical practice was a more elaborate statement of God's faithfulness (vv. 5-10a). This prescribed confession emphasized God's faithfulness and the wonderful way God cared for Israel. The wandering "Armean" in verse 5 was Jacob. God heard the cry of his oppressed people and brought them out of Egypt. So this confession emphasizes God's marvelous involvement in every turn of their history. As a proper response, the people tithe, offer the first fruits, and confess the wondrous ways their God cared for them and brought them to this land of "milk and honey."

New Testament Lesson   Romans 10:8b-13   *First Christian Creed*

First we have attention to the response of the heart and an inward certainty that God did save us through the Christ. Then verses 9 and 10 issues in the confidence of the Lordship of the Christ. It is only after this we can move toward right living.

Verse 11 is a quotation of Isaiah 28:16 and tells us that our faith is founded in God's mercy and is unlimited. Faith makes us equal. Verse 12's use of "Lord" means Christ.

Verse 9 and 10 give us the foundation for the first Christian creed. William Barclay states these three things are necessary: 1) a person must say Jesus Christ is Lord, 2) a person must believe that Jesus is risen from the dead, and 3) a person must not only believe in his/her heart; he/she must confess with his/her lips. "Christianity is belief, plus confession." Now that will preach.

The Gospel   Luke 4:1-13   *The Temptation Of Jesus*

These experiences in the "wilderness" follow right after Jesus' baptism by John in the Jordan. Perhaps they can best be described as Jesus, after becoming convinced at his baptism of who he was and that he had a very special mission and ministry to carry out, now needed to retreat to the wilderness to figure out what that ministry ought to be like.

He was tempted to make it a ministry of political power (v. 6).

He was tempted to make it a ministry of fantastic feats for his own glory (v. 9).

And we must remember these were not just one time temptations. These Jesus faced over and over and over his entire ministry. Notice verse 13, "... until an opportune time."

One more thought. Could it be that this "wilderness" was a nickname for the Qumran community into which John may have been baptizing folks, including his cousin? And that Jesus retreated to Qumran to read the Old Testament scrolls in order to figure out his mission thus being tempted to do these various styles of ministry? A few scholars would say so. I lean that way as well.

Preaching Possibilities

A. I doubt we can get by without preaching on the temptations of Jesus in the wilderness; but, all three readings this First Sunday in Lent are strong and will stand alone. I really like the Deuteronomy possibilities. We can emphasize tithing, first fruit giving, and confessing God's faithfulness. It is a great opportunity to talk about stewardship of 1) our money, 2) our natural resources, and 3) God's love for us.

B. The Second Reading is a chance to talk about creeds: Paul's (v. 9), the church's (apostles), and our own (often more lived out than spoken). Also, this Romans passage is easily organized into a three-point sermon:
   1. Our lips often reveal what we believe in our heart (v. 8b).
   2. It is essential to believe Jesus is Lord and God raised Jesus from the dead (v. 9).
   3. The old distinction between Jew and Greek no longer applies. God saves all who ask (v. 12).

C. We could use all three considering the person writing the message.
   1. Moses lays down some rules to live by when God gives us promised land: tithing, first fruits giving, and confession of God's greatness.
   2. Paul tells us who is saved: those who confess Jesus as Lord and that God raised him from the dead.
   3. Luke wants us to know that even Jesus was tempted — so are we.

Possible Outline Of Sermon Moves

A. Begin by reminding your hearers what happened just before today's gospel story. Jesus was baptized and it became clear to him he had a special ministry to carry out because he was no less than God's own son.

B. Move to today's text stating now that he had his "ordination" into ministry these temptations were part of his figuring out how that ministry should shape itself. There were three shapes it shouldn't take:
   1. Using his divinity as a miracle worker caring most for himself.
   2. Using his divinity for political power and gain.
   3. Using his divinity for spectacular stunts and calling attention to himself.

C. Move to considering the positive forms Jesus' ministry did take on:
   1. A ministry of servanthood and loving the unlovely.
   2. A ministry of modeling how the person of God ought to live here on earth.
   3. A ministry of humility and self-sacrifice for others.
   4. A ministry of following God's will and going to the cross for others' sins.

D. Move to story telling using one of the stories below.

E. Move to your own ideas about what this Gospel says to us about our congregation's activities and observance of Lent this year.
   1. We ought to do a ministry of servanthood in our community. Big Brother, feed the hungry, and so on.
   2. We ought to live differently than the rest of the world, modeling how God wants us to love each other.
   3. At least these forty days of Lent we ought to find a way of sacrifice for church and others.
   4. Our worship ought to be frequent and our devotion intense, admitting our sins and celebrating our cross-provided forgiveness.

F. Move to a kicker telling of the fact even Jesus was tempted! So we can expect temptation, too. And we can expect Jesus to understand when we are tempted and to be willing to help us resist.

G. Frame your sermon in the terms of a new season of the church year called Lent. After his baptism Jesus had his forty days, and now so shall we have ours.

Prayer For The Day

Help us in this holy season of Lent, dear Holy Parent, to resist temptation like Jesus did and to ask for your forgiveness when we don't resist as we should. We would make this holy season one of special devotion and sacrifice. Please show us the way to do it in our busy secular culture in which we now live. In Jesus' name. Amen.

Possible Metaphors And Stories

In the construction of Park Place, a seventeen-story apartment complex, I noticed there was a man standing on the top of the structure relaying the instructions from the ground to the man operating the crane. A pastor sometimes has the awesome responsibility of relaying a person's message to God through prayer and also confession.

At the Jack and Jill supermarket where I asked for a copy of *The National Enquirer*, the woman at the checkout counter said, "Father, you don't want to read that kind of smut!" I wanted the paper to see the account of Roger Williams' wedding in which I had participated. Look at this double standard. We clergy must live up to those high standards but also encourage the laity to do the same.

In order to install cable for television in a trench, the utility company has to come out and mark where electric, gas, and telephone wires are buried. They use little red flags; the trench for the cable can then be dug. As we mature as Christians, we need to mark where the power for our lives is, as well as the dangers.

In the movie *Schindler's List*, Schindler is on the balcony of the home of the commandant of a prison camp where for sport the commandant would shoot prisoners walking in the prison yard. Schindler said to him, "Real power is when you have the power to shoot them if you want to, but you do not." When we have the power to get even and do not is when God's power of love and forgiveness is most real.

Second Sunday In Lent

Revised Common	**Genesis 15:1-12, 17-18**	**Philippians 3:17—4:1**	**Luke 13:31-35**
Roman Catholic	**Genesis 15:5-12, 17-18**	**Philippians 3:17—4:1**	**Luke 9:28-36**
Episcopal	**Genesis 15:1-12, 17-18**	**Philippians 3:17—4:1**	**Luke 13:(22-30) 31-35**

Seasonal Theme   Jesus and his disciples move toward Jerusalem and the cross.

Theme For The Day   The undeserved love of Christ for us and the intention with which he went to the cross for our sins.

Old Testament Lesson   Genesis 15:1-12, 17-18   *God's Covenant With Abram*
The promise of 12:2-3 is confirmed as God forms a covenant with Abram after the blessing from Melchizedek. With the covenant was a warning that there would be many years of enslavement (15:13). Notice that as soon as the Lord promised Abram a reward, Abram mentioned he did not have his own son. And the Lord promised he would have an heir and that his offspring would be as many as the stars of heaven. We read of Abram's faith because it is the basis for making the covenant. To seal the deal Abram cut in half (v. 10) the animals. Egypt like the birds of prey opposed the deal.
In verses 17-21 God reveals God's self in the fire of a torch and even as it passed between the pieces of slaughtered animals. Even the geographical boundaries of the promised land are given in verse 18.

New Testament Lesson   Philippians 3:17—4:1   *Citizenship In Heaven*
Paul steps up his advice to those in the congregation causing a problem and tells them to follow him. Paul calls these trouble makers a sarcastic "enemies of the cross." And they have physical appetites which have become their God.
Then this wonderful thought that our citizenship is in heaven (v. 20). So the goal and guide of our Christian lives is more than time and space. It is from heaven that the Christ comes and transforms us — perhaps Paul's "spiritual body." Paul tells us that the resurrection of Jesus means that we will have a transformation of our bodily existence. See 1 Corinthians 6:13 and 1 Corinthians 6:20.
The metaphor Paul uses for a Christian being an athlete for Christ is meaningful. He says after that Damascus road experience he is forgetting the past, not taking glory in the past, and always looking forward, reaching out for those things ahead. The Greek word is *epekteinomenos* which is the word for a racer stretching forward for the tape. So he is running full speed for the finish line!
Barclay believes Paul is writing against the anti-nomians who denied that there "was any law at all in the Christian life. They declared that they were within the grace of God; therefore, it did not matter what they did. God would forgive." Paul says we must never ease up or relax our standards — but run flat out towards the finish line, until the end.

The Gospel   Luke 13:31-35   *Lament Over Jerusalem*
Not all Pharisees hated Jesus. I wonder if these two who warn Jesus might have been Nicodemus and Joseph of Arimathea.
Jesus calls King Herod a fox. He was not willing to shorten his work even one day to escape from an earthly king. Verse 34 probably tells us that Jesus was often in Jerusalem and had great affection for the city. He had tried to offer his love only to have it spurned. That must have been a continuing bitter disappointment to him. But Jesus still comes to people offering to love them only to have them reject him.
The metaphor in verse 34 of a hen gathering her brood is often pointed to in feminist theology as one of God as female rather than the traditional male image. It's a lovely image, regardless.

Preaching Possibilities

A. The Gospel account of Jesus pressing on into the city of Jerusalem will connect with Paul's claim of an athlete pressing on toward the goal, but it is not a strong connection after those two points.

B. Of course each reading will stand alone, too.

C. The Old Testament and Abram's covenant probably won't work well at this time of Lent unless we would emphasize Abram's covenant and our covenant with God for which Jesus had to go on to the cross.

D. The imagery in Paul's Philippians will preach if we haven't previously used the Christian athlete and race metaphor. One could ask some very pointed questions as moves in the sermon:
   1. What in us could we invite others to imitate?
   2. How are we sometimes enemies of the cross?
   3. What is our God and our glory? And what earthly things do we have our minds set on?
   4. What are the implications for us now because we have our citizenship in heaven?
   5. How might we be Paul's joy and crown, too?

Possible Outline Of Sermon Moves

A. Begin with a story from your own (or someone you know) experience of trying over and over to love someone but always being rejected.

B. Move to Jesus' words about Jerusalem which becomes your text. Read from a visible Bible Luke 13:34.

C. Move to explain about the warning from Pharisees to get out of the neighborhood and how it might have been Joseph of Arimathea and Nicodemus, as they later claimed the body after the crucifixion.

D. Expand this idea of how we all get a chance from time to time to stand up for Jesus when everyone else is taking the opposite view.

E. Move to the intention of Jesus going to a certain death on the cross.

F. Tell a story to illustrate going toward the cross.

G. Move to Jesus loving the people of Jerusalem even if they were going to crucify him. Now apply that same undeserved love toward us when we reject him.

H. Give your own witness as to what this undeserved love has meant to you in:
   1. your life,
   2. family life,
   3. congregational life, and
   4. your own ministry.

I. Tell your people what you believe this means for your congregational program and ministry.

J. Frame your sermon by returning to your opening story and finish it with "the rest of the story."

Prayer For The Day

In this sacred season of Lent, dear Holy Parent, we have assembled here again today to marvel at the way you sent your Son into Jerusalem and the cross for our sins. We look with amazement at the way you love us when we really don't deserve it. Teach us what our response ought to be today as a congregation, like little chicks whose mother hen wants to gather them under her wings. In Jesus' name. Amen.

Possible Metaphors And Stories

An article in the *Arizona Republic* told of a two-month-old boy whose mother accidentally left him on top of her car. He fell off when the woman drove away, tumbling face down into a busy intersection.

The infant, who was strapped into a car seat, suffered some cuts and scrapes, but was not seriously injured. "The baby had abrasions to the head, but it doesn't look serious," Police Sgt. Gene Klimek said. "It looks like the baby seat really did its job."

On *CNN News* the story was continued to say that a semi-truck driver reported seeing the child on the road and then stopped his rig to protect it. Another had driven on by, just missing the infant by inches. That second trucker was certainly that baby's savior.

There is a scene in the movie *The Mission* in which Mendoza has killed his brother and Father Gabriel has dragged up the steep waterfalls a bag full of heavy metal armor. Finally at the top, the Jesuit missionary is freed by the cutting of the rope which was weighing him down. A beautiful picture of the heavy weight of sin and the freedom of believing in our Lord Jesus Christ.

In the liturgy of the Jewish bat mitzvah of Julie and Valerie Glauberg was this beautiful prayer: "In a world torn by pain, a world far from wholeness and peace, a world waiting still to be redeemed, give us, Lord, the courage to say: 'There is one God in heaven and earth.'"

On a recent airline trip I saw the Columbus control tower hold up the takeoff of our 727 stretch for a tiny two-seat Cessna 140 to land. About the same time an "expedite crew" brought one late bag out from the dock and loaded it on board a United 737 aircraft. Large is not always the factor in the kingdom. God expedites our salvation and cares for us like important people.

George A. Buttrick tells in the *Upper Room Pulpit* about a picture painted by the French artist, Paul Flaudin. The picture is titled, *Christ Mourns Over The City*. "But the city in the canvas is not Jerusalem. It has tenements, spurting flame from blast furnaces, and a pall of smoke. Cathedrals, too, but they seem to be dark as the day dies. Christ stands on a cliff looking down on the city. He gazes fixedly, motionless, sad, compassionate. 'How often have I desired to gather your children together! Yes, he could gather that whole city ...' '... and you were not willing!'" (*Speakers Illustrations for Special Days*, edited by Charles L. Wallis).

Third Sunday In Lent

Revised Common	Isaiah 55:1-9	1 Corinthians 10:1-13	Luke 13:1-9
Roman Catholic	Exodus 3:1-8	1 Corinthians 10:1-6, 10-12	Luke 13:1-9
Episcopal	Exodus 3:1-15	1 Corinthians 10:1-13	Luke 13:1-9

Seasonal Theme   Jesus and his disciples move toward Jerusalem and the cross.

Theme For The Day   The patience of our God in dealing with our lack of good works.

Old Testament Lesson   Isaiah 55:1-9   *Invitation To Abundant Life*
     Similar to Proverbs 9:1-6, we have here a call to a banquet to attain life. Yahweh is the speaker in this poem. Food and drink indicate that the relationship between Yahweh and the people is good. The danger is not to accept the food and seek elsewhere for food which does not satisfy. That is a mistake. Verses 6 and 7 are the prophet's words encouraging them to seek Yahweh and abandon sin. Seeking Yahweh in this passage is to ask for forgiveness and to quit a way of life which is without God.
     We are also invited in this passage to share in the world mission of the Messiah. Verse 7 is a call for repentance. The negative is to forsake and the positive is to return to the Lord. These are great words which will preach: "everlasting covenant," "witness," "forsake," "return to the Lord," "mercy," "abundantly," "pardon," and "steadfast." Still, perhaps the most compelling word in this reading is "... come." We have an hospitable invitation to come.

New Testament Lesson   1 Corinthians 10:1-13   *Warnings From History*
     God will judge the Corinthians like God did Israel years before, after caring for them so well in the exodus. Like Moses was the deliverer of the Israelites, so Jesus was the deliverer of the Corinthians. Paul pleads with them not to repeat the dreadful mistakes of the past. Four things are forbidden: 1) idolatry, 2) sexual misconduct, 3) testing God, and 4) grumbling. He warns these self-contented Christians that they also face the temptation to compromise and sin. They are not exempt.

The Gospel   Luke 13:1-9   *Repent Or Parish And No Figs*
     Two incidents are used to refute the Jewish idea that a disaster has caused the sins in those who are hurt. First is the butchering by Roman soldiers of some pilgrims while giving their sacrifice in the Temple. The second, some people were crushed to death by the falling of the tower of Siloam (v. 4). Instead, Paul says that as a whole the Jewish nation was sinful and all would suffer unless they repented.
     The nation was like a fig tree which didn't bear fruit. It was only fit to destroy. But God is ready to grant more time for repentance. The fig tree represents Israel as also in Hosea 9:10. According to the *New Bible Commentary*, "Fruit could not be taken from a tree the first three years (Leviticus 19:23) hence this tree was presumably six years old."

Preaching Possibilities
     We could use all three readings today under the theme of "An Invitation." The Old Testament is an invitation to an abundant life with enough. The New Testament is an invitation to learn from history and repent, and the Gospel is an invitation to bear fruit and accept God's patient mercy.
     The Isaiah lesson can stand alone as beautiful descriptive poetry about our invitation to come to a loving God. And it is about the invitation we are to extend on God's behalf to others. It's lovely stuff which instructs us how God wants to relate to us.
     Verse 13 of 1 Corinthians 10 lends itself to an evangelical sermon dealing with "When life is hard" or "When we are tested," we have these assurances. Many of them are going through testing, like us. God will not let the struggle be more than what we can endure. And with the struggle, God will provide

a way through. Word after word it is jam-packed with assurances for our many hearers who need to hear them. And perhaps what we need to hear as well.

A Possible Outline Of Sermon Moves

Title: A Parable About God's Patience

Text: Luke 13:6-9

A. Begin with a plant you have nurtured which never did produce (or bloom) and how you got impatient with it and cut it down, and so on. A rose in the back yard or a fruit tree, etc., will do.

B. Move to the parable for today. Tell how fig trees were planted and no fruit harvested for three years — but this one at year 6 had still not produced.

C. Move to the plea of the gardener (who can represent Jesus) to give it another chance. A little more time. Explain how Jesus from the cross makes that plea for us also.

D. Move to the cultivation of the tree and how we can be enriched to produce fruit, too.
   1. There is cultivation by Christian education.
   2. There is cultivation by other Christian's encouragement.
   3. There is cultivation by the Holy Spirit.

E. Apply this to the corporate ministry of your congregation.
   1. We must cultivate (make a climate) which helps each one of us produce fruit. That fruit might be companionship for others, social justice in the community, witness to others, tithes of our income, loving the unlovely, and so on.
   2. We must cultivate the vineyard to protect and nurture the young, newer plants (children).
   3. We must harvest the fruit-producing love and prune out the hate and bigotry and self-centeredness of each other.
   4. And we must be patient with each other as God is, and has been, patient with us.

F. Frame your sermon now by returning to your story of impatience with something you tried to grow with which you began the sermon.

Prayer For The Day

Help us to be patient, O God, as you have been patient with us. And let the fruit of all-inclusive love, good works, ministry to others, compassion, stewardship, witness, and meaningful prayer always be in this, your vineyard called (*your congregation's name*). Our prayer today is in the name of Jesus the gardener who has saved us. Amen.

Possible Metaphors And Sermon Stories

In the recent Special Olympics held in Hong Kong, twelve physically challenged young people started the race. One fell after just a few yards and began to cry because of hurting his knee. The other racers stopped, turned around, and went to him. One offered to "kiss it to make it better" and the others helped him up. Then they all walked the rest of the race hand in hand. The crowd gave them a four-minute standing ovation.

My daughter, Bethany Allison, gave me a shirt to wear in Hong Kong where I was teaching. She had embroidered it with two Chinese characters. Paul Lau, upon seeing it at a distance, thought it said, "God is angry." But another student read it more carefully, "God forgives." Now we have it right!

C. R. Findley, speaking of patience, quoted the famous preacher Henry Ward Beecher, who told of a woman who prayed for patience, and God sent her a poor cook.

In my favorite Shakespeare play, *Othello*, we have the words: "How poor are they that have not patience! What wound did ever heal but by degrees?"

Fourth Sunday In Lent

Revised Common	Joshua 5:9-12	2 Corinthians 5:16-21	Luke 15:1-3, 11b-32
Roman Catholic	Joshua 5:9-12	2 Corinthians 5:17-21	Luke 15:1-3, 11-32
Episcopal	Joshua (4:19-24) 5:9-12	2 Corinthians 5:17-21	Luke 15:11-32

Seasonal Theme   Jesus and his disciples move toward Jerusalem and the cross.

Theme For The Day   The gracious forgiveness of God and our acceptance of each other.

Old Testament Lesson   Joshua 5:9-12   *Preparation For Warfare*

This is after being free from the disgrace and indignity of slavery in Egypt. "Place" in verse 9b is a holy place or sanctuary. This is the first celebration of the Passover in the land — it's a transition from being on the way to arriving and conquering Jericho. Gilgal also is a part of the stories of Samuel and Saul. It became a rallying point in the days of Samuel for the priest who retreated there and built a sanctuary.

The manna in verse 12 was a substance excreted by two species of insects on the tamarisk tree branches. And the phrase, "... land of Canaan," is first used here. So here is the final remaining event in the mobilization of the Yahweh army for the takeover of Canaan: Passover. Begun in Exodus 12, the family-centered celebration would be successful as a mark of the believer. They are now ready to go to war.

New Testament Lesson   2 Corinthians 5:16-21   *Ambassador For Christ*

We have here a partial realization of the hope for a new order of things in a new world. The new here makes us see people differently and our own change from self-concern to others. All this is from God through Christ. God brings about our reconciliation. We then have this "... ministry of reconciliation." It's our message to others also (v. 19). We can tell others about the Christ working it out that our sins will not be held against us. The term for us in verse 20 is "ambassadors for Christ" (v. 20). This is the technical term for a legate of Caesar. This person not only speaks on behalf of Caesar, but also in place of Caesar. So we are witnesses on behalf of Jesus, representing him and speaking on his behalf.

The Gospel   Luke 15:1-3, 11b-32   *The Parable Of The Loving Father*

The dividing up of the property was not unusual. The younger son did have initiative! But he was the center of his own life. In Winston Churchill's novel *A Far Country*, the far country is the loss of standards and ideals. According to *The Interpreter's Bible*, "Edwin McNeill's interpretation is that the father was also a prodigal. He was a materialist, casual and worldly in rearing his sons, sentimental in his forgiveness, shallow always in bourgeois mind." It would be a very different take on this parable.

The return is all joy. I can almost cheer as the father runs to meet his lost returning son. I have been there, God. But hold on a minute, there is another prodigal son! He had stayed home. I wonder if he had not helped to cause the younger son to leave home in the first place. This fellow found out that coldly respectful code of living isn't enough. He must have secretly coveted what his brother had done and gotten. This elder son can be a picture of the church. Again, from *The Interpreter's Bible* a wonderful comment: "If the younger son returning home had met his brother before he met his father, he might have turned right around and been thankful for the far country(!)"

I wonder if Jesus knew this father and his sons and if they might have even been neighbors of his in Nazareth? And all this seems to be a parable about God's undeserved graceful forgiveness and our responsibility to practice it toward our sons and daughters. Notice it is God who takes the initiative as he runs to meet his returning son.

Preaching Possibilities

A. The connection of the Old Testament Lesson and the Gospel would be the mutual celebration of returning home. For the Israelites, it's going in to their promised land, and for the prodigal son and family, it's the celebration of a lost member of the family returning to his home.

B. I'm not sure we can do it, but I would like to preach on the New Testament Reading from Paul.

C. However, the Gospel story is so strong and liked that the congregation may not like ignoring it. So here is what we could do with the 2 Corinthians 5:16-21 reading:

   1. *Title*: Saint Paul's Advice for the Christian Life

   2. *Text:* 2 Corinthians 5:16-21

   3. Begin by telling about a situation which you used to see in one way, but now see quite differently.

   4. Move to how Saint Paul once lived life as a radical Jew, even killing Christians, but now is a different person who sees life in a different, a new way.

   5. Read verse 17 and then explain the new and very different way Paul advises us to live.

     a. See people not just as human animals but as brothers and sisters in Christ.

     b. It's time for us to get rid of old ways which are self-centered and move to new ways which are God centered.

Old	New
Get even	Love
Accumulate	Share
Demand your rights	Humbly serve
Hate	Love unconditionally

     c. We have a ministry of reconciliation. As Jesus reconciled us to God we must carry out a ministry of reconciling others to God, to us, and to each other.

     d. We are ambassadors for Christ. We must share and invite others into this new reconciled life with God. It will change us to new people, help us see things differently, and provide the possibility of a new life for others.

       Example (from *These Will Preach: Life in Christ*): "Sometimes when there is a typhoon in the Philippines some trees survive and are still standing, even with green leaves. But those who know will say, 'That tree is already timber,' meaning even though it doesn't look like it, it is dead" (An old man interviewed on *CBS News*).

       "We also can look like we are living but already dead. In the Christ there is new life."

   6. Frame the sermon by returning to your opening story of when you saw something in a new way; then list your points A through D in reverse order.

Possible Outline Of Sermon Moves

   Here is an excellent opportunity to do interesting narrative preaching which will invite your listeners to take part in the parable. Like many movies and television shows, we'll begin in the middle and then later return to the beginning in a "flashback."

A. Begin by relating the situation of a bewildered father giving a party to celebrate his young son's return home. The older son is outraged because in a self-centered way he resents all the attention given to his younger brother.

B. Move to how we can have similar feelings about those who join our fellowships late in life and a lot of fuss is made over them.

C. Continue by saying what you think was wrong with the older son's attitude. Self-centered, selfish, jealous, and so on.

D. Move to the beginning of the story. Tell about the young brother wanting to leave home for the far country.

E. Define the "far country" back then and name the far countries that you and I are tempted to go to — drugs, wealth addiction, self-centeredness, sexual promiscuity, hedonistic living, and so on.

F. Move to the father. Here is the one character in the story Jesus wanted to represent God. This father longs for his son's return and is gracious and joy-filled when he did.

G. Draw a couple of conclusions
   1. God wants us to return home.
   2. The church might be a place of celebration for the return of those in the far country.
   3. God's radical grace is the glue which holds us together.
H. Finish by returning to the father's party for the son and make it one of celebration for the faithfulness of the oldest, as well as of the youngest son.

Prayer For The Day

We are thankful, dear God, that you make us new people and ambassadors with a ministry of reconciliation. And we celebrate here today the gracious loving way you receive us back home again and again. Give us your divine protection in our far countries and the invitation over and over to return to you. In Jesus' name. Amen.

Possible Metaphors And Stories

Scott Hamilton is quoted in the *America West* magazine as saying, "A champion is someone who has faced their demons and come out better in the process. It's nothing to do with beating other people. It's about meeting your own expectations." Ice skater Hamilton won sixteen consecutive championships, including four U.S. and World titles.

Michael Leach is quoted by Bishop Robert Mattheis as follows: "Catholicism means throwing a party for everyone. The church is not a country club; it's a family. Dissent doesn't kill families; disinterest does ... The church as a family fills its tables to bursting for prodigal sons and daughters — morning, noon, and night. Such a church refuses to condemn or even compare one family member to another. It takes Jesus' words to heart: Luke 15:31."

On a television sitcom, *One Day At A Time*, Mrs. Ann Romano said after a tough day with the children: "All of this for a Whitman Sampler on Mother's Day."
To be a parent and Christ-like is not easy but worth much more than an annual box of candy.

Fifth Sunday In Lent

Revised Common	Isaiah 43:16-21	Philippians 3:4b-14	John 12:1-8
Roman Catholic	Isaiah 43:16-21	Philippians 3:8-14	John 8:1-11
Episcopal	Isaiah 43:16-21	Philippians 3:8-14	Luke 20:9-19

Seasonal Theme   Jesus and his disciples move toward Jerusalem and the cross.

Theme For The Day   A disciple's extravagant sacrificial love and adoration of Jesus.

Old Testament Lesson   Isaiah 43:16-21   *Deliverance Old And New*
    We have here another fresh deliverance of Israel which is written in terms of the Exodus from Egypt long before. But in verse 17 the exiles are to forget the Exodus long ago — because the future one predicted will be even greater. The passage serves to affirm God's divine purpose for God's chosen people. And there is praise never far from the writer's thoughts (v. 21).

New Testament Lesson   Philippines 3:4b-14   *New Righteousness Found*
    Paul claims he has seven reasons to be even more confident in Judaism than others (v. 5). He states in verse 7 that he really discounted all their reasons for his confidence and that he had discovered a much better way. The single gain of knowing Christ outweighed all these other claims. His righteousness doesn't come from him or God — it comes through faith in Christ (v. 9). And now he wants to live identified with Christ crucified and risen. He says there is a power of Christ's resurrection which he wants to share (see 2 Corinthians 4:7-12).

The Gospel   John 12:1-8   *Mary Anointing Jesus*
    John has combined the two anointing traditions into one. It's a combination of an emphasis of preparation for his burial (Matthew 26:12) and an emphasis on the woman's love and respect for Jesus (Luke 7:44-47) evoking Jesus' forgiveness for her sins (Luke 7:48-49). The verb used to wipe his feet is the same one used to describe Jesus' wiping of his disciples' feet at the foot washing in John 13:5.
    The New Interpreter's Bible describes it beautifully! "Through Mary's act, the stench of death that once lingered over this household has been replaced by the fragrance of love." There is definitely an attempt by John to try to link Mary's anointing with the events of the farewell meal. And notice this: Mary's act of devotion was really extravagant. This perfume was worth a year's wages. In the washing of the disciples' feet by Jesus and the last supper and Jesus' burial, faithful discipleship is revealed. It is defined by acts of love and demonstrated first by a woman.

Preaching Possibilities
    While it can always be done by enough stretch of the imagination, the three lessons for today probably best stand alone. Any of the three will preach.
A. The Old Testament — We are delivered by God still again.
B. The New Testament — Righteousness is ours for the accepting.
C. The Gospel — The woman Mary, one of the first disciples to demonstrate unrestrained love.
        The New Testament Philippians text is rich in theology and lends itself to a teaching homily. It could go something like this:
    1. Introduce the reading by telling of Paul's situation at the time of writing. (He was in prison and wrote this to Christian friends in Philippi thanking them for their love and support.)
    2. List Paul's virtues he could rely on (v. 5).
    3. Tell Paul's lack of confidence in these and that he insisted he is relying on faith in Christ which provides a righteousness from God (v. 9).

4. Explain Paul's belief that there is a power of Jesus' resurrection and the privilege of sharing Jesus' suffering.
5. The kicker is: We also shall attain resurrection from the dead (v. 11).

Possible Outline Of Sermon Moves

A. Begin by telling of Judas' complaint that waste was taking place among the disciples.
B. Tell of when you thought there was waste among the contemporary disciples in your church.
C. Return to the story and retell what Mary had done.
D. Now list the reasons you think John told this story here in his Gospel:
   1. to foreshadow the last supper;
   2. to foreshadow the washing of the disciples' feet; and
   3. to foreshadow the killing of Jesus on Calvary.
E. Draw the conclusion that in our discipleship there are times for extravagance and even what some would call waste.
F. Make the point that discipleship is defined by acts of love and one's response to Jesus. Mary's act would be commanded in the washing of feet as mandatory for those who will be his disciples.
G. Return to the story with your own opportunities to love Jesus and anoint him with a fragrance which can be smelled in your home, church, workplace, place of rest, and neighborhood. And one which will be sweet smelling to others.

Prayer For The Day

Show us the ways, O God, to love Jesus like Mary of Bethany did. Direct us in our discipleship that we might be extravagant in our love of you and of your people. And help us from becoming another grumpy, stingy, and complaining disciple like Judas. In Christ's name. Amen.

Possible Metaphors And Stories

On the sitcom *Night Court*, Dan Fielding was in the hospital, had been close to death, and had partially recovered. Fielding said, "In order to love, one must be able to give — so no one will love me because I can't give. I love you, Harry. There, I said it." Harry replied, "Yeah, you said it. Now why don't you say it again to yourself."

Jesus tells us to love one another. We must also love one another as one of God's family whom God treasured.

I was buying chemicals for use in our hot tub when the woman asked if I wanted a fragrance. I asked, "Which one smells religious?" She smelled three before realizing it was a joke. How does religion smell? Can you smell kindness, mercy, gentleness, forgiveness, humbleness, precious love?

Marvin Kalb on NBC interviewed an old man who had the grazing rights for his cows on the land where the pope would preside at a mass. Kalb asked, "Would the cows mind not having this grass to graze on tomorrow?" "No," was the answer, "and their milk will be all the sweeter because the pope was here."

Sacrifice makes life richer and more worthwhile.

Sunday Of The Passion (Palm Sunday)

Revised Common	**Isaiah 50:4-9a**	**Philippians 2:5-11**	**Luke 22:14—23:56 or Luke 23:1-49**
Roman Catholic	**Isaiah 50:4-7**	**Philippians 2:6-11**	**Luke 22:14—23:56**
Episcopal	**Isaiah 45:21-25**	**Philippians 2:5-11**	**Luke (22:39-71) 23:1-49 (50-56)**

Seasonal Theme   Jesus and his disciples move toward Jerusalem and the cross.

Theme For The Day   The entrance into Jerusalem and an emphasis on what Jesus accomplished there for us.

Old Testament Lesson   Isaiah 50:4-9a   *The Teaching Servant*

This servant has been taught by Yahweh and has the gift of speaking. So there is an alertness and comprehension of God's message. Second Isaiah, a talented poet, gives us, with eloquent words, God's message.

Here is a great message for us preachers. As Isaiah comforted the frustrated people, so we must speak encouragement to our healers (v. 4). Verse 6 tells of inevitable antagonism vented on Isaiah because he was sensitive to God's prophetic words. However, the disciple of Israel is given help (v. 7). He is sustained by this confident assurance.

New Testament Lesson   Philippians 2:5-11   *Initiating Christian Humility*

Verse 8 is the center of this passage which describes Jesus' humility in his passion and death for us. We have an early Christian hymn in verses 6-11. Its theme is the humiliation and exaltation of Christ. It could be one of the earliest descriptions of Jesus' career: his pre-existence, his ministry on earth, and his eventual exaltation. The hymn, according to *The International Bible Commentary*, is based on the Servant Song of Isaiah 52:13—53:12. These things Jesus did:

1. Being in the form of God did not regard equality with God;
2. Made himself a slave (see also Isaiah 53:12); and
3. Being born in human likeness, and ... in human form, he humbled himself. Because of all this he is worshiped in his divine supremacy. This is honor that is paid to God (Isaiah 45:23). Verse 11 contains the earliest creed of the church and the confession of the World Council of Churches: "Jesus Christ is Lord."

The Gospel   Luke 22:14—23:56   *Luke's Account Of Jesus' Passion*

For this traditional "Palm Sunday" now named "The Sunday of the Passion" we have Luke's account in Cycle C of the international lectionary. It moves from Maundy Thursday's Lord's Supper to the death and burial of Jesus. *The New Revised Standard Version* describes the story in the following way: any one of the topics is a good subject for preaching, depending on what other services you will hold during Holy Week.

Luke 22:14-23	The Institution of the Lord's Supper
Luke 22:24-30	The Dispute about Greatness
Luke 22:31-34	Jesus Predicts Peter's Denial
Luke 22:35-38	Purse, Bag, and Sword
Luke 22:39- 46	Jesus Prays on the Mount of Olives
Luke 22:47-53	The Betrayal and Arrest of Jesus
Luke 22:54-62	Peter Denies Jesus
Luke 22:63-65	The Mocking and Beating of Jesus

Luke 22:66-71	Jesus Before the Council
Luke 23:1-5	Jesus Before Pilate
Luke 23:6-12	Jesus Before Herod
Luke 23:13-25	Jesus Sentenced to Death
Luke 23:26-43	The Crucifixion of Jesus
Luke 23:44-49	The Death of Jesus
Luke 23:50-56	The Burial of Jesus
Luke 24	... to be continued, Easter

Preaching Possibilities

This is the one Sunday of the church year when it is better not to preach, but to let the scripture tell the story. Please don't just read (or have read) this scripture. Put some real effort into rehearsing a group of women and men so it might be done well. Give each reader character parts and one person the part of narrator.

You might also consider the singing of hymn verses in between segments and/or a prayer about that which has just been read. An example might be:

1. Read Luke 22:14-30
2. Sing "Love Consecrates the Humblest Act" (in *Lutheran Book of Worship* number 122).
3. Pray — Dear Jesus, we thank you for giving us the Holy Supper for your presence with us now. Help us to shed all ambition of greatness in your kingdom here or in eternity. Amen.
4. Read Luke 22:31-53.
5. Sing, and so on.

Possible Outline Of Sermon Moves

While strongly encouraging you to let the scripture be the highlight and focus of this day, I will still offer one suggested outline of sermon moves. If you use the New Testament Reading, here is a suggestion:

Title: Out Of Our Mind

Text: Philippians 2:5-11

A. Begin by telling about Paul being in jail when he wrote this letter thanking his Christian friends for their love and support.
B. Move to the three things Paul said as advice to his friends:
   1. Have Jesus' mind (not yours) when you make decisions for this life.
   2. Here is what Jesus did for us: did not try to be equal to God; emptied himself; was born like a human; was humble and went to his death on the Cross.
   3. Tell what this means now. Because he did what we heard about in the Gospel, Jesus is revered, witnessed to, and worshiped around the world.
C. Move to the creed in this passage: "Jesus Christ is Lord." Some see him as a miracle worker, others as an example of a godly person, and still others as a great prophet. But for Paul in prison, he was Lord, the one who dominated our lives and is ruler over all.
D. Return now to Paul in prison and tell your hearers what you would have written from that Philippian prison, concluding by asking them what they would have written. And still Paul claims: read Philippians 2:9-11.

Prayer For The Day

Help us to initiate your humility and treat you as our Lord and Savior, O God. And on this day you entered Jerusalem to work forgiveness and a new kind of fellowship for your disciples, prepare our hearts to observe this holiest of weeks with devotion and contrite hearts. In Jesus' name. Amen.

Possible Metaphors And Stories

The author of *Ironweed* states: "It's a short distance from the 'Hallelujah' to the 'hoot.' " So it is we can come down fast and hard and painfully.

On ABC's *World News Tonight*, Charles Gibson said of retirement, "When you retire you go from 'Who's Who' to 'Who's that?' " Jesus went the other way: from "Who's that?" to "Who's Who."

All Bataks of Sumatra can tell you their Bona ni Pinesa (village of origin). Even if gone for years, they return, visit, and greet old friends, relatives, and family. No matter where they are in the world, they still have their village of origin. Many ballads are composed about it. Toba Bataks often return to Samosir Island of the Lake Toba area.

Dean Zimmerman of the Lutheran Theological Seminary where I teach in Hong Kong announced at the daily chapel service that "the Coming of the Savior for today has been canceled due to the professor's illness." But no cancellation this Palm Sunday — our Savior heads into Jerusalem toward torture and the cross.

Maundy Thursday/Holy Thursday

Revised Common	**Exodus 12:1-4 (5-10) 11-14**	**1 Corinthians 11:23-26**	**John 13:1-17, 31b-35**
Roman Catholic	**Exodus 12:1-8 (11-14)**	**1 Corinthians 11:23-26**	**John 13:1-15**
Episcopal	**Exodus 12:1-14a**	**1 Corinthians 11:23-26 (27-32)**	**John 13:1-15 or Luke 22:14-30**

Seasonal Theme   Jesus and his disciples move toward Jerusalem and the cross.

Theme For The Day   Maundy Thursday we observe communion, Christ is present, and we love each other in humility.

Old Testament   Exodus 12:1-4 (5-10) 11-14   *The First Passover Instituted*

Because this is "Maundy Thursday," the night Jesus began the practice of communion and celebrated the Passover in the upper room, the church officials selected this passage from Exodus 12 which describes the beginning of Jewish Passover. This is the foundation of communion for Christians. Passover was (is) basically the celebration and remembrance of the deliverance of the Israelites from Egypt. Many Old Testament scholars believe this was originally an ancient pastoral festival and that here it is given a new significance. Interesting — because Jesus gave it yet a new meaning in the upper room. The writer of Exodus certainly had in mind the passing over by the angel of death of the homes of Israelites who had placed blood on their door posts (v. 7).

New Testament Lesson   1 Corinthians 11:23-26   *The Institution Of The Lord's Supper*

Here is the earliest account of the Lord's Supper in the Bible. Paul's letters circulated even before the Gospel accounts were published. As the Passover in the Old Testament Lesson is a memorial of the people's deliverance from Egypt's slavery, so the Supper becomes an act of remembrance of Jesus' work on the cross and presence with us now. Lutherans and Roman Catholics take, "This is my body," seriously and claim the "real presence" of Jesus' body and blood in this sacrament. A new covenant is celebrated (v. 25). Instead of keeping all the rules, we now believe in God's grace in Jesus' life, death, and resurrection. For preaching I like the new take on verse 26 when Jesus tells disciples that whenever they observe this sacrament of the altar they are proclaiming again Jesus' death. So communion has an element of not only Jesus with us really, but also a witness to his saving and forgiving us.

The Gospel   John 13:1-17, 31b-35   *Jesus Washes The Disciples' Feet*

The name "Maundy Thursday" is based on verse 34 where it says Jesus gives disciples a new mandate — to love one another. Jesus' humbleness is well pictured in the story. In verse 14 Jesus must be talking of all disciples to have fundamental cleansing. This is often done in serving and loving humbly each other. I would have liked to hear Jesus speak the words of verse 34. Jesus will leave them soon, so he is telling them the only bond which will keep them together is love. I wonder if there were tears in Jesus' eyes when he said it. And there is a flip side in verse 35. Just like Paul claims in the New Testament Lesson that when disciples take communion it is a witness to Jesus with us, so Jesus says that when we love one another people will know we are disciples. It will preach!

Preaching Possibilities

A. All three readings connect well today. The Old Testament is the background of communion, the New Testament is the earliest account, and the Gospel adds the mandate to love each other as they participate in Jesus' real presence in the sacrament of the altar.

B. Each reading will stand alone as well. The Old Testament Exodus account will lend itself to describing the ancient season and method of Passover and then telling of the new meaning Jesus gave it in the upper room.
C. The New Testament can lend itself to instructing our people about why we have communion and what it means when we do it.
   1. It is a remembering.
   2. It is a time of fellowship with Jesus really there.
   3. It is a thanksgiving for God's grace gift of forgiveness and eternal life.
   4. When we do it, it proclaims to others what we believe.
D. The Gospel also stands well alone and is a great lesson on humbleness.
   1. We are to serve each other humbly as Jesus did.
   2. We are to love each other, which will bind us together.
   3. If we do this, we will be known to others as disciples of Jesus.

Possible Outline Of Sermon Moves

A. Begin by giving your own memories of the observance of Maundy Thursday in your home church and what you wondered about at that immature age.
B. Move to your understanding now of this day when we
   1. learn the history of the sacrament of the altar,
   2. learn the meaning of the sacrament to disciples, and
   3. learn the new mandate which accompanies the sacrament.
C. Move to a look at the Exodus account and explain the history of Passover.
D. Move to a look at the 1 Corinthians reading and just what communion has meant to Christians down through the years.
E. Move to the John story of foot-washing and how it teaches us humility and love for each other in our discipleship.
F. Apply the above teachings to your congregation's ministry and worship practices.
G. Frame the sermon by returning to your memories as a child of Maundy Thursday.

Prayer For The Day

We give thanks, O God, for the way you have always provided a way out for us in our suffering, even as you did with the Israelites from Egypt's slavery. And we pray we might cherish this sacrament when you are here with us and help us make a witness to others. We would ask you to teach us humility as you demonstrated when you washed the disciples' feet this night. And above all, teach and help us to love one another as you have loved us. In your name. Amen.

Possible Metaphors And Stories

Kellogg's Corn Flakes used to advise on their television advertisements: "Kellogg's Corn Flakes, taste them again for the first time."

Taking the bread and wine can be like that. Let's not lose the newness of it.

Boston Market used to advertise its food like the "Boston Carver" and ends the television ad with a woman saying, "Don't mess with dinner." What could we Christians say should not be messed with? Don't mess with the Word. Don't mess with the table of the Lord where we commune with our God in the bread and the wine.

In the movie *Starman*, an alien crash lands right into the life of a widow, Jenny. He hears her use the word "love" and asks her to define it. She replies, "Love is when you care more for someone else than you do for yourself." Jenny came very close to God's love which we have for another.

The Marines had an advertisement on television during a San Francisco '49ers and New Orleans Saints football game: "The few, the proud, the Marines." What might be an ad for disciples of Christ: "The few, the humble, those who serve, Christ's disciples."

Good Friday

Revised Common	Isaiah 52:13—53:12	Hebrews 10:16-25 or	John 18:1—19:42
		Hebrews 4:14-16; 5:7-9	
Roman Catholic	Isaiah 52:13—53:12	Hebrews 4:14-16; 5:7-9	John 18:1—19:42
Episcopal	Isaiah 52:13—53:12 or	Hebrews 10:1-25	John (18:1-40)
	Genesis 22:1-18		19:1-37

Seasonal Theme Jesus and his disciples move toward Jerusalem and the cross.

Theme For The Day The complete forgiveness worked for us by Jesus on the cross by our God who loves us that much.

Old Testament Lesson Isaiah 52:13—53:12 *The Suffering Servant*

The New Jerome Biblical Commentary has an interesting description of this fourth Servant Song of Isaiah. "The style is heavy, sobbing, and recurrent with a frequent intoning of *u* and *o* vowels, *h* and *l* consonants, the sounds of a dirge." Appropriate for Good Friday, isn't it? So we have the portrayal of the suffering servant in this passage and then Jesus in the New Testament combined this suffering servant image with the messianic concept of the son of man. Looking back from the Good Friday event, we can read into this passage all kinds of predictions, many of which were really not there. Consider these:

1. "he shall startle many nations"
2. "despised and rejected by others"
3. "a man of suffering"
4. "he has born our infirmities"
5. "he was wounded for our transgressions"
6. "upon him was the punishment that made us whole"
7. "by his bruises we are healed"
8. "you make his life an offering for sin"
9. "he shall bear their iniquities"
10. "he bore the sins for many"
11. "and made intercession for the transgressions"

The servant is innocent; still he suffers with those who are sinful and puts his goodness into their attitudes.

New Testament Lesson Hebrews 10:16-25 *Forgiveness Of Sins And A Call To Persevere*

In plain words the author seems to be saying to the Good Friday event that God is making a new covenant through the crucifixion. After this event there is no longer the need for rites and offerings for our sins. Jesus did this once and for all on the cross. Verse 17 even claims God won't even "remember" our wrong doings — we are forgiven! And it's Jesus' blood which has been the final offering — not that of bulls and scapegoats. Now we can approach the temple cleansed, "sprinkled clean." So we can hold fast to our faith and encourage each other to respond to the new covenant by meeting together and doing good deeds.

The Gospel John 18:1—19:42 *The Arrest And Crucifixion*

We have the story of betrayal, arrest, trial, denial, crucifixion, and burial of Jesus as related in John. It's a very familiar story. Let me just point out a few things which are a bit surprising.

1. It is surprising that Peter was carrying a sword (18:10).
2. The "... another disciple" in verse 15 may have been John.

3. The third person to question Peter was a relative of the person whose ear Peter had cut off (v. 26).
4. It seems like Pilate allowed the scourging as an alternative to crucifixion.
5. Pilate's "Here is the man" (19:5) was much more meaningful than he knew. Jesus was the representative man, standing in our place.
6. Actually, the Jews had no power to crucify Jesus. So Pilate's comments in verse 16 are puzzling.
7. John sees a fulfillment of Psalm 22:18 when the guards took Jesus' clothing.
8. The words, "It is finished," John claims for Psalm 69:21.
9. Verse 35 seems to refer to the author John seeing it.
10. John's account of the burial is important for he names Nicodemus. Both he and Joseph of Arimathea were members of the Sanhedrin (see John 3:1-15).
11. Perhaps to fulfill Psalm 16:10 — it was a new tomb.
12. Jesus did not come into contact with corruption. Usually those condemned for sedition would have been thrown into a common grave ... perhaps Pilate never did believe the verdict.

Preaching Possibilities

A. I hope you will offer your people the ancient Tenebrae service today instead of preaching. It follows the custom of dividing the passion story into seven parts and extinguishing one of seven candles each time you read a portion of the story. A verse of a hymn may be sung in between as well. Each time a candle is extinguished, lower the light in the sanctuary until it is completely dark after the final reading. Pause, and then make a cymbal crash representing the opening of the tomb. Carry out the new paschal candle to its place in the chancel and bring up the lights just enough for people to exit in silence.

B. Of course if you must preach, there is much, much rich material. Those who selected these three readings must have wanted us to present the New Testament Reading as what was accomplished, and the Gospel as the narrative of how it actually took place in Jerusalem.

The three key verses could be:
1. Isaiah 53:5, he is wounded for us.
2. Hebrews 10:18, forgiveness and no more offering for sin.
3. John 19:30, Jesus finishes the mission alone.

Possible Outline Of Sermon Moves

Title: Here Is The Man
Text: John 19:5

A. Begin by telling what seeing a cross today means to you.
B. Move to what the sight of a cross meant to those who lived in Jerusalem. Compare with hanging noose, electric chair, firing squad. Tell how even Pilate seemed to try to avoid Jesus going to a cross. Use clues from the scripture.
C. Move to asking what it is that Jesus did on the cross this day which so changed its symbolism.
    1. He worked our forgiveness once and for all.
    2. He demonstrated how much God loves us.
    3. He made a new covenant with us based on God's grace.
    4. He took our place and punishment.
    5. He worked an atonement for us with God.
D. Return to your opening remarks about the meaning of a cross to you and wonder out loud what it meant to Pilate after he turned over Jesus to hang on it.

Prayer For The Day

You have worked a wonderful sacrifice for us today on the cross. We are sorry for our sins which made it necessary for you to hang there, dear Jesus. Help us always to revere the cross in our lives and to celebrate your love which it symbolizes. In your name. Amen.

Possible Metaphors And Stories

A letter from missionary friends Barry and Alice Lang in Madan, Papua New Guinea, said, "Bilum is what people here use to carry all their personal possessions. The color and so forth indicate membership in a particular tribe. Mothers put their babies in them and hang them from a tree branch. The breeze rocks the infant to sleep. Jesus Christ carries his bilum of our heavy loads, mistakes, sins, worries, and problems. In many of our Lutheran churches, bilum is carved on the inside or outside as a constant reminder that Jesus carried our cross. We ought to help carry one another's burdens."

While on my way to a speaking engagement, I was worried about parish problems. The security machine at the airport went off because of my crucifix in my suit coat pocket.

There's the answer. We serve the Christ and it is he who sets the direction and our mission.

In the movie *The Crying Game*, the captive says to the captor who belongs to the Irish Republican Army, "There is a story of a frog and a scorpion. The frog carries the scorpion across a river on its back. Halfway across the scorpion stings the frog and the frog asks why. The scorpion replies, 'Because it's my nature.'"

Our nature is to sting rather than to love. Only with God's help can we change.

Retired Bishop Ronald Diggs of Liberia was arrested and told to stand trial on Good Friday. So all the Monrovia churches scheduled their Good Friday services for the court where he was to appear. On Thursday, they dropped the charges. The cross of Good Friday ought to free us — from sin, from guilt, from fear, and from shame.

An Introduction To The Easter Season

The season of Easter, which we now begin, runs from the Easter vigil on Easter eve until Pentecost. After the resurrection of Jesus we have a number of appearances of Jesus (all from John) alive and out of the grave until the Ascension story forty days later. The First Reading is always from Acts and records for us the activities of the disciples after Easter and the beginnings of the early Christian Church.

Gospel Readings

John 20:19-31	Jesus appears to the disciples
John 21:1-9	Jesus appears to seven disciples
John 10:22-30	Jesus rejected by the Jews
John 13:31-35	The new commandment
John 14:23-29	He will be leaving them
John 17:20-26	Jesus' prayer for his disciples

The First Readings from Acts

Acts 5:27-32	Apostles are persecuted
Acts 9:1-6 (7-20)	Conversion of Saul to Paul
Acts 9:36-43	Peter in Lydda and Joppa
Acts 11:1-18	Peter's report to the church at Jerusalem
Acts 16:9-15	Paul's vision of the man of Macedonia
Acts 16:16-34	Paul and Silas in prison

Please notice that the Sundays in this season are named Second, Third, Fourth, Fifth, Sixth, and Seventh Sunday *of* Easter. It continues to be an Easter celebration and *not* Sundays *after* Easter.

Heads Up Alert

After the celebration of the Resurrection of our Lord on Easter Sunday, we now move into seven weeks of Easter. I would like to suggest giving a sermon series for these seven weeks based on the First Reading, all coming from Luke's book of "The Acts of the Apostles." You can obtain additional help from the Comments on the First Lesson for each of these seven Sundays.

The selection of these accounts of the activities of the early Christians is to give us a peek at the early church shortly after its inception at Pentecost. They complement the Gospel accounts of Jesus alive and out of the grave by presenting the church as the alive Christ in the world through his church.

Notice that these are not *after* Easter Sundays, but rather are *of* Easter Sundays. So a possible sermon series for this season on "God's Easter people."

Easter 2	Acts 5:27-32	Easter people have courage in the midst of opposition
Easter 3	Acts 9:1-6 (7-20)	Easter people know conversion and a new way of living
Easter 4	Acts 9:36-43	Easter people know healing and good works
Easter 5	Acts 11:1-18	Easter people are all-inclusive people
Easter 6	Acts 16:9-15	Easter people have a call to go over and out
Ascension Day	Acts 1:1-11	Easter people have a power of joy
Easter 7	Acts 16:16-34	Easter people can sing in prison

Each week ought to begin with a brief review of the "Easter people" before the one for that particular Sunday. A variation can be to end the sermon with a summary of the previous sermon in the series.

A variation on the same First Readings could be the following: "The Bible's Easter People"

Easter 2   Courage for Peter
Easter 3   Conversion for Paul
Easter 4   New life for Dorcas
Easter 5   Salvation for us Gentiles
Easter 6   Baptism for Lydia
Ascension   Power and joy for the disciples
Easter 7   Freedom for a mad woman or Joy for a Philippian sailor

If you are going to do such a series, it would be good to announce it Easter Day when you have your largest attendance and oft times many visitors.

The Resurrection Of Our Lord (Easter Day)

Revised Common	Acts 10:34-43 or	1 Corinthians 15:19-26 or	John 20:1-18 or
	Isaiah 65:17-25	Acts 10:34-43	Luke 24:1-12
Roman Catholic	Acts 10:34, 37-43	Colossians 3:1-4	John 20:1-9
Episcopal	Acts 10:34-43	Colossians 3:1-4	Luke 24:1-10

Seasonal Theme   The resurrected Christ becomes a physical presence in the world again.

Theme For The Day   The day of victory over death for God's Son and for us. And the anticipation of Jesus alive with us here.

First Lesson   Acts 10:34-43   *The Gospel To The Gentiles*

This is Peter's sermon and a summary of Jesus' life, work, and interaction with his disciples. He was explaining the gospel to Gentiles, Cornelius in particular. Jesus told the disciples upon Ascension mountain that they were to make disciples of all nations. Perhaps they thought it meant to make them all Jews first. Now Peter was accepting table fellowship with the Gentiles. In this passage are more of the facts of Jesus' life than any other Acts speech. Verse 39 is especially powerful in that the disciples claimed first person eyewitness and also by the use of the very word *martyrdom* testify, witness, preach — there is a commission there for all who follow even today.

Second Lesson   1 Corinthians 15:19-26   *First Fruits*

It would not have been an easy thing for those of a Greek background among the Gentile converts to accept. The historical resurrection of the Christ, and our resurrection as well, is fundamental to the Christian faith. To deny it is to place Jesus in a martyr's grave, and remove from us the hope of eternal life.

The first fruits of verse 20 refer to the first sheaf of the harvest which was always brought to the temple as an offering of thanksgiving to the Lord. See Leviticus 23:10ff. Jesus is that first fruit (Revelation 1-18; Romans 6:9) in anticipation of those of us who die but will be raised to be with him (1 Thessalonians 4:16, 17). Verse 26 is especially appropriate because this is Easter. It makes the Easter claim that the resurrection is victory over death's power for us who are in Christ. Paul doesn't concern himself with the unbelieving dead here — I won't either! This is Easter, the day of resurrection, and we ought to concentrate on its effect for believers.

The Gospel   John 20:1-18   *Mary Magdalene And The Empty Tomb*

We are given two pictures through which we can get a handle on the resurrection: the empty tomb and Mary's experience of meeting the alive-again-Jesus in the garden. In John's account there is only the empty grave and some of Jesus' burial clothing. Yet John believed in this evidence. He already was confident of Jesus and his promises. So all it took was an empty grave and those clothes and John was sure Jesus had beaten death just as he said he would. We all need to take notice of this story before we move on in the Easter season to accounts of the risen Christ's appearance. Verses 11-18, Mary Magdalene in the garden with Jesus is a marvelously poignant narrative of grace and joy in Easter resurrection. Jesus' promise is kept; he would see them again and their grief would turn into joy (John 16:20-22; 14:18-20). Notice she is to tell them of the "Logos" in Jesus' return to God.

Cross/resurrection/ascension says *The New Interpreter's Bible* "... is the decisive eschatological event for the Fourth Evangelist, because it forever changes the way God is known in the world and makes God's new age a reality."

I cannot resist pointing out how this story of Easter garden and empty tomb portray Mary Magdalene as one of the early disciples. Verse 18 paints her as the first one to announce the fact of the resurrection and what Jesus told her. The two names she uses to speak of Jesus (vv. 11-18), Rabbouni and Lord, remind us of his farewell words in John 13:13. This also proves her discipleship. Let's be sure to say it in this Easter message. There were women disciples as well as men.

Preaching Possibilities

A. There are many possibilities for sermonizing today. One could use all three readings:
   1. Acts 10:34-43 — Easter for Peter: a message for everyone
   2. 1 Corinthians 15:19-26 — Paul's Easter: a matter of first fruits
   3. John 20:1-18 — Easter for Mary Magdalene: a matter of promises kept. Easter for John: the empty tomb was enough.

B. Any of the three readings will work separately as well; however, the John account is what your people have come to hear and experience again this year. I think a comparison of the beloved disciple John's believing by just seeing the empty tomb with Mary Magdalene's having to see Jesus face to face is worthwhile.

C. If you prefer to go with a single text and an exegetical sermon, these look strong and promising to me:
   1. Acts 10:34 — God shows no partiality
   2. Acts 10:39 — We are witnesses
   3. Acts 10:40 — God raised him on the third day
   4. 1 Corinthians 15:20 — The first fruits
   5. 1 Corinthians 15:22 — We die in Adam and live in Christ
   6. 1 Corinthians 15:26 — The last enemy: death
   7. John 20:8 — Seeing and believing
   8. John 20:18 — I have seen the Lord

Possible Outline Of Sermon Moves

The Easter Gospel from John begs for a simple narrative sermon. Here is an idea.

A. Begin by describing in your own words that which leads up to Easter Day.
   1. Driving out the money changers in the Temple
   2. Maundy Thursday foot washing and communion
   3. Good Friday's crucifixion
   4. Saturday's day of death and waiting

B. Retell in your own words John 20:1-9.

C. Talk about the difference between John (beloved disciple), and Peter. John believed first on the evidence of the empty tomb because he already believed (v. 8).

D. Tell your people how Easter's empty tomb has enabled many disciples to believe ever since.

E. Give your own witness as to what the empty tomb means to you:
   1. At times of death
   2. At time of a life crisis
   3. When having doubts about your faith

F. Move to the story of Mary Magdalene in the garden. Tell in your own words. Explain she wasn't expecting Jesus, so she did not recognize him when he came to her.

G. Talk about how our expectations affect what takes place in our seeking the Christ.

H. Give your witness as to what it means to you that Jesus appeared first to a woman disciple.
   1. Jesus appeared to those he loved and they were common salt-of-the-earth folks.
   2. He will come to us also if we look beyond the empty tomb expecting his alive presence to be here with us.

I. Explain what our witness ought to be today. Use 17b, "But go ..." and 18, "Mary Magdalene went and announced...." So should we.

J. Frame the sermon by returning to the events of Holy Week and telling how this event cast them in a whole different light. Not only for Mary and John. But also for us.

Prayer For The Day

We thank you, dear God, that you brought your crucified Son out of the grave and that we might come here and celebrate it as glorious Easter. Help us to believe like John and go and tell like Mary Magdalene, and keep us full of expectation. In the Easter Christ's name. Amen.

Possible Metaphors And Stories

There is a small church called Saint Peter in the Parish of Saint Andrew about one half hour from Kingston, Jamaica, near Fort Charles, where the tombstone of one Lewis Gladly reads as follows:

> *Here lies the body of Lewis Gladly who departed this life in Port Royal the 22nd of December, 1739, aged 80. He was born in Montpelier in France, but left that country for his religion and came to settle in this island where he was swallowed up by the great earthquake in the year 1692. By the providence of God was he by another shock thrown into the sea and miraculously saved until a boat took him up. He lived many years after in great reputation. Beloved by all that knew him and much lamented at his death.*

We also have a new life in Christ available to us.

Five grown children kept the remains of their mother in her bedroom more than eighteen months after she died, filling the room with presents and flowers in the belief that she would be resurrected. Blanche Riley, 56, died in March, 1990, in a second-floor bedroom. A niece of Mrs. Riley in Florida grew suspicious about the family's claim that she was unavailable and had been sleeping a lot. Family members cleaned the remains daily, changing the bedclothes and disinfecting the room to mask the odor (*Oakland Tribune*, September 22, 1991).

Easter people have a better hope!

There is a story told of a White House employee calling Woodrow Wilson in the middle of the night and saying that an IRS employee had died in the middle of the night and asking if he could take his place. Wilson said, "It's all right with me, if it's okay with the undertaker."

Jesus took our place on Good Friday and Easter through resurrection.

On *CBS News* with Connie Chung, she called it the Lenin problem: "What to do with a god who failed." They have Lenin on display. I saw him. Now what do you do with him? Bury ... traditionalists say no.

Our God is one who won in the Easter victory. Not on display in a glass tomb, embalmed and preserved. No need to display a dead preserved body. Ours is alive through us and the church. We are the Easter people.

Second Sunday Of Easter

Revised Common	Acts 5:27-32	**Revelation 1:4-8**	John 20:19-31
Roman Catholic	Acts 5:12-16	**Revelation 1:9-13, 17-19**	John 20:19-31
Episcopal	Acts 5:12a, 17-22, 25-29	**Revelation 1:(1-8) 9-19**	John 20:19-31

Seasonal Theme   The resurrected Christ becomes a physical presence in the world again.

Theme For The Day   It's still Easter and we celebrate Jesus with us just like those first disciples did.

First Lesson   Acts 5:27-32   *Apostles Before The Council*

In this account of Luke, Peter gives a marvelous explanation and defense and witness before the Sanhedrin. The apostles were accused of not following the decree of this body today (Acts 4:18). They were suspected of getting even for the death of their leader. So on behalf of all the disciples Peter claims:

1. Disciples had to obey God rather than any human authority (v. 29).
2. They had killed the very one God had raised up for them, Jesus (v. 30).
3. The one they had killed had come to give forgiveness to them (v. 31).
4. The disciples and God's Holy Spirit were witnesses to the above truths (v. 32). This was probably a reference to Pentecost.

While Peter's defense enraged those who heard it (v. 33), still it was a fine model of a disciple's utterances in a public gathering like the Sanhedrin.

Second Lesson   Revelation 1:4-8   *Alpha And Omega*

During this Easter season we are using passages from the book of Revelation as our Second Reading. The author, John, is writing in order to encourage Christians to resist the pressure to worship the emperor and to warn them that the showdown between God and Satan will be soon. They were important words to these faithful Christians, who were faced with choosing between the emperor or Jesus as their Lord.

Today's reading is the first of seven letters to seven churches in the province of Asia, which are identified in verse 11. Jesus is presented as a faithful witness in order to encourage the readers to be faithful in their own witness as well. Verse 5b is a reference to Psalm 89:27, firstborn being Christ's status in resurrection.

While the Alpha and Omega of verse 8 are tempting to center on, I like verse 6 and the idea that we are a kingdom of priests of God (see Isaiah 61:6). So in the New Testament we, having been freed from our sins, become a "kingdom of priests." This may have been a concept already familiar to early Christians.

Of course Alpha and Omega are the first and last of the 24 letters in the Greek alphabet. Maybe John is also saying that the end will be as the beginning was. What other metaphors might we come up with? *A* to *Z*? Everything but the kitchen sink?

The Gospel   John 20:19-31   *Another After-Easter Appearance*

The International Bible Commentary makes an interesting homiletical point. "Each of the resurrection appearances of Jesus fulfills a special purpose. For Peter it was the proclamation of victory; for Mary it was the satisfaction of love; now for the rest it is the calming of fear." In verse 22 we have an old friend in the scripture, "the breath of God" (Genesis 2:7; Ezekiel 37:9f). Here Jesus breathed on them and they were changed from timid men and women to bold witnesses. And this new spirit-filled church can pronounce on sin as certain as Jesus said it could (v. 23). The disciple who always demanded factual proof got to then make the first confession of faith which occurred after the day of resurrection. And verse 29 is a great one! It is as if Jesus is affirming all those who believed before such evidence, as Easter resurrection was available to them. So we don't see this as scolding but celebrating those who came to faith with less evidence.

Preaching Possibilities
A. We can put all the readings together under the theme "It's Easter Again."
    1. Acts: It's Easter again and we can be brave.
    2. Revelation: It's Easter again and we can be faithful witnesses.
    3. John: It's Easter again and we too have a spirit of peace.
B. Individually we have power in all three readings.
    1. The Acts account bears telling in narration form in your own words about what Easter meant to those first disciples and what it means to you now. Then what it can mean to this, your congregation.
    2. The Revelation account could stress the things which we are pressured to worship and then talk about the meaning of Alpha and Omega and the meaning of "kingdom of priests." How does that affect our congregational and individual behavior? Two major questions need to be answered. What does it mean to be a priest? And what does it mean to be part of a kingdom?

Possible Outline Of Sermon Moves
Text: Gospel for today
Title: Could be "Easter Continued" or "Easter, Part II"
A. Begin by telling how your Easter went last Sunday and the relief when Holy Week and Easter were *over* again this year.
B. Wait a minute! This is Easter 2. It's still Easter. We aren't finished yet! Relate to a movie, second part, like *Rocky 2*. Now tell in your own words the story of John 20:19-31. Here also is a continuation of the story. In fact, every first day of the week year round is a "little Easter."
C. Consider with your congregation what the second celebration teaches us.
    1. For Peter it was a victory, and we have a victory also.
    2. For Mary it was love satisfied, and now it pictured her misfit son in a whole new light.
    3. For the other disciples, it meant calm for their fears, and it can do that for us, too.
    4. For doubting Thomas and us, it meant concrete proof.
D. Like an encore we have it played again to our unrestrained, standing ovation. Jesus is alive, out of the grave, and with us here and now.
E. Frame your sermon by returning to your telling of last week's Easter and relief that it was over. But not really!

Prayer For The Day
We celebrate again today, O God, your coming out of the grave so we might one day also know our own resurrection. We rejoice in our victory, your love, calm for our fears, and proof of your alive presence with us still. In Christ. Amen.

Possible Metaphors And Stories
A mother brought her son to a concert to hear a great pianist. At intermission the little boy broke away, went up on stage, and began to play "Chopsticks" on the grand piano. A spotlight was placed on the little lad and the crowd got quiet. The boy became very afraid. The maestro saw it from the wings of the stage, came out and sat on the bench with the boy, and began to play the upper part of "Chopsticks." He leaned over and whispered, "It's all right now, son. I'm with you."

God comes and sits with us and sees us through.

Mercedes Benz has an advertisement on television in which a big, new, black Mercedes crashes into a wall for research safety. When asked why they share the scientific information with other auto manufacturers worldwide, the researcher responds, "Because some things in life are too good not to share." So, too, the gospel — just "too good not to share."

A ballplayer for the Pittsburgh Pirates said he was not afraid. His parents had taught him: "No matter what, God still loves me. My parents still love me, also." To be assured of being loved is one of the greatest gifts life can give us. It is one of the most profound shaping forces in any person's life.

On the NBC *Nightly News*, Tom Brokaw told of a man in East Germany who said, when asked why he liked Mikhail Gorbachev, "Because for the first time in my life, I am not afraid." Our Emmanuel promised, "Be not afraid; I am with you always to the end of the age!"

Third Sunday Of Easter

Revised Common	Acts 9:1-6 (7-20)	Revelation 5:11-14	John 21:1-19
Roman Catholic	Acts 5:27-32, 40-41	Revelation 5:11-14	John 21:1-19
Episcopal	Acts 9:1-19a	Revelation 5:6-14	John 21:1-14

Seasonal Theme   The resurrected Christ becomes a physical presence in the world again.

Theme For The Day   Our call to follow Jesus by tending and feeding Jesus' loved ones and following him as he appears to us.

First Lesson   Acts 9:1-6 (7-20)   *The Conversion Of Saul*

On that lonely, week-long, 140-mile walk no doubt Saul thought much about how Stephen had faced his death with such bravery and calm. So we have here not so much a spontaneous conversion, but rather a sudden giving in to that which had been nagging at him for quite a while. It's perhaps one of the best known conversion stories. Saul had the authority from the Sanhedrin to persecute the early Christians. He would extradite them from Damascus and bring them back to Jerusalem.

Barclay tells us that violent thunder storms were common here as the cold air of the mountains hit the hot air of the plains. There would be lightning, and Christ spoke to Saul in it. The struggle to understand those he tormented was over — he gave in finally to the Christ. This story will continue, for he will enter the city a changed person.

Second Lesson   Revelation 5:11-14   *The Lamb Is Worthy*

In verse 12 we have the vindication of the Lamb. The victim finally gets its place, and in the vision it is next to the one seated on the throne (v. 13). So Jesus is identifying with the victims of his society and then he became the victim (Lamb). *The New Interpreter's Bible* calls this "... an alternative story — in which the side of the victims is taken." John describes seeing the heavenly hosts and affirms the Lamb's validity.

Here this hymn of praise to the Lamb moves to ever-widening circles: from elders to all the heavenly hosts (v. 11) then to all creation (v. 13). It's all sealed by the word and adoration of the four living creatures and the elders.

The Gospel   John 21:1-19   *Jesus Appears To The Seven Disciples*

This is the third appearance of Jesus since the Easter resurrection (v. 14). The first was in the garden to Mary Magdalene. Because she was a woman, no doubt the Gospel writer didn't count this one. So another first appearance is recorded in John 20:19ff. It took place in the upper room. The second would be a week later in verses 20:26ff. This time Thomas is there in the upper room. Now — we have the third (or fourth) today. The disciples had gone fishing back at familiar Galilee. Jesus told them where to catch fish after a dismal all night trying. And he cooked their breakfast of fish and bread for them. Then there was a marvelous commissioning of Peter after confessing he loved Jesus. Peter is to care for the sheep. This is a recommended Gospel passage often used in ordination and installation services of pastors. Some commentators claim the three times asked of Peter if he loved Jesus is corresponding with Peter's denial three times of Jesus.

Augustine thought the 153 number of fish to do with the commandments and the gifts of the spirit. I believe that to be unnecessary guessing and allegorizing.

Verse 19 summons us to a loyalty that might lead to death. Homiletically, the readings will divide up with three narratives:

1. The advice to try again on the other side of the boat to catch fish.
2. The preparation of their breakfast by Jesus.
3. The dialogue with Peter about love and shepherding sheep.

Preaching Possibilities

I am not certain the three readings for today connect very well. They all are rich on their own.

A. The Acts account and the John passage could go together as representation of Jesus' appearances out of the grave and in the world.

B. Still, I would argue for either the conversion experience on the road to Damascus or Jesus' advice of where to fish and his breakfast dialogue with good old Peter. Consider this for the Damascus road conversion:
1. Begin by telling of something you believed deeply and then completely changed your mind about.
2. Describe Saul's long walk from Jerusalem to Damascus, including what he must have remembered from holding the robes of those who stoned Stephen.
3. Describe lightning on that road.
4. Illustrate how we still use the phrase that something "strikes us."
5. Talk about what this conversion story teaches us.
   a. Jesus still wants to appear to those who persecute him and forgive them and change their minds.
   b. No one is beyond the concern and conversion of Jesus.
   c. Saul told Paul he was going his own way and going the way Jesus directed him.
   d. Often we within the church still need a conversion, like from greed to sharing, hating to loving, and so on.
6. Tell about the conversions of such as Martin Luther also in a thunderstorm, Wesley in a worship service, Joan of Arc, and so on.
7. Tell of Paul's missionary service after this Damascus road conversion.
8. Frame by returning to your opening narration about your own conversion from one point of view to a radically different one.

Possible Outline Of Sermon Moves

A. Introduction: For those of us who demand proof, the witness of the Bible relates numerous times when the after-Easter alive Jesus appeared to the disciples.

B. Relate in your own words the appearances of Jesus:
1. To Mary Magdalene
2. To those gathered in the upper room
3. To Thomas in the upper room
4. And today to seven of the disciples who had gone fishing
5. And so alive and present, he cooked breakfast for them

C. Tell how these stories of Jesus' appearance affect your faith.
1. Gets rid of doubts
2. Instructs me to look for his alive presence in my own life
3. Tells me it's when I am with other believers I am most likely to know his presence

D. Move to the Jesus and Peter dialogue. Tell it in your own words. Say why Jesus asks three times.

E. Ask us disciples what it means for us to tend Jesus' sheep and feed Jesus' sheep. Who are these sheep for your congregation? In what ways are we both tended to and fed? And where will it lead us if Jesus says the same words to us that he did to Peter: "Follow me"?

F. Frame by giving your relief that we have these accounts of Jesus' appearance and perhaps state where you think we might be likely to see his resurrected presence now.

G. Pray for that presence.

Prayer For The Day

Dear Easter Jesus, please appear to us like you did your first disciples. In our gardens, in our homes and upper rooms, along our shores, and even at our breakfast tables, come to us also. And show us the way to feed and tend your sheep here in your community and how to follow you. We pray all this as your Easter people and in your name. Amen.

Possible Metaphors And Stories

There are several scenes in the movie *Cocoon* which speak of new life. Bernie tries to take his dead wife into the pool and Walter says: "It's too late, Bernie, the life is gone." Sin is pictured when one regressed into being unfaithful to his wife again. Life in the water — a beautiful picture of baptism and the new life we have in Christ.

"Florida city drained by Virgin Mary pilgrimage." An article in the *Contra Costa Times* newspaper of January 5, 1997, claimed that in Clearwater, Florida, the crowds coming to see an image resembling the Virgin Mary on a glass office building are costing the city big bucks.

"The faithful have numbered 450,000 — four and one half times the city's population — over the three weeks since the image was first noticed. And a city report put the tab at $40,000 to deploy police to handle the crowds and direct traffic." The document also tells of easily riled worshipers and votive candles that started fires, including one that burned a police officer.

"A city panel, dubbed the Miracle Management Task Force, decided to scale back crowd and traffic control efforts over the weekend.

"Meantime, the image is still on the side of the Seminole Finance building and its owners have no plans to try to remove it."

Al Haversat, a Lutheran clergyman, told of a man calling the florist and giving specific directions to prepare flowers for a casket with an extra wide ribbon, and so forth. When he got them, he was astounded to find the directions on the ribbon; so it read: "Rest in peace on both sides and if there is room, we'll meet in heaven."

We have peculiar ideas about heaven being a sort of better-than-here place.

Oral Roberts, Robert Schuller, and Billy Graham all died at the same time and went to heaven. There wasn't room for them for a few days, so they temporarily had to go to hell and wait until their place was ready. The Devil soon called and asked Saint Peter to get them out of there because Roberts had healed everyone, Graham had saved everyone, and Schuller had raised enough money to air condition the place!

Fun humor, but is it not so that our task as God's disciples is to do just that: to heal, to save, and to make conditions better for the less fortunate?

Fourth Sunday Of Easter

Revised Common	Acts 9:36-43	**Revelation 7:9-17**	John 10:22-30
Roman Catholic	Acts 13:14, 43-52	**Revelation 7:9, 14-17**	John 10:27-30
Episcopal	Acts 13:15-16, 26-33 (34-39)	**Revelation 7:9-17**	John 10:22-30

Seasonal Theme   The resurrected Christ becomes a physical presence in the world again.

Theme For The Day   We have absolute assurance from our God of our eternal life with God and all the Saints.

First Lesson   Acts 9:36-43   *Peter In Lydda And Joppa*

The names Dorcas in Greek and Tabitha in Aramaic mean a gazelle or deer. Notice we are told that Peter prayed (v. 40). So we see that Peter healed using the power of Jesus and not his own. (See Matthew 10:8.) The word *saint* is used previously in verse 32 and here in verse 41. Paul often used this word to describe church members. William Barclay tells us that the root word for this (*hagios*) means *different*. It is a marvelous word homiletically. These saints were both holy and different. They had been saved to serve and not for any great privilege. That is different! What a picture: the widows and different church members gathered around Peter, wearing and showing him the things Dorcas had made with her own hands as acts of kindness. Yes, it is really different. Please take special note that Tabitha was called a disciple (v. 36). We often present disciples in the Bible as all men. This is the only place the Greek word for *disciples* is used. Later in the second century in the Gospel of Peter it is used again and this time it is for Mary Magdalene. The raising of Dorcas is important because it is the first miracle like this by an apostle.

This woman's good works of charity have inspired women's groups around the world to be named the Dorcas Circle or Tabitha Class, and so on.

Second Lesson   Revelation 7:9-17   *Many From Every Nation*

Let's consider some of this imagery. The white robes stand for purity and resurrection glory. The palm branches stand for victory and joy. The washed robes represent forgiveness of sins through faith in the Christ who died for us. Verses 6 and 7 are drawn from Isaiah 29:8 and 49:10.

We can approach the passage several homiletical ways. John sees our forgiveness in verse 14. Verse 16 lists the hardships of their earthly life and promises that it will not be so in heaven. Verse 17 pictures Jesus as our guide and shepherd. And then comes 17b with a beautiful assurance that our sadness will be no more. All together it is a nice picture of life beyond this one. God is counting on our arrival, rejoicing in our forgiveness, relieved of our earthly worries, a shepherd to lead us, and no more pain and grief. It will preach and comfort all the Easter people.

The Gospel   John 10:22-30   *Jesus Rejected By Jews*

The Festival of Dedication celebrated the rededication of the Temple in 164 B.C. There would be many lighted lamps in the houses around the Temple and in the Temple itself.

The question the Jews asked Jesus meant they were not a part of his flock. Verse 30 simply says Jesus' and God's will are the same. It's not an attempt to explain the Godhead. In verse 27 we have a nice mutuality. He knows them and they follow him. I have seen shepherds call out for their sheep in Palestine from a common fold and the sheep separate themselves out and follow their own shepherd whose voice they recognize.

In reading this passage one has to question if these Jews really wanted to know the answer to verse 24 or if they simply were trying to trap Jesus. Verse 25b seems to offer Jesus' answer to such a question: "Watch what I do and you will be able to know who I am."

Preaching Possibilities

A. We could use all three readings under the theme: "After Easter Saints." They tell us about what it is like and what our assurances are as one of the saints of God.
   1. First Lesson — We are to do good things for others, including miracles of healing. And women are also disciples!
   2. Second Lesson — We have a much better life beyond the grave than this one. It is assured by Jesus' death on the cross for us and by the compassionate love God has for us!
   3. The Gospel — God leads us like a shepherd right into eternal life where we are secure as Easter people.
B. For Protestants who are so shy about good works, the First Reading is an excellent opportunity to speak about doing acts of charity as Jesus' disciples (male and female) and about the natural love of the saints who do them.
C. As for me this year, I will use the Second Reading by itself and talk about our hope and promise of eternal life as John's Revelation lays it out.

Possible Outline Of Sermon Moves

A. Begin by relating a funeral you had to conduct of a real, dear saint of the church.
B. Relate how "after Easter Christians" have in today's Second Reading some promises and assurances which helped you preach at this funeral.
C. Move to read Revelation 7:9, 14b, 16, and 17.
D. Explain the Promises:
   1. 7:9: God knows we'll be there and it will be a large gathering of all sorts of races, colors, and nationalities.
   2. 14b: Jesus' sacrifice on the cross assures us that we are forgiven of all our sins.
   3. 16: The earthly struggles we have now will all be gone.
   4. 17: Jesus will be our guide and lead us to a satisfaction like we never will know here; a loving, forgiving God will remove the grief of our earthly life.
E. Relate the first story told below in Possible Metaphors And Stories.
F. Frame your sermon by returning to your story about having to conduct a funeral for a very dear saint of the church. Then remind your listeners of your main points by repeating them in reverse order — 4, 3, 2, and 1.

Prayer For The Day

Dear God, we who are the Easter people are here again today celebrating your alive out of the grave presence with us. And we are enjoying the assurances you give us about our own eternal life. We are thankful you lead us to heaven to join all the Saints praising you. In Jesus, the Christ's, name. Amen.

Possible Metaphors And Stories

On an episode of the popular television sitcom *Night Court*, Mac, the court bailiff, said to a woman covering for her husband's suicide by confessing to murder: "Beyond a man's limit is a place where God doesn't want us to be alone."

So God's Emmanuel, the Holy Spirit, is with us.

For my class in advanced preaching, Roger and I wheeled a casket past a seminary classroom and into the chapel. It caused quite a stir in the class. Perhaps eschatology needs more emphasis in all our theological studies. The casket brought the discussion very close to the ground! It was for my students to use for practice in preaching a funeral sermon.

It's especially true that the awareness of life's brevity brings an awareness of life's gift nature.

Staples, the office supply store, had a television advertisement which always ended with the slogan, "Yeah, we've got that." What are people shopping so desperately for in their lives? Grace, forgiveness, peace, friendship, salvation ... "Yeah, we've got that."

We walked five miles from Totota, Liberia, to a little bush village. The little dried mud and stick church was "full plenty" and we had to move outside. Each person brought a lantern or flashlight, and several hundred sat on the ground to hear the gospel proclaimed under the starlit and moonlit night. They held a flashlight on my face and Pastor Manawu translated my sermon into Kpella. We were God's people and witnesses to God's word. Halfway around the world from home and church, but under the same stars and the same moon, we prayed and praised God.

Fifth Sunday Of Easter

Revised Common	Acts 11:1-18	Revelation 21:1-6	John 13:31-35
Roman Catholic	Acts 14:21-27	Revelation 21:1-5	John 13:31-35
Episcopal	Acts 13:44-52	Revelation 19:1, 4-9	John 13:31-35

Seasonal Theme   The resurrected Christ becomes a physical presence in the world again.

Theme For The Day   After Easter disciples love each other. It is also a witness to those outside the church who see it.

First Lesson   Acts 11:1-18   *Peter's Report*

Christianity escapes being another sect of Judaism by overcoming this renewed criticism of Peter for baptizing the uncircumcised Gentiles. We actually read this story twice in Luke's book of Acts. It was a real milestone for the Christian Church when the decision is made to include the Gentiles.

Notice in verse 3 the first criticism against Peter was his eating with Gentiles. Peter just states the facts. The Holy Spirit had come upon Gentiles as well as Jews. You could not argue with that.

Barclay says the number of six witnesses in verse 12 is important, because with Peter, it makes seven. This is the number of witnesses which were necessary in Egyptian law to prove a case. Peter says here are the facts and there are seven witnesses to prove them. Few, if any, are ever argued into the kingdom — but witness, now that will work!

Second Lesson   Revelation 21:1-6   *A New Heaven And Earth*

Let's take these six verses one at a time.

Verse 1 — We have an introduction to the new earth and heaven that replace the older ones which have passed away. (See Isaiah 65:17.)

Verse 2 — Repeated again in verse 10 this serves as an introduction to more detailed 21:9—22:9. The word *bride* represents the church. Some scholars maintain that the New Jerusalem symbolizes the saints.

Verse 3 — This loud voice is not necessarily Christ or God. "The dwelling place" refers to Ezekiel 37:27. For God to be with us can mean victoriously or a wish or prayer.

Verse 4 — This repeats Revelation 7:17 and is an allusion to Isaiah 25:8. This elimination of death is apocalyptic and often occurred in early Christianity as death being conquered through Christ.

Verse 5 — Look at Isaiah 43:19. The short speech in verses 5-8 is God and is the only such speech in this book with a brief self-disclosure in 1:8. Then comes the emphasis on the revelation being truthful.

Verse 6 — Similar to Jesus' final words on the cross (John 19:28). The divine title "Alpha and Omega" is used several times in Revelation — an emphasis on the absolute power and sovereignty of God or of Christ.

Also we have here an allusion to Isaiah 55:1. There is a nice homiletical link between the invitation to drink and the living water.

The Gospel   John 13:31-35   *A New Commandment*

Jesus is speaking to those most precious to him and calls them "little children" (used seven times in 1 John). Like a dying father, he gives his most intimate thoughts to his children. It's a new mandate (thus Maundy Thursday) to love each other. This radical new kind of love begins a new age and is the mark by which Jesus' disciples are known (see Acts 4:33). We see in this passage a conclusion to what it means to be in a relationship with Jesus (vv. 1-5) and it provides a final definition of Jesus' "own." To love one another as Jesus loves us according to *The New Interpreter's Bible* "... is to live a life thoroughly shaped by love that carries with it a whole new concept of the possibilities of community." I like that!

In some ways it's easier to love one's enemies than to love friends who are there most of the time.

I like the idea that the way we love each other will be a symbol to others that we are really his disciples.

Preaching Possibilities

A. All three readings can work together if you have not yet addressed the theme "After Easter Disciples."
   1. First Lesson — After Easter disciples are inclusive, including all kinds of people.
   2. Second Lesson — After Easter people anticipate having a victory over death and their life begins and ends in Christ.
   3. The Gospel — After Easter people have a radical undeserved love for others and each other.
B. The First Reading is also rich with homiletical probabilities. Verse 18b will make a powerful proclamation of the good news that race and gender are not barriers for the Holy Spirit and salvation.
C. Or one could creatively preach from the negative. Those criticisms of Peter that he ate with the Gentiles and that he baptized and made Christians from other than his own people are for today, too. We could put the story in a contemporary setting to make it relevant and close to the ground. Verse 3 might read: "Why did you go to gay and lesbians and eat with them?" Notice the first paragraph under Possible Metaphors And Stories.
D. A quite different approach would be to focus on the Holy Spirit in baptism using verses 15 and 16. Baptism could be presented as much more than special water and a magic Trinitarian formula of words.
E. Another possibility for this Sunday would be a "letter sermon" based on the First Reading. It could be a letter from Peter to his brother Andrew, telling him about the criticism he faced from Jewish Christians and his own reasons for doing what he did. It will preach!

Possible Outline Of Sermon Moves

A. Begin by relating a time someone uttered very important words just before they died. If you heard them, it makes the story even more relevant.
B. Move to the Gospel for today explaining that Jesus said some very important words to people important to him before leaving them.
C. Read John 13:33, 34.
D. Move to what's new about this mandate.
   1. This commandment transcends the ten given by Moses, which are much more legalistic.
   2. This love is one we ought to have for others who don't even deserve it.
   3. This love has a model in Jesus on the cross to demonstrate God's love for us.
   4. This love is a gift that post-Easter people have because of their common discipleship.
   5. This love is only possible because of God's Holy Spirit.
E. Move to verse 35 and read, holding the Bible from which you read it in your hands for all to see.
F. Tell your listeners that the promise is that when we love each other in this way those who see it will know we are disciples, so here is a powerful witness to what life in a discipleship community is like.
G. Frame your sermon by returning to your opening story, then giving 1 through 5 above in reverse order.

Prayer For The Day

Teach us to love each other, dear Jesus, and to do it without any expectation of being loved in return. And may we love each other in such a gracious manner that others seeing it will want to be a part of our fellowship. In the Easter Jesus' name, we pray. Amen.

Possible Metaphors And Stories

The famous evangelist Dwight L. Moody often told the story of his trying to join a very prestigious church in Boston. Because he often had brought "street people" into their worship service, the elders tried to postpone his membership as long as possible. They told him he should pray about it for a month and then re-apply for membership. After the month, Jesus told Moody not to be upset — that he had been trying to get into that church for years!

The headline in the *South China Post* was: "Bombing Victim's Father Preaches Forgiveness for McVeigh." Bud Welch whose daughter was killed in the Oklahoma City bombing was crusading in the U.S. Congress and audiences across America by stating: "There is no healing from killing people." The rest of the relatives of those 168 killed were asking to see the execution on television. "They think they will get some type of healing," Welch said. "There is nothing about killing that's going to heal them."

Springing up on Pentecost and Calvary, the church flows through the ages like a river — that same river, and no other, will flow unchangingly on through the ages until that great day when it will empty completely into the formed sea of eternal blessedness (Wilhelm Loehe, Neuendettelsau, Germany).

In the television special *Wallenberg*, a Lutheran, who was a member of a wealthy family in Sweden, saved many Jews from the Nazis in Poland and Hungary. He said to his driver upon seeing a death march, "What shall we Christians say about this thing?" The driver answered, "I don't know. I'm not a theologian." Wallenberg responded, "Perhaps we are witnessing the death of God." What horrible things we humans do to each other.

Sixth Sunday Of Easter

Revised Common	Acts 16:9-15	Revelation 21:10, 22—22:5	John 14:23-29
Roman Catholic	Acts 15:1-2, 22-29	Revelation 21:10-14, 22-23	John 14:23-29
Episcopal	Acts 14:8-18	Revelation 21:22—22:5	John 14:23-29

Seasonal Theme   The resurrected Christ becomes a physical presence in the world again.

Theme For The Day   Important words Jesus said before ascending, including the gift of peace, God's love, and the Holy Spirit.

First Lesson   Acts 16:9-15   *A Call From Macedonia*

On this missionary journey, Paul and Timothy got as far as Troas. After Paul's dream of a man pleading for them to go to Macedonia, the narrative changes to the plural (v. 10) so that it sounds as if the author Luke joined them at this point. Perhaps he was, in fact, the man from Macedonia. Or perhaps Paul had a vision of Alexander the Great, who had conquered much of the world. Now Paul sets out to conquer the world for Christ.

In verses 11 to 15 we have Lydia, the first convert in Europe. Paul went to the riverside because in this Roman colony there would be no synagogue from which to start his evangelism. Lydia was from the upper class. Notice she at once offered hospitality to Paul (v. 15). Paul often described the Christian as one who offered hospitality (see Romans 12:13). Peter stressed this idea as well in 1 Peter 4:9. I wonder if there are not two great transitions here for the Christians faith: 1) it moves into Europe and 2) it moves into the upper class.

Second Lesson   Revelation 21:10, 22—22:5   *The New Jerusalem*

The author describes a lovely vision of Jerusalem, the holy city (see Ezekiel 40:2). There are some interesting ideas about this new Jerusalem. Because it is where God lives, there is no need for a church (v. 22). There will be no need for a sun or moon — God's glory will be its source of light (see Isaiah 60:19f). Verse 24 is interesting because we can gain the idea that those dwelling in this holy city will be a blessing to those outside (see Isaiah 60:5ff and Psalm 72:10). Then comes this vision of openness and welcome in verse 25 with gates always opening and the promise that night will no longer inhibit them, as God's shining on them will be continuous (check out Isaiah 60:11).

Homiletically one can imagine what heaven is like from this passage. However, this is still Easter and we ought to talk about being alive and out of the grave. So if we do use this passage, we probably should use it to illustrate the Easter theme of a new day, a new presence of the risen Christ, and a new people of God community.

The Gospel   John 14:23-29   *The Advocate Will Come*

The monologue of Jesus is in response to a question Judas (not Iscariot) asked of him. In it Jesus gives the disciples some truths they remembered.

1. If they love Jesus, they will follow his teachings.
2. God will come to them and live with them.
3. Jesus' words are not his own but from God.
4. The Advocate (Holy Spirit) will come to them in order to teach them.
5. Jesus blesses them with a peace which means much more than the worldly view of peace, which is the absence of trouble. Here it is a comfort and inner strength for the time they would be under severe pressure and distress.
6. They should celebrate his departure, because in a strange way this is how he will be with them always.

7. Jesus comes from the Father and is one with God.
8. He tells them all this ahead of time so when it happens they can believe it.

Jesus is really saying that he has made a start but there is much more to learn. The Advocate (Holy Spirit) will continue the teaching and take them even further. Christ is really telling them of his legacy for all disciples.

Preaching Possibilities

A. We have another opportunity to talk about after Easter discipleship using all three readings:
   1. First Lesson — All disciples are called to ministry and we invite all economic strata into the kingdom.
   2. Second Lesson — Things are different after Easter. We have a new dwelling place.
   3. The Gospel — We have the risen Easter Christ with us in spirit and we still have a lot to learn in our discipleship.
B. If by now we have well covered the "Easter people" theme, there are a number of individual topical sermon texts today.

The call of God	Acts 16:9
The global mission of the church	Acts 16:15
A likeness of heaven	Revelation 21:22-25
Wide open gates to the church	Revelation 21:25
The coming of the Spirit	John 14:26
The gift of peace	John 14:27
There is more to learn	John 14:26

Possible Outline Of Sermon Moves

Text: John 14:23-29

A. Begin with a story of preparing to leave to travel somewhere.
B. Introduce the Gospel account as Jesus preparing to leave the disciples in bodily form.
C. Make the point that when we know we may not see someone ever again, we choose our words carefully.
D. List what Jesus was communicating which young John wrote down.
   1. Those who love Jesus will try to follow his teachings (v. 23) and God will love them.
   2. We do not face our discipleship alone. Our help is the Holy Spirit (v. 26).
   3. The gift of peace is ours — a peace different than the world knows (v. 27).
   4. We have Jesus' help in believing (v. 29).
E. Use an illustration from below at the end of each of the above moves.
F. Pray after each of the four above teachings. Here are some suggestions:
   1. We know you love us, dear God, and we pray today that knowing you love us will help us follow your teachings. Amen.
   2. Holy Spirit, continue to inspire and instruct us in our discipleship. It's so good to know you are rooting for us here and in heaven. Amen.
   3. We thank you, dear God, for the gift of peace you bestow upon us. And we pray we might be a channel through which others are given peace, as well. Amen.
   4. We rejoice in the advance notice you gave the disciples so they could believe; now help us believe, too. Amen.
G. Frame your sermon by returning to your opening story about someone preparing for a departure.

Prayer For The Day

In this Holy Easter season, when we are so mindful of your resurrected presence with us, dear God, help us through your Holy Spirit to hear our call to discipleship and to be part of the global mission of the church. Refresh our vision of the New Jerusalem in our lives and give us your blessed peace. In the risen Easter Christ's name. Amen.

Possible Metaphors And Stories

My daughter Sarah used to live in Washington, D.C. She agreed to meet me where the metro lines meet in the center city. It worked and we found each other. The old song goes: "Meet me in Saint Louis, Louis, meet me at the fair." Where shall we meet as God's people? Where love and consideration for others intersect.

The strip of highly colorful and decorative cloth given as a special gift of friendship by the Bataks of Sumatra is called an *ulos*. At a wedding reception it is wrapped around the bride and groom, binding them as one. It is symbolic of deep, rich friendships kept warm in the future. Often woven into the cloth is "God's Peace." Like a blanket, it is used to keep warm at night and to carry a baby slung over the shoulder in what is named a *parompa*.

We have a comfort of peace also and it's sometimes called the Comforter, the Holy Spirit, which keeps us warm in spirit and peace-filled in struggle.

At the installation of a chaplain to the homeless at People's Park in Berkeley, the invitation was extended to offer the peace to each other. A large black dog snapped at a man who kicked it in the teeth.

Peace seems so temporary, artificial, and elusive.

At the Kennedy Space Control Center there are signs which come on telling of the many countdown checks. Then at about fifteen seconds before lift-off the sign reads: "Commit." So too, in landing a plane, there is a time when it's too late to abort the landing and the pilot "commits."

Perhaps there are times like confirmation (affirmation of Baptism) when we are to commit with the help of the Holy Spirit.

The Ascension Of Our Lord

Revised Common	Acts 1:1-11	Ephesians 1:15-23	Luke 24:44-53
Roman Catholic	Acts 1:1-11	Ephesians 1:17-23	Luke 24:46-53
Episcopal	Acts 1:1-11	Ephesians 1:15-23	Luke 24:49-53

Seasonal Theme   The resurrected Christ becomes a physical presence in the world again.

Theme For The Day   The power of the Ascension, and Jesus becoming the Christ in heaven for us on earth, and witnessing.

First Lesson   Acts 1:1-11   *The Promise Of The Spirit*

This book of the Acts of the Apostles seems to be the second book written to Theophilus (v. 1) by Luke. First came the life and teaching of Jesus in the Gospel of Luke, then this one relates how it went after Easter and the ministries of the Apostles in the early church. The events went like this:

1. Jesus gave the apostles the Holy Spirit.
2. Jesus appeared to them many times after Easter to give them proof of the physical resurrection.
3. Power is promised for witnessing.
4. Jesus ascends.

Two messengers told them Jesus had ascended and would return in a similar fashion.

Notice in verse 4 the disciples are ordered to *wait* for the Spirit. Waiting is one of the toughest struggles for this author. It seems a waste of precious time. Actually it is empowering and encouragement for the task (Isaiah 40:31).

Verse 8 is the one all missionaries use when preaching back home and when meditating on their mission and ministry overseas. God's spirit helps us witness. And a witness can state for sure something is true. Our witness is often most effective in our action rather than our words. In Greek the word for *witness* is the same one for *martyr* — we are faithful even if it means death.

Verses 9-11 tell us that it's not easy to explain this story of the ascension. Only Luke writes about it (Luke 24:50-53). Jesus couldn't just gradually fade away, so there needed to be a definite conclusion to his physical resurrected presence. Luke provides that and adds an equally difficult idea to explain — the second coming. I'll leave that idea alone because to speculate on it is even more than Jesus did (Mark 13:22).

Just notice out of this complicated story that the disciples were happy when they returned to Jerusalem. Something very powerful and joy-filled appeared!

Second Lesson   Ephesians 1:15-23   *Paul's Prayer*

I like Paul's comments to a former congregation here. What joy he must have written to them that he had heard they were faithful and loved the saints. He then prayed that they would be given wisdom and revelation. It's verse 18 that I find so intriguing —"eyes of the heart." If it were not Ascension and those gathered expecting a homily about the curious event on a hill outside Jerusalem, it's the heart I would talk about. *The Interpreter's Bible* says, "For that citadel of the soul which stands guard over love and hate, loyalty and treachery, trust and mistrust, we still have no better word than heart." See the following references to heart: Matthew 5:8, Mark 7:21, 1 Samuel 16:7, and 1 Peter 3:4. When the heart has been moved by gifts from God we are enlightened — that's worth much more than intellectual brilliance (Matthew 6:33).

In the next portion of this verse and that following, Paul lists some of the results of an "enlightened heart": hope, glorious inheritance, and his power for us believers.

Wow, there is power here! Paul says God used power to raise Jesus from the dead and place him in heaven with God (no doubt this passage was chosen for Ascension Day) and God has made Jesus the head of the church which is Jesus' body. This much power God gives to us believers as well! Now *that's* power! So this passage is a prayer by Paul, that Christians may know God's purpose and power.

There are some rich metaphors: Spirit of wisdom and revelation; the eyes of your heart; riches of his glorious inheritance; seated at the right hand; put all things under his feet; head over all things; and the church, which is his body.

The Gospel　　　　　　　　Luke 24:44-53　　　　　　　*The Ascension Of Jesus*

A number of appearances of Jesus after the Easter resurrection took place in the upper room. It must have been a gathering place for those frightened believers. But now that Jesus is about to leave them physically, he tells them this:

1. He has now fulfilled what the Old Testament writers claimed would happen.
2. The major thought here is that the Christ will suffer and rise from the dead.
3. And they are witnesses to this Good News and must leave the security of the upper room and take this message to all nations (v. 48). They will have God's help in the doing of it!

Verses 50 to 53 are Luke's first take on the Ascension of Jesus as no longer the physical incarnate God-man from Nazareth. He now becomes the Christ of heaven. How this happened is not at all describable. Whatever happened that day on the Mount of Olives across Kidron Valley overlooking the Temple mount, we know it was all a part of our God's plan to end the physical earthly presence and begin a new spiritual relationship which could not be severed. Paul understood in Romans 8:38, 39. The joy of the disciples (v. 52) comes from knowing that Jesus was in heaven and remained their advocate and friend there.

Preaching Possibilities

Because of the theme of Ascension *today* we must go with Luke's account of this mysterious event in the First Reading and the Gospel. That means the Second Reading from Ephesians written by Paul probably can only be used in support of the two accounts of the Ascension.

The connection, it seems to me, is Ephesians 1:20-21 and God's power put to work in relocating the raised crucified Jesus to the Christ seated at the right hand of God. (I once knew an old pastor who loved to ask how we knew if God was left-handed? Then he would quote verse 20 and say it was because Jesus sat on his right hand!)

If we preached on the Second Reading alone, we could ask the question: "What does Paul tell us about the Ascension?" Because Jesus ascended to return to God, we can love each other (v. 15), we can have the spirit of wisdom and revelation (v. 17), deep in our heart we have enlightenment (v. 18), we have hope and are called (v. 18b), we inherit God's power (v. 19), and Jesus becomes the head over the church (v. 22).

Possible Outline Of Sermon Moves

The homiletical plot will be to start with Luke's narrative of Ascension, then move to the Acts account and then move to Paul's witness, finishing with what this all means for us now in the twenty-first century.

A. Begin by retelling in your own words Luke 24:50-53, if the scripture has already been read.
B. Move to a confession that it is hard for us to explain how this all happened. If you want to take a risk for the sake of humor, you might even mention that today Jesus would need a "mission control" to avoid all the other stuff flying around earth.
C. Tell why Luke put this story here.
　1. To transition from earthbound incarnate Jesus from Nazareth to the Christ of heaven always there for us.
　2. To see Jesus as the fulfillment of all God promises us in the prophecy.
　3. To encourage his readers to take seriously their role as witnesses.

D. Move to Luke's account in Acts and point out that Ascension is all about God's power.
   1. The Holy Spirit gives us power: the power to forgive on God's behalf, the power to heal, the power to love the unlovely, and the power to witness.
   2. Both accounts of Luke emphasize the responsibility we disciples have to witness to the gospel (Acts 2:8 and Luke 24:48).
   3. Paul in writing to his Ephesian church talks of power also (Ephesians 1:19). We believers still have it even if we haven't used it for a long time.
E. Move to what all this means for us now.
   1. We have a Christ in heaven who cares about us and so we never must face our lives alone.
   2. We have an untapped power God wants to give us to help us live life victoriously.
   3. We are to be witnesses and we all know those to whom our witness can be life changing.
   4. We have a global mission to make this witness wherever the gospel has not been proclaimed.
F. Finish by using Luke 24:52. When they returned it was not with sadness, but with joy. This is a joy that is not the same as happy, for that is too fickle. This is a joy which is the opposite of unbelief. We can have this joy also.

Prayer For The Day

Ascended Christ, we are filled with great joy just like those earlier disciples, because we know you are now our friend in heaven. We rejoice in the way you fulfilled all the Old Testament promises of crucifixion and resurrection for us that we might have forgiveness and also life with you and beyond the grave. Give us power that we might be effective witnesses every day of our lives and whenever the opportunity presents itself. Amen.

Possible Metaphors And Stories

A man by the name of William Quinn was in jail in San Francisco, accused of sending letter bombs. He is supposed to have planted explosives in a hollowed-out Bible. The Bible can be that explosive without humans stuffing it with dynamite. (The root word for dynamite is *dinimus*, used a number of times in the New Testament.) Loving neighbor and enemy, going the second mile, turning the other cheek, forgiving seventy times are indeed radical and explosive!

On the outside of the Anthropological Museum in Mexico City are the words: "God is as invincible as the night and as untouchable as the wind ... They were able/knew how to dialogue with their own heart" (Aztec).

In Wittenberg-Lutherstadt they told me the story about a large statue of Christ in front of the Castle Church. A group of Nazi youth on a Sunday afternoon beat it to pieces with clubs and then painted these words on a nearby fence: "The reign of Christ is over." Later a Christian youth group saw what had been done and took the paint brush and can and stuck the pieces of the statue back together. Then they added three letters to the sign: "all." "The reign of Christ is over all."

Seventh Sunday Of Easter

Revised Common	Acts 16:16-34	Revelation 22:1-14, 16-17, 20-21	John 17:20-26
Roman Catholic	Acts 7:55-60	Revelation 22:12-14, 16-17, 20	John 17:20-26
Episcopal	Acts 16:16-34	Revelation 22:12-14, 16-17, 20	John 17:20-26

Seasonal Theme   The resurrected Christ becomes a physical presence in the world again.

Theme For The Day   Jesus prayed for his disciples and us to be one in God and each other.

First Lesson   Acts 16:16-34   *Paul And Silas In Prison*

The slave girl would have been called a Pytho, which was a mad person who did fortune telling. It is interesting that those who exploited her were angry because she no longer could make money for them. No joy here because of the healing. Whenever something cuts our profits, we are tempted to rail against it no matter how good and compassionate the cause. And these owners of the slave girl played on the hatred of the Jews by Romans when they appealed to Roman pride and had Paul and Silas arrested for actually doing a very loving act of healing. Christianity had attacked vested interests and brought lots of trouble. Certainly the Christian business persons must always ask if by earning their profit they are exploiting other people.

Look at the characters in this midnight story: the Roman jailer who would have to pay with his own life if he lost any of his prisoners; the slave girl who was of the lowest social class and Lydia who was from the highest; Paul and Silas in jail, beaten, in stocks, singing hymns. How I wish I could have heard them! Notice Paul baptizes the very one who had imprisoned him. It's a radical love.

Notice also the whole household was baptized, which probably included all ages even infants. And one wonders if there was water enough for an immersion?

Then we have again something often related in the ministry of Jesus and the Apostles. There is an immediate response to the healings and/or saving. This jailer-Christian washed their wounds and fed them!

And earthquakes. They often happen in this part of the world, as archaeological evidence reveals.

Second Lesson   Revelation 22:12-14, 16-17, 20-21   *Jesus, Come Soon To Us Saints*

With this Second Reading we finish our series of readings from the book of Revelation. Phew! This reading begins with an announcement that the Lord will come soon and people will get what they deserve. This is also written in 2:23, 20:12, 1 Corinthians 4:5, and Ephesians 6:8. The Alpha and Omega is repeated again. The robed saints who have washed in the sacrificial Lamb's blood may enter through the gates to the New Jerusalem. All others look out!

Then in verses 16 and 17 we have established that it is none other than Jesus in the promised lineage of David, the Morning Star, who provided the angel's message to the churches. (See Numbers 24:17.) Also see 2 Peter 1:19 where the word is better translated "Light-bringer."

In verse 17 we have an invitation for the Lord to come. Then again, it may be the Spirit is the spirit of prophecy. So the spirit and the bride are the prophets and the saints.

Jesus is the one who "testifies" in verse 20. Verse 21 is a familiar New Testament benediction. Some use "with God's people" in place of "all the saints."

So we might summarize this reading like this: Jesus is coming soon and people will be judged according to their works on earth. Jesus is all of life from the beginning to the end. However, we who have salvation through Jesus' sacrifice will walk right into heaven. We, the saints, invite Jesus to return soon, and it is Jesus himself who has sent this word through his angel to us. God's grace be with us all. Marana-tha.

The Gospel John 17:20-26 *Jesus' Prayer For His Disciples*

This passage is usually interpreted as a prayer for the entire church. In order for people to recognize Jesus as God incarnate, unity is important. The purpose of this savior — prayed for — unity is to make it possible for God's love to be known. *The International Bible Commentary* states: "That companionship, which had begun a few years earlier, the Lord wishes to take into eternity. He will derive the greatest joy from knowing that they will behold this glory. This vision of the father will also be satisfied." It seems to me there are several unities prayed for here. Jesus prays that, just like he was one with God, his disciples might be one with God. And he prays just like he and his disciples were unified so might the disciples be unified. And he prays that the whole church would be unified with God and with each other. This is one of the most quoted texts in the scripture, often used to plead for organic union of all denominations and Christians. But I wonder if it were not meant by Jesus to be more of a oneness with God, like the oneness he had with God. You decide.

Preaching Possibilities

Now that we have celebrated the Ascension it seems a little redundant to return to Jesus' after Easter appearances. Perhaps we ought to rename this Sunday "Ecumenical Sunday" or "Church Unity Sunday" or for the more liturgical-minded it could be "The Sunday after Ascension."

A. Since it is the last Sunday of the Easter season, I hope you will consider a summary of these seven Sundays of Easter beginning with Easter itself and continuing through this seventh Sunday. An outline might look like this:
1. What a great Easter day it was when we gathered here and celebrated Jesus' coming out of the grave and how Mary Magdalene and young John and Peter bore witness to the resurrection.
2. Our second Sunday we considered how Thomas doubted and they saw the alive Jesus face to face.
3. The third Sunday we heard how Jesus calls us to follow him and care for his people.
4. The fourth Sunday we heard Jesus assure those disciples of their eternal life with him.
5. The fifth Sunday Jesus is teaching the disciples to love each other and how we do that will affect those who see it.
6. The sixth Sunday we have Jesus promising the gift of the Holy Spirit and that they must continue to learn about discipleship.
7. Then this seventh Sunday we hear Jesus praying for all disciples that they might be unified and that God's love might be in them.

B. Of course the First Lesson is such a powerful story it calls for good spellbinding narrative preaching. The slave girl story of "When our faith cuts into the profits" will work.

C. Or the midnight earthquake freeing Paul and Silas in the Philippian prison. This lends itself to addressing conversion, witnessing, and baptism. We might also approach this story through the eyes of Christian joy even in persecution.

D. If you have been preaching the recommended series on the Acts First Readings during this season, today would be a time to frame the series using the outline on page 92.

Possible Outline Of Sermon Moves

A. Begin by telling about a prayer you heard prayed which really was moving to you.

B. Move to the prayer Jesus prayed for his disciples contained in the Gospel for today. If you have not read the Gospel yet in the service, do it now.

C. Move to listing out what Jesus prayed for:
1. He prayed his disciples would be one in God.
2. He prayed his disciples would be united with each other.
3. He prayed that all those who would believe would be one.
4. He prayed that this obvious unity lived out would help others believe in Jesus.
5. He prayed that just like God sent Jesus on a mission the disciples might consider they were sent by Jesus on a mission as well.

116

D. Move to a review of this Easter season and the lessons we have learned by the appearances of Jesus recorded in Acts and John these seven Sundays.

E. Tell a story to illustrate from the Possible Metaphors And Stories below.

F. Frame by returning to your opening story about a very meaningful prayer you heard or prayed.

Prayer For The Day

We thank you, dear God, for this season of Easter when we might know for certain your out-of-the-grave presence with disciples of all ages. Keep us aware of your sacrifice for us on the cross and your glorious resurrection to win the victory over death that gives us hope and comfort even today. We who are your Easter people rejoice. In Christ's name. Amen.

Possible Metaphors And Stories

In his election concession speech, Al Gore quoted his father with the phrase, "Shake the soul and get the glory out."

"Four toast Henry" (Siang Kung) was asked about returning to Myanmar. He replied, "I would not return to that hardship except many missionaries here left their bones in our ground and I must return to honor them."

On NBC's made-for-television movie, *Going Home*, Bobby is dying of cancer and asks his father, "What's going to happen to me when I die? Where will I go?" The father replies, "Son, I don't know." Bobby says, "Grandpa knows; he talks to God." Grandpa had said after finding out that Bobby was dying: "You think tears dry up when you get old? Everything dries up but that!"

Life here hurts, but those who speak to God get through.

At a community Thanksgiving service at the First Methodist Church, Des Moines, the Drake University Choir sang the *Messiah*: "... he shall reign forever and ever ..." and left the sanctuary before the sermon.

The "forever" got shortened up a bit.

In the poem, "The Rape of Lucrece," Shakespeare has the words, "One for all, or all for one we gage." (Gage means "pledge.")

An Introduction To The Pentecost Season

We begin the second half of the liturgical year with the festival of Pentecost. We have just completed *Our Lord's half year* when we heard Luke's accounts of Jesus' life. Now we move into the *Church's half year* when we read the accounts of Jesus' miracles, ministry, and teachings.

This is the longest of the seasons and will take us through Christ the King Sunday up to the first Sunday in Advent. So here comes a period of instruction when we study the implications of having a Holy Parent, Savior, and Spirit-presence with us. We apply the teachings and example of Jesus' life with us in our church's ministry and practice — and to our own witness out in the world now.

The liturgical color for this season of growth and learning is green after we observe Pentecost (red) and Holy Trinity Sunday (white).

Heads Up Notice

Please note that in the first six weeks in Ordinary Time after Pentecost (Propers 4-9), the Second Reading is from Galatians beginning with the first verse and essentially reading in order until 6:16. Consider preaching a series on these strong passages Paul wrote to Christians who were puzzled about what to do about the Old Testament ceremonial practices now that they were Christians. In general, the letter defends the New Testament truth that we are justified by faith in Jesus Christ. And that we have the power of the Holy Spirit working in us. An outline for a series might look like this:

First week	Galatians 1:1-12	Freedom from the present evil age
Second week	Galatians 1:11-24	From persecuting to proclaiming the faith
Third week	Galatians 2:15-21	Justified by faith in Jesus Christ or Christ living in me
Fourth week	Galatians 3:23-29	All one in Jesus Christ and Abraham's offering
Fifth week	Galatians 5:1, 13-25	Freedom in Christ or indulgence in self?
Sixth week	Galatians 6: (1-6) 7-16	Bear one another's burdens or let us not grow weary

The title for the above series could be "Pastor Paul's advice for Christians like us."

Pentecost Day

Revised Common	Acts 2:1-21 or Genesis 11:1-9	Romans 8:14-17 or Acts 2:1-21	John 14:8-17 (25-27)
Roman Catholic	Acts 2:1-11	Romans 8:8-17	John 14:15-16, 23-26
Episcopal	Acts 2:1-11	1 Corinthians 12:4-13	John 20:19-23 or John 14:8-17

Seasonal Theme   The teachings, miracles, and earthly ministry of Jesus.

Theme For The Day The birthday of the Christian Church and the coming of the Holy Spirit upon the disciples.

First Lesson   Acts 2:1-21   *The Coming Of The Holy Spirit*

The Day of Pentecost gets its name from the fact it was on the fiftieth day after the first Sunday after Passover when the first of the barley harvest was brought to the temple. I like an alternate name used then: "the day of first fruits" (Numbers 28:26; Exodus 23:16a). The wind represents the Spirit of God (Ezekiel 37:9-14). John the Baptist had announced that the one coming would conduct a baptism of wind and fire (Luke 3:16-17). Like in the burning bush for Moses, the fire represents divine presence.

This was not the last time the disciples were filled with the Holy Spirit (see 4:8, 31). And when the descent of the Spirit on the disciples took place, it was natural that prophetic speech would follow. See Paul's advice in regard to speaking in tongues in 1 Corinthians 12:10, 28-30, 14:2-9. Here the message was "the mighty deeds of God" (v. 11). There is a great list of countries from which the crowd came.

Peter then preaches. He begins by making light humor of the charge made in jest that the disciples were drunk. It's just too early in the day for that!

Peter continues by quoting Joel's prophecy of what will happen in the "last days." The person to come was Jesus and his time is now. The last days have begun: We have the day of the Lord and the day of God's salvation to all who call upon his name described here. Verse 20 could be interpreted as what took place in Jerusalem on God's Friday.

Second Lesson   Romans 8:14-17   *Through The Spirit We Become God's Children*

This reading connects well with the Spirit in the Acts account of Pentecost. Lots of spirit here! The Spirit God gives is not of fear but of adoption into God's family. This gives us a very special relationship to Christ, the unique Son. We can cry aloud to our Holy Parent. Christ has already shared in the inheritance of God's glory and we can count on sharing that glory one day, too. And in verse 17b there is a connection between Christ's passion and his resurrection. So, according to Paul, we are adopted by God into the family, can call on him like a loving parent, and can share with God's unique Son God's glory.

The Gospel   John 14:8-17 (25-27)   *Jesus — The Way To The Father*

The center of this reading must be verse 9b: "Whoever has seen me has seen the Father." It's Jesus' answer to Philip's question in verse 8. Jesus' answer is that God is in him, and so when they see him they are getting a glimpse of God. Also (and here is the kicker), if you can't accept this answer, then simply watch what I *do* (v. 11). And if they believe they will do these good works of compassion also, then the promise of verses 13 and 14 is so great. When Jesus is in God, he has promised to do whatever the disciples asked of him if it is in his name.

Somehow, those disciples did not understand what we now call the *incarnation* as the ultimate revelation of God. Three times we have the word *believe* as we move from Jesus' revelation of God to their accepting it.

A new teaching begins in verse 12 with the "Very truly I tell you...." To love Jesus is to keep his commandments. In verse 17 we have the first use of *paracletos* — the Paraclete in the Fourth Gospel. Some words which help designate the full range of meaning in this word, *paraclete*, are to exhort and encourage; to comfort and console; to call upon for help; and to appeal.

There are many English translations of the noun, according to *The New Interpreter's Bible*: comforter (KJV), advocate (NRSV), counselor (NIV), and paraclete (NJB). The point here is not so much on those who refuse to accept the paraclete; but rather, on the gift of the paraclete by Jesus to his disciples. We have it, too! This whole passage tries to answer the question of whether the disciples can continue to love Jesus after he is gone, as well as future generations who never lived with him.

Preaching Possibilities

A. On the Sunday of Pentecost we will just about have to go with the biblical account of Pentecost and the coming of the Spirit on the disciples in Jerusalem's square, as described in the Acts account.

B. There is a strong connection, however, between that account and the Second Reading and the Gospel. It is the Spirit, the Paraclete.
1. In the Acts account, the Spirit begins the church.
2. In the Romans account, the Spirit makes us God's daughters and sons.
3. In the Gospel of John, the Spirit is our advocate/paraclete here and in heaven. It will preach.

C. Of course, if you just wanted to preach on the reading from John you could organize your homily around either or both of the lists above of the various translations of *paraclete*, telling your listeners of the truth revealed by each one. It could be framed in a story of your own experience of "The Spirit of the Thing" like a team sport or a deeply moving religious experience.

D. Another approach to the Gospel Reading from John would be to use verse 9b and concentrate on what disciples saw Jesus do and be, which revealed the Holy Parent to them:
1. He had great compassion;
2. He loved the unlovely;
3. He was willing to be sacrificed for them;
4. He brought healing to the sick and infirm;
5. He fed the hungry and went the extra mile;
6. He defeated death on Easter; and
7. He gave them help in heaven for on earth living.

Possible Outline Of Sermon Moves

A narrative sermon on Pentecost from Acts 2.

A. Begin by relating a very happy birthday you celebrated and what made it so.

B. Move to the birthday of the Christian Church on Pentecost in Jerusalem. Tell the story in your own words.

C. Move to listing for your hearers what in this account serves as a preview of how this church shall be.
1. It will be a spirit-filled church (v. 2).
2. It will be a witnessing and bold church (v. 4).
3. It will be a unique fellowship of changed people (v. 13) (use the Gospel Reading here).
4. It will be a church of many languages and color (v. 4).
5. It will be a church which amazes and astonishes other people (v. 7) (use the Second Reading here).
6. It will be a scripture-centered church (v. 16).

D. After each of the above moves, you can relate it all to your congregation and if you are living out the church of Pentecost. Or you can wait and just reflect one or two of the above and apply it to your congregation, starting with the "second birthday"* of your congregation when it began.

E. Talk about the vision of those who gathered to begin your congregation from your congregational history.

F. Frame the sermon by returning to your opening birthday narrative.

Prayer For The Day

We rejoice and give thanks on this day of Pentecost and birthday of your church in Jerusalem for all those who have gone before us equipped by your Spirit as your sons and daughters. Keep us faithful here at (*your congregation*) to the Spirit-filled vision of what we ought be and what, with your Paraclete, we can be. Give us your Spirit just like you did those first disciples and bless our unique fellowship like you did theirs. Amen.

Possible Metaphors And Stories

That first Pentecost must have been something else! Three thousand baptized. Pity the poor altar guild who prepared the font, and think of the church secretary who had to get all the certificates in order. The usher must have had quite a time parking the chariots and camels. The property committee probably rebelled at cleaning up the parking lot after that long service. The acolyte had to hold 3,000 burning candles. That next week when the other Jerusalem pastors met for text study, they were heard saying, "Yes, but the theology is weak there, and besides they probably will go out the back door as fast as they came in the front."

The local parish church was on fire and a crowd gathered. The pastor spotted an inactive member and commented: "Joe, this is the first time I have seen you at church for a long time." Joe responded, "Well, Pastor, this is the first time I have seen this church on fire!" Yes — let the Pentecost fire set our congregations ablaze!

My asthma is especially bad today. I breathe but get little effect from doing so. I think it can be so in the church as well. The Spirit's wind of Pentecost blows, but we get very little effect from it.

Nissan cars have run an advertisement on television that I like a lot. An old farmer looks at this dilapidated pick-up and says: "She's been good to us, but I reckon it's time to go into town and get a new one." He returns driving wildly into the barnyard doing "doughnuts" and shouting with glee as he drives his new Nissan. His wife asks, "Wilfred, what's got into you?" He answers, "I don't know, but I like it!" Oh, that we might celebrate Christian joy and let the Spirit get in us. The promise is, we'll like it. "Life is a journey; enjoy the ride."

———————

*The first birthday being Pentecost in Jerusalem and the second birthday being the beginning of your congregation.

Trinity Sunday

Revised Common	Proverbs 8:1-4, 22-31	Romans 5:1-5	John 16:12-15
Roman Catholic	Proverbs 8:22-31	Romans 5:1-5	John 16:12-15
Episcopal	Isaiah 6:1-8	Revelation 4:1-11	John 16:(5-11) 12-15

Seasonal Theme   Jesus' acts of compassion and teaching ministry.

Theme For The Day   Jesus has sent a Paraclete we can ask for help, inspiration, and presence.

Old Testament Lesson   Proverbs 8:1-4, 22-31   *Wisdom At Creation*

In this collection of wisdom from the ancient world, we have wisdom presented as a woman at the city gates and at the crossroads announcing her concerns. And her message is for "... all that live" not just Israel. Then we move to verses 22-31. We have a foundation here for a belief of a cosmic wisdom (Wisdom of Solomon 7:22-81) and for the New Testament idea of Logos, which helps us understand Christology.

It's an interesting picture of Wisdom standing by God's side at the time of Creation. And the bonus is that Wisdom standing by God is a "she." *The Interpreter's One-Volume Commentary* claims: "... it seems probable that the conception derives ultimately from a Canaanite source and that 'wisdom' was originally a pagan goddess of wisdom." Whatever its reason, perhaps here is an opportunity to use the feminine in presenting God and God's work of creation and wisdom.

So Wisdom, according to verse 30, is present with the Lord at creation. We must ask what she is doing there. Perhaps there are several answers:
1. She is a child who plays before him (v. 31) or
2. She is helping with the creation task as a crafts (wo)man, (v. 3:19), or a "master worker."

While this passage was no doubt selected to help present the Triune God on this special Trinity Sunday, it may do more to confuse than to elucidate.

New Testament Lesson   Romans 5:1-5   *Results Of Justification*

Paul lays out for us the results of being justified, which can easily be our outline of sermon moves as well. Because:
1. We are justified by faith (v. 1);
2. We have peace (v. 1);
3. We have obtained access to God's grace (v. 2);
4. We share God's glory (v. 2);
5. We can endure our sufferings (v. 3);
6. We always have hope (v. 5);
7. Our hearts are full of God's love (v. 5); and
8. We have been given the Holy Spirit (v. 5).

I like the first best of all. It describes a new relationship with God as peace which is now available to us. Notice verses 3 and 4. Sufferings produce character. Verse 2 is also marvelous. We have access to God: see Ephesians 2:15 and 3:12 and Hebrews 7:25 and 9:24 for additional support of this idea that Jesus worked for us access to God. This means really that God is willing to love and deal with us sinners. Now *that's* good news!

The Gospel   John 16:12-15   *Promises Of A Continual Presence*

In this portion of John's Gospel we learn much about the Paraclete. The text is often called Jesus' farewell discourse. Here we have the function of the Paraclete among the believers. The disciples' future was very uncertain — they will be tested, but they will not be alone. Jesus is the truth and thus the

Paraclete is the "Spirit of Truth" (v. 13). The Paraclete is also described in similar terms in John 7:16-17; 8:26, 40; 12:49-50. Also in verse 13 the Paraclete will help them in the future for which Jesus cannot prepare them before he departs. It's because of the changing times in which they live and carry out their mission and ministry.

In verse 15, we have what Jesus spoke of many times during his ministry (vv. 5:19-20). The Paraclete is a full part of the revelation of God and the proclamation of that fullness to those disciples who follow after them.

From John's Gospel we can say two basic things about the Paraclete:
1. Jesus continues his presence in the early church and among the congregations of believers after his ascension through the Paraclete, and
2. The Paraclete is our witness and our teacher.

Preaching Possibilities
A. If on this Trinity Sunday we go with the theme of Jesus' continued presence through the Paraclete, we can look at John's teachings about the Paraclete. Here are the passages: 14:16-17; 14:26; 15:26; 16:7-11; 16:12-15.

One could use a theme like "The love of God continues ..." and then develop the idea of Jesus sending out the Paraclete so the incarnate God's love continues through the faith community.
B. This is the one and only Sunday named for a doctrine of the faith rather than for an event in the life and teachings and ministry of Jesus. So we ought to consider seriously doing a doctrinal sermon teaching about our concept of God as Trinity. An outline could be:
1. Wrong ideas about the Trinity, like "... three Gods";
2. The scripture's foundation for the concept of the Trinity;
3. The Trinity as an explanation of God's presence with us in different times and conditions:
   a. As our creator God
   b. As our savior Jesus
   c. As God's presence with us now to inspire and instruct.
4. The implications for us as individuals and for us as a community of faith now:
   a. We treat all creation with reverence, as we know it comes from, and still is, God's;
   b. We celebrate our forgiveness and salvation and invite others into the kingdom of the sacred;
   c. When we are hard-pressed, afraid, struggling, and have doubts, we have help through the Paraclete who is God's presence now.
5. Relate a story regarding the Trinity found below.
C. The Old Testament also gives us an opportunity to speak forcefully about women in the church and in God's plan of creation and redemption. Then one could move to the Romans reading, making the point that the benefits Paul lists that we have because we are justified are for women and men alike. We believe that there is no difference. Then list out how we as individuals and as a congregation ought to practice complete equality in our ministry and mission. And if there are sexist abuses, hold them up for all to see. Finish with female Wisdom being there at creation from the Proverbs account.
D. One more possibility for Trinity Sunday.
1. The Old Testament Lesson — God as creator.
2. The New Testament Lesson — God as our savior.
3. The Gospel — God as spirit presence with us now.
It's a perfect three-point and three-story sermon.

Possible Outline Of Sermon Moves
A. Begin with the first illustration below.
B. Move to the scripture reading: read John 16:13.
C. Move to the background of why Jesus said this. He was leaving the disciples and they needed some assurance he would be with them in spirit even after he left bodily, and so on.

D. Move to explain what this having a Paraclete means to us as a congregation. We must take seriously the Spirit with us in our worship, and in our life together. And we can be that presence of Jesus to others with this Spirit's help.
E. Move to what the Paraclete meant to those disciples back then and what it means to us now.
    1. We don't face our suffering alone.
    2. We have help to believe.
    3. Jesus' words are dynamic and can be applied to all ages and situations.
    4. We have help beyond what the world can ever provide.
F. Move to your own testimony.
    1. When is it God's Paraclete is most felt by you?
    2. When is it you most need this help?
    3. How does the Paraclete help you as a preacher?
G. Frame your sermon by returning to the opening story and rereading John 16:13.

Prayer For The Day

Holy Spirit, come upon and with us here today as you promised you would. Give us courage when we need it; lift us up, warming our hearts with a knowledge of your love and presence; and teach us how to obey Jesus' words and live together as disciples. In the name of God, our Holy Parent and Creator; of Jesus, our loving and forgiving Savior; and of the Holy Spirit, God's presence with us now. Amen.

Possible Metaphors And Stories

Herbert W. Chilstrom, former Bishop of the Evangelical Lutheran Church in America, said: "Perhaps William Barclay is most helpful of all when he suggests 'paraclete' is derived from a term used by the Greeks to describe a very special person who went to war with the soldiers. He carried no weapons. His purpose was simply to be with the men as a source of wisdom, common sense, and encouragement. When the battle went badly, it was his task to remind them that only a battle had been lost and not the war. When they did well and came home heady with pride and overconfidence, it was his task to remind them they had only won a battle, not the war. In this role, 'the paraclete' was often the key to victory. His help at the right moment, his word of encouragement, his wise counsel were often the difference between victory and defeat." It is the role the Holy Spirit would play in our lives as well. (See John 15:26-27.)

On a car at Methodist Hospital parking lot were two stickers: "Things go better with wine," and below: "Christians have more fun, especially later." Great to give out that kind of message about being a Christian; however, I would want to say about the second message: "Christians have more fun, especially right now." We often give the impression our faith is mostly for eternal life, while we have the Holy Spirit to equip us for life here and now.

According to the Batak *adat* of Sumatra, they have what is called the laws of *dalihan natohr*. It means it takes three stones put under the cooking pot to hold it in right position. If one of the stones is missing, the pot falls down and the people couldn't cook.

The Indonesian Batak word *sahala* means a concrete power belonging to important and powerful people, such as a *raja* (who is a chief) and a *datu*, a religious person. And they will tell you the signs of a *sahala*: worldly success, large and fruitful fields, many cattle, many children, and the ability to be a leader. Now, what can we who live in an English-speaking country say are the signs that we have God's Paraclete with us?

Corpus Christi

Roman Catholic   **Genesis 14:18-20**   **Corinthians 11:23-26**   **Luke 9:11-17**

Theme For The Day

Corpus Christi is a great mass held in honor of the Holy Eucharist. The name comes from the Latin, *Festum sanctissimi Corpus Christi*. In German the title is *Fronleichnamsfest*, which is the feast of the Body of our Lord. It all began with a pious Augustinian nun named Juliana of Liege about 1209, who reported a vision that said there should be a feast in honor of the sacrament. It was first known as *Festum Eucharistiae* and spread rapidly through the church in the thirteenth century. One could say it is a Holy Thursday without the sadness.

The Corpus Christi Procession, which first appeared in Cologne, has been a part of the observance since the fourteenth century. In Europe this Holy Parade was held like a triumph of Christ the King. First the host was carried in a covered chalice, then in a reliquary, and then in a special container designed for that purpose.

It is my sincere hope that Lutherans and other denominations will discover the richness and pedagogical benefits of observing this meaningful festival. Let's now consider the scripture readings for the day.

Old Testament Lesson   Genesis 14:18-20   *King Melchizedek Gives A Banquet For Abram*

Melchizedek, who was priest-king of Salem, received Abram after he had won a battle and laid out a banquet of celebration for him. He then gave Abram a blessing and Abram returned the favor with a tithing of all the booty he had captured in the fight. In the New Testament, Melchizedek is seen as a sort of "Christ," and thus this passage for the Corpus Christi celebration.

New Testament Lesson   1 Corinthians 11:23-26   *Words Of Institution*

This is the earliest biblical recording of the "words of institution" for the consecration of the elements at the Eucharist. They were written to a congregation in Corinth that was abusing the Lord's Supper. (See verses 17-22.) Paul tells them this is the tradition he received from the Lord and had given to them when he was there in Corinth with them. Notice in verse 25 the promise of a "new covenant," which we can first find in Jeremiah 31:31. This supper proclaims the Lord's death until his second coming. Of course, we can see why this was chosen as the Second Reading for the day we observe the mass as our special blessing from God.

The Gospel   Luke 9:11-17   *Feeding The Five Thousand*

In this Gospel Reading we relate how Jesus was the giver of bread from heaven, which can connect with the theme for the day of bread being the body of Christ in the Eucharist. Perhaps when Jesus prayed before the distribution of the bread he may have used the very ancient Jewish table prayer: "Blessed are you, O Lord, our God, King of the world, who brings forth bread from the earth."

The ideas here that we can use to connect with the Eucharist and body of Christ are the distribution of bread, hungry people, blessing of bread, and plenty for everyone.

If we were preaching on this text separate from the Corpus Christi emphasis, I would take a very different tack, such as:

1. In Jesus' hands even the little can be made great.
2. Prayer made the difference.
3. Send them away who have needs, or organize them and feed them.
4. The flip side of the miracle is that Jesus got 5,000 men to sit down and share what they may have already had with them.
5. There is a stewardship of leftovers, too.

Preaching Possibilities

Because of the nature of this festival, we must prepare our message as one that instructs and teaches respect for the Eucharist.

A. If we use all three readings, a single outline might be as follows: Three great banquets
   1. The Old Testament — Here is a celebration of a victory banquet.
   2. The New Testament — Here is a Passover banquet that proclaims Christ's sacrifice for us.
   3. The Gospel — Here hungry people are fed with the bread of life. For a treatment of this miracle see *The Miracles Of Jesus And Their Flip Side* (Schmalenberger, CSS Publishing Company, 2000), whose metaphors and stories following the Prayer For The Day will work to illustrate the homily made up of the three points.
B. Of course the Second Reading is the heart of the matter, and it will stand alone to talk of the body of Christ and what it means for us today.

Possible Outline Of Sermon Moves

A. Begin with a story of what communion would look like to someone who had never seen it before.
B. Move to retell the Holy Thursday evening passion story in the upper room.
C. Read the scripture 1 Corinthians 11:23-26.
D. Talk about Christ's body and what it means for us:
   1. Born as God incarnate in Bethlehem;
   2. Modeled what a godly body ought to live like, doing acts of mercy and compassion like healing and feeding;
   3. Took a beating and was crucified for our sins;
   4. Came out of the grave to beat death so we might also; and
   5. Returned to God to prepare a place for us.
E. Tell your hearers about Nun Juliana and how she thought we should take a time each year to celebrate the importance of Jesus' body, all he did on earth in it, and the fact we can have it present with us in the Eucharist.
F. Frame your sermon by returning to your opening comments about what the Eucharist might look like to someone who never saw it before. Contrast this with what it means to you.

Prayer For The Day

On this festival of Corpus Christi we give thanks for Sister Juliana, who would remind us over and over what a precious gift you have given us in your real body which is with us even today in the Holy Eucharist. Help our hearts to bow in reverence and sing in joy for this gift we adore today. In Christ Jesus' name, we pray. Amen.

Possible Metaphors And Stories

Jesus had compassion on the many hungry listeners
And taught the wary disciples an unforgettable lesson
Of response to need and how little becomes so much;
At his prompting they all participated in new sharing.

(JLS)

"Upon such sacrifices, my Cordelia, the gods themselves throw incense" (King Lear).

Samuel M. Shoemaker wrote in *Pulpit Digest* years ago, "During the war I remember seeing the picture of an altar set up for Holy Communion, which was simply an actual workbench. After it ceased to be used for obviously religious purposes, it went back to being a workbench again. I like to think that the boards which upheld the sacred vessels later felt the hammer-blows of people making doors and window-frames and shelves for houses."

The Jacobites of Scotland never met one another on the mountain path, never sat down to a table of council and conference, without lifting a cup to pledge the return of their king and prince, Charles. In every celebration of the Lord's Supper, since that last and first night in the upper room, the followers of Christ have lifted the sacramental cup as a token of their faith that their King shall come. And when he comes he shall come not to bring pain and suffering, as did King Charles to unhappy Scotland, but to bind up all wounds, to set at liberty all captives of sin, to wipe away all tears from all eyes (Clarence E. Macartney).

Proper 4, Pentecost 2, Ordinary Time 9

Revised Common	1 Kings 18:20-39	**Galatians 1:1-12**	**Luke 7:1-10**
Roman Catholic	1 Kings 8:41-43	**Galatians 1:1-2, 6-10**	**Luke 7:1-10**
Episcopal	1 Kings 8:22-23, 27-30, 41-43	**Galatians 1:1-10**	**Luke 7:1-10**

Seasonal Theme   Jesus' acts of compassion and teaching ministry.

Theme For The Day   The compassionate healing Christ who responds at a distance for one of a different race and religion.

Old Testament Lesson   1 Kings 18:20-39   *Elijah's Test For God*

Up on Mount Carmel, Elijah took a big gamble. He called for a trial to see whose God was real: Baal or Yahweh. It's a dramatic story about the prophets each praying to their God to bring down fire and burn the offering placed on the altar. There is some humor in verse 27. The first two phrases could mean Baal was relieving himself! Verse 28 means the priests of Baal were doing a sort of frantic prophesying and actually hurting themselves. Verse 36 reminds us that this is not just a God of nature, but also a God of history and people to whom Elijah prayed. And the prayed-for fire came ... and the people responded to such a demonstration of power. Homiletically, we must ask pointed questions about this story:
1.   Should we test God like Elijah did up on Mount Carmel?
2.   If the fire had not come down, does this mean Yahweh is not really our God?
3.   How about we who have not seen the fire come — can we believe also without such an experience?

I believe the most poignant verse is 29: "... was no voice, no answer, and no response." Those prophets of Baal are not the only ones who have times like that when it just seems as though God is not paying attention to us.

New Testament Lesson   Galatians 1:1-12   *Direct From God*

Right at the opening of this letter Paul lets us know his authority. He considered himself an apostle by direct divine intervention. His authority comes from God. The letter goes to those churches he founded on his first missionary journey. In verses 3-5, we have the focus of early preaching. Some of these Christians were deserting the true faith for a perversion of the faith as Paul had presented it to them. Then in verses 11 and 12 we have sort of an announcement of the focus of his thesis — through a revelation of Jesus Christ, Paul received this gospel he now proclaims. Not from humans did this come, nor from a Professor of Theology at an Association of Theological Schools approved Seminary. This came direct from God! That belief of Paul must have been the engine which drove his missionary zeal.

The Gospel   Luke 7:1-10   *Healing A Centurion's Servant*

There is a similar story in John 4:46-53. In that account it's an official in Capernaum whose son is ill. What we can't miss homiletically here is the strong faith of this centurion. And notice his sense of stewardship. He made a big donation, even though a Gentile, to build the Jewish synagogue. Then he tries not to waste Jesus' time. And he was a good steward of his servant's health as well (vv. 6, 7). He sensed somehow that Jesus had a higher authority than he did. That authority was none other than God. But it's the faith of the man which moves me. He just knew all Jesus had to do was to "... speak the word" and his servant would be healed.

Preaching Possibilities

I have published a sermon on this parable in my book *The Miracles Of Jesus And Their Flip Side* (CSS Publishing Company, 2000).

A. It would be possible to talk about miracles today using the Old Testament Lesson and the Gospel as literal ones and the Second Reading as a miracle of change of heart in Saul of Tarsus to Paul the Apostle.

B. Of course this Sunday could also be the first in a series of sermons based on Galatians as outlined above.

C. If we first go with the Elijah story, we could say something like this:
1. God can still light fires in our lives.
2. We also have proof of God's power and presence.
3. What shall we do when, like the prophets of Baal, there seem to be "... no voice, and no answer" (v. 26c).
4. Our response ought to be like the people's response in verse 39.

Possible Outline Of Sermon Moves

A. Begin by telling the Luke story, putting it in a contemporary setting. "A Muslim once sent word to an ordained Christian medical missionary that his domestic worker was ill and near death...."

B. Move to the scripture account in Luke and read it, explaining that it is a similar situation.

C. Move to what you think this miracle of healing at a distance says to you today.
1. God will heal us at a distance also.
2. God would have us be concerned about the health and well being of those who serve us.
3. Our importance doesn't count for much when disaster hits.
4. Faith makes a bigger difference than our ethnic background or churchly loyalties!

D. Move to a different take on this parable as we consider the stewardship principle.
1. The Centurion was a good steward of his servant's health.
2. The Centurion was a good steward of his wealth as he shared it for the building of a synagogue.
3. The Centurion was a good steward of Jesus' energy. "Just speak the Word."
4. The Centurion was a good steward of the gospel that Jesus can do all things.

E. Move to what the implications are for your congregation.
1. We have a ministry of prayer and healing.
2. We have a ministry of compassion for others, often those much less fortunate than we are.
3. In our congregation those of power and those of no power are all God's people and should be treated with respect.
4. We have a ministry of stewardship of our health, our money, and our energy.

F. Frame your sermon by returning to the opening story and finish the story similar to the way Luke finishes it.

Prayer For The Day

Help us to be good stewards and bless the ministries you have given us of healing and compassion. And here in (*your congregation*) help us all to respect each other no matter what our status or lack of it. And for those of us who have the capacity to give, show us how to bless others with the gift. In Jesus' name. Amen.

Possible Metaphors And Stories

Morgan Stanley/Dean Witter has used a slogan on television: "Move your money; get well connected." It is similar to Jesus' words in the Sermon on the Mount: "Do not store up for yourself treasures on earth ... but store up for yourselves treasures in heaven" (Matthew 6:19, 20).

Now that is really connected!

Dan Rather told of the rising water in Great Salt Lake, twelve feet higher in the year 1987. Christians got together and prayed. Engineers built a viaduct and pumped it out to another lake in the desert! There is a time to pray and a time to be the instrument through which God answers prayers. Get up off your knees and get busy!

Sir Philips Gibbs in his book *The Cross of Peace* wrote of modern civilization: "Modern progress has made the world a neighborhood. In the days of dividing walls of race and class and creed we must shake the earth anew with the message of the all-inclusive Christ, in whom there is neither bond or free, Jews or Greek ... but all in one."

We relocated the thermostat from the drafty hall to the living room today. There is a big difference between a thermostat and a thermometer. One feels the temperature and takes the necessary action to change it. The other just tells you the temperature but does nothing about it. It's the difference in the way we often respond as well: complain and do nothing to help make the necessary improvement.

Proper 5, Pentecost 3, Ordinary Time 10

Revised Common	1 Kings 17:8-24	**Galatians 1:11-24**	Luke 7:11-17
Roman Catholic	1 Kings 17:17-24	**Galatians 1:11-19**	Luke 7:11-17
Episcopal	1 Kings 17:17-24	**Galatians 1:11-24**	Luke 7:11-17

Seasonal Theme   Jesus' acts of compassion and teaching ministry.

Theme For The Day   Jesus and our ministry of compassion and miracles on God's behalf.

Old Testament Lesson   1 Kings 17:8-24   *The Widow Of Zarephath*

There are two miracles recorded here. Elijah provided the widow of Zarephath, who had so little, with a jar of meal and a jug of oil which would not run out. And in verses 17-24 Elijah also revived from death the widow's son. Good work, Elijah! No doubt this reading was selected to partner with Jesus' healing of another widow's son at Nain. Interesting in this story of Elijah and the widow that the widow was a Phoenician, a worshiper of Baal — and a widow, which means she was extremely poor. Add to these facts that the city of Zarephath was in extreme drought. This is also the homeland of Jezebel, who became the champion for Baal in Israel after marrying Ahab (16:31). There may be a strong homiletical contrast between God using the ravens to feed Elijah and this widow to feed him.

Next in verses 17 and 24, we have the resuscitation of the widow's dead son. Here, it seems to me, is another attempt to claim that Elijah's God, the God of Israel, is truly a God of life and power — even the dead can be revived! So we have a number of attempts to establish that not Baal, but Yahweh, Elijah's God, is real:

1. The lighting of water-soaked wood on the mountain;
2. The feeding of Elijah, using ravens;
3. The widow's bottomless container of food; and
4. The bringing back to life of the widow's son.

And maybe best of all, this widow was not a worshiper of Elijah's God — yet she received these marvelous gifts from God through Elijah. If we think of Elijah as a forerunner of Jesus and Elijah's ministry as foreshadowing Jesus, we really have something here to preach about.

New Testament Lesson   Galatians 1:11-24   *Paul's Authority*

First a chronology of Saul to Paul:

1. Saul is persecuting the church.
2. Saul gains high position in the Jewish faith.
3. Saul, however, was elected even before his birth to be an apostle to the Gentiles.
4. Saul has a vision on the Damascus road.
5. Paul goes on retreat into Arabia.
6. Paul returns to preach in Damascus.
7. Paul visits Peter and James in Jerusalem.
8. Paul preaches in Syria and Silesia.

So the great missionary begins his ministry of evangelism to the Gentiles. Paul now begins his argument which will continue through chapter 2. He tries to establish his authority and thus prove the validity of his message. Like verses 11 and 12 state, the gospel he preaches didn't come from humans — but through Jesus' revelation to him. I wonder if he isn't also trying his best to explain that this rabid Jew who was persecuting Christians now wants to be their spokesperson of the gospel.

There are three such resurrection miracles done by Jesus in the Gospels: this widow's son, Jairus' daughter, and Lazarus. Raising the dead is one of the signs of the Messiah Jesus called attention to in 7:22. Some of the language this event uses is the same language as the Elijah account we have in the Old Testament Lesson for today. Verse 13 is the first time Luke calls Jesus "... the Lord." His power over death evidenced that which must have caused the title to be used.

Perhaps in both resurrection stories today we have best the power of compassion for those who grieve as much as the power to bring back to life a dead corpse.

Preaching Possibilities

A. Of course the Old Testament Lesson and the Gospel will work well together, especially with the theme of compassion for the poor, giving, and the ability to have and give new life. What fun it could be to tell the story in your own contemporary context. "A Christian pastor was on her way to a Rotary Club meeting when she came across a crowd weeping and watching pall bearers loading a casket into a waiting funeral coach ..." (be sure to use the local funeral home's real name).

B. The New Testament Reading will stand alone very well with the theme of where the Gospel comes from.

C. It would be a stretch, but one could call this "Miracle Sunday" and use all three readings, organizing them around the Old Testament Lesson and the miracle of food for the hungry; then the New Testament Reading with the theme of a miracle of conversion; then the Gospel with a miracle of compassion and new life for dead bodies.

To prepare for such an emphasis you might want to call three or four members and ask them what miracles Jesus has performed in their lives.

Possible Outline Of Sermon Moves

A. Begin by reading a contemporary and imaginary newspaper article about "a local funeral director and mourners were astounded last Tuesday as Pastor (*Name*) brought back to life a little son of local widow." And so on.

B. Move to reading the account of the event at Nain's gate from the Bible.

C. Move to mention the other two resurrections in the Gospels.

D. Explain how they were motivated as acts of compassion because Jesus had the power to help, not to prove Jesus' power to do them.

E. Use the revival of the widow's son in 1 Kings to illustrate how Jesus' example and forerunner had demonstrated this same compassion years before.

F. Tell your people about some of the miracles you have witnessed in your life.

G. Follow with what you think this all says to us in the church today.
   1. God wants us to feed the poor, like Elijah.
   2. God wants us to give new life, like Elijah.
   3. God wants us always to have compassion, not just for "our own," but for all people who are in pain and suffering.

H. Frame the sermon by returning to your opening imaginary newspaper story and add how this miracle affected the local church and community.

Prayer For The Day

We celebrate today the warm concern you have for us and for all people whether they are your disciples or not. Show us the way to be instruments of your love in the world to all those who have need of your compassion. And hear our thankfulness today as well, that we might invite others to be fed and given new life here and eternal life beyond this one. In Jesus' name. Amen.

Possible Metaphors And Stories

Andy Rooney on *60 Minutes* was looking through many travel brochures. He asked, "Why isn't it ever raining in any of these pictures? And there are never any crowds either. When you get there, everyone is dressed just like you."

We do romanticize life and often think it far better somewhere else.

At the Cathedral of the Virgin of Guadalupe in Mexico, there is a long narthex hall full of hand-painted plaques representing the miracles occurring in individual lives. An example is a picture of a boat on fire, or a car hitting a pedestrian, or a person getting out of a hospital bed.

What miracles of our members could we paint on the walls of our church narthexes?

Atlanta's Dion James hit a baseball in Shea Stadium which hit and killed a dove on the fly. He got a double and thus set it up for the Braves to win the game. A fly ball to left field had been turned into a double. It was the first time this had ever happened in Major League baseball. Shortstop Rafael Santana had to pick up the dead bird and bring it to the bat girl, who didn't want it.

Life is as fickle for us as for the bird. Death comes any time. Our finest efforts can kill.

At the funeral of Ruth Walthall, Pastor William Zimman told of falling asleep on a trip as a child and waking up the next morning in his own bed. Heaven must be a similar experience.

For a sample sermon on today's Gospel see *The Miracles Of Jesus And Their Flip Side* (Schmalenberger, CSS Publishing Company, 2000).

Proper 6, Pentecost 4, Ordinary Time 11

Revised Common	1 Kings 21:1-21a	Galatians 2:15-21	Luke 7:36—8:3
Roman Catholic	2 Samuel 12:7-10, 13	Galatians 2:16, 19-21	Luke 7:36—8:3
Episcopal	2 Samuel 11:26—12:10, 13-15	Galatians 2:11-21	Luke 7:36-50

Seasonal Theme Jesus' acts of compassion and teaching ministry.

Theme For The Day God's grace and forgiveness in the story of Mary Magdalene.

Old Testament Lesson 1 Kings 21:1-21a *Naboth's Vineyard*

What a problem King Ahab had! His wife was none other than the infamous Jezebel who was the daughter of a Phoenician monarch. Ahab understood and obeyed the laws of Yahweh and, while unhappy about it, did not take by force the vineyard he and Jezebel so much wanted for Jezebel. It was strange to her that her husband's desires were not satisfied because of the ancient laws of a God. So she worked it out in a more devious way, seeing that the vineyard's owner was falsely accused and then executed so Ahab could confiscate his vineyard. The charge pertaining to the owner comes from Exodus 22:28. However, Jezebel and Ahab also broke the laws listed for them in Exodus 20:13, 15-17.

Elijah jumped on this behavior by predicting the disaster of Ahab's house. Ahab is a pitiful sight. He let his wife muscle a man and he had already caused Israel to sin (v. 22) by going after idols (v. 26). Ahab really did have a problem.

New Testament Lesson Galatians 2:15-21 *Troublesome Laws And Grace*

Paul is making his case over the conflict in Antioch. His reputation was under attack for rebuking Peter. So Paul describes the incident with his take on it in verses 11-14. His argument is:
1. By placing their faith in Jesus they acknowledged that the law could not make them right with God.
2. Paul claims the giving up on the Jewish ceremonial observance does not make the gospel an instrument of sin.
3. Paul says it's the law which led him to this radical action (v. 19). Perhaps he is getting ready to make his point in 3:17-25.
4. Paul answers why he speaks so strongly (vv. 20-21). It's about grace and the worth of what Jesus did on the cross. And if we get righteousness by keeping the law, we have no need for Christ's death on the cross.

The Gospel Luke 7:36—8:3 *A Sinful Woman Forgiven*

This is a story about the religious of the day being very upset by Jesus' acceptance of a prostitute in a rather embarrassing fashion. Jesus' response to Simon's criticism was clear in the parable he told him. The more we are forgiven the more we ought to be able to love on God's behalf. This woman had gone out of her way to welcome Jesus; Simon had been hospitable but had not gone out of his way to do so. For Jesus, this proved she had been forgiven for lots of sins. Notice that in the parable the love follows the forgiveness.

In verses 8:1-3 we have listed a number of disciples who were women and traveled with Jesus. Mary of Magdala (a village on the sea of Galilee) is mentioned and appears to be the one mentioned in 7:36-50. Women disciples are mentioned so rarely in our readings. I do hope today you will call attention to Herod's steward Chuza's wife, Joanna, and Susanna. A wife of a steward to the king just must be addressed.

Preaching Possibilities

A. This is the perfect Sunday to talk about Mary Magdalene as a disciple. We shall return to that later in the Possible Outline Of Sermon Moves. The connection of the Gospel and the Old Testament Lesson is obvious: A woman, Jezebel, and her relationship to her husband, King Ahab, and Mary Magdalene and her loving relationship to Jesus. One haughty, arrogant, and conniving; the other humble, penitent, and receiving forgiveness. The former's outcome is disaster and the latter's is loving discipleship.

B. Then there is the big idea of stewardship and a woman who is the wife of Herod's steward. It's a little stretch but one could imagine what it is like being married to one who takes Christian stewardship seriously today.

C. In Paul's letter we have a key text which could be used as an exegetical sermon based on Galatians 2:16, 17, and 20. Then this grace is illustrated in the Gospel in the forgiveness of the prostitute.
   1. Jezebel and Ahab illustrate how sinful we are.
   2. Paul witnesses to justification through Christ by grace.
   3. Mary Magdalene is a great example of this grace acted out by Jesus the Christ.

Possible Outline Of Sermon Moves

Title: Mary Magdalene Lives At (*your church*)

A. Technique: Have a woman (if you are male) come into the pulpit and read your sermon manuscript for you. You might even want to have her dressed in appropriate dress of women in Bible times. Even a scarf over her head will help.

B. Write a manuscript in first person using the following information:
   1. Born in Magdala on the shore of Galilee
   2. Became a "woman of the night"
   3. Was healed of demon possession by Jesus
   4. Came to Jesus for forgiveness for her past
   5. Story in today's Gospel of anointing retold
   6. Is at the cross at crucifixion
   7. Jesus appears to her in the Garden
   8. Tells the disciples of the resurrection
   9. Life changed because of knowing the Christ
   10. An invitation for those hearing the sermon to know Jesus and change their lives also

Note: Any Bible dictionary will be helpful in writing such a first person sermon. I like *Harper's*.

Prayer For The Day

In many ways, dear Jesus, we have not lived as we should have, and we ask for your graceful forgiveness, just like you forgave Mary Magdalene. Help us to demonstrate our love for you like she did and to have a thankful heart like she had as well. We pray in Jesus' name. Amen.

Possible Metaphors And Stories

In 1719 the king offered what was called an "Act of Grace" to all pirates in the Caribbean. If they would give up their pirate's life, the king would give them amnesty and some land to settle on. Calico Jack, one of the most notorious, took the offer. It is an offer Jesus works on God's behalf from the cross.

In an HBO movie *Tell Me What You Want*, Max Herschel's daughter tells him, as he tries to keep track of what his lover had done and was doing, "Don't keep books on people you love."

I recall the first time I got a glimpse of the pyramids of Giza on the outskirts of Cairo, Egypt. I made the van driver stop so I could take a picture, but after a while as we got closer, I asked that he stop again for another shot. Several times we went through the same process as the three grand pyramids opened up before us.

Grace is like that. It opens up wider and wider, more and more grand. Our first glimpse seems so small compared with now.

Barbara Walters of *20/20* interviewed Mr. and Mrs. John Hinckley, Sr., parents of John Hinckley, Jr., who shot Press Secretary James Brady, two secret service agents, and President Ronald Reagan.

When asked if they had any words to James Brady and the secret service agents shot in the assassination attempt, his parents replied, "Yes, we are very sorry." Then asked if they had any words to their son who shot the men, "Yes, we love him very much."

Love the sinner; *hate* only the sin.

Proper 7, Pentecost 5, Ordinary Time 12

Revised Common	1 Kings 19:1-15a	Galatians 3:23-29	Luke 8:26-39
Roman Catholic	Zechariah 12:10-11; 13:1	Galatians 3:26-29	Luke 9:18-24
Episcopal	Zechariah 12:8-10; 13:1	Galatians 3:23-29	Luke 9:18-24

Seasonal Theme   Jesus' acts of compassion and teaching ministry.

Theme For The Day   Jesus' compassion and power over the demonic and the danger of the powers which oppose God's will.

Old Testament Lesson   1 Kings 19:1-15a   *Elijah Flees From Jezebel*
King Ahab's wife, that Jezebel, was a real problem! She threatened to kill, or have killed, Elijah, just like he had killed the priests of Baal (v. 40).

It's an interesting story that can be told from the pulpit in a dramatic way: Elijah under threat of life on the run and then meeting no less than God, not in the loud and dramatic things of life, but in a little gentle voice out of sheer silence (v. 13).

Notice Elijah did not even pause in Judah. Jehoshaphat's son, Jehoram, was married to Athaliah, the daughter of Ahab and Jezebel. That makes the King of Judah a son-in-law of scheming Jezebel (v. 3).

In verse 8, we see Elijah going to Sinai where the covenant was first established. So he connects his ministry with that of Moses. Yahweh's coming was announced by such as hurricane, fire, and earthquake — but not this time. This time it's much more intimate, in a gentle breeze. Marvelous pictures to paint and words to speak from our poetic pulpits today. Contrast the experience of God with that portrayed in Exodus 19:18; Psalm 18 (v. 17).

New Testament Reading   Galatians 3:23-29   *All Children Of God*
In general Paul makes the proposition that before Christ, we were imprisoned by the law, which became our disciplinarian. After Christ, faith takes us to a new freedom because we are justified and made children of God. The word *disciplinarian* in verse 24 is sometimes translated "custodian" and other times "pedagogue." Both describe a superior slave who took a young boy through the streets to his schoolmaster. It's a good metaphor to describe the role of the law.

In verse 27 we learn that baptism is putting on Christ and even more. Verse 28 is one of the great statements of Paul: Because we are all baptized into Christ, we have unity and even better, spiritual equality. Let racists and sexists put that in their pipe and smoke it! All the baptized are God's children and thus equal brothers and sisters and heirs as well!

The Gospel   Luke 8:26-39   *The Gerasene Demoniac*
We find this story in Mark 5:1-20 and Matthew 8:28-34. Luke seems to have improved on Mark's original telling of the story. In Luke's Gospel this is the only time Jesus goes out of Jewish territory. In early Christianity this miracle of healing must have meant:
1.   Jesus had compassion on a man from outside Palestine;
2.   Jesus had power over demons; and
3.   There is a connection to the victories over the demonic by the apostles (Acts 8:9-24; 13:6-12; 16:16-18; 19:11-20). No doubt stories like this demonstrated the power of Jesus and brought out faith.

We, however, must find a way to apply this passage for hope for those who in our day suffer from anxiety, depression, and compulsive behavior. The idea in verse 30 that his name was "legion" is an interesting one. Those who suffer with mental disorders will understand. For they have lost their individuality and inside them there is a war going on of conflicting forces. Here we have a story of such

137

great compassion of Jesus that he would cross Galilee and go into a foreign territory to whip the demons in a man not Jewish!

Now, an idea on the flip side of this miracle: perhaps some or much of the cure was in telling others how much Jesus had done for him. Maybe the telling was as good as Prozac and Zoloft for healing.

And then, there are those poor pig farmers! What had they done to deserve the loss of all that pork? (v. 33). Perhaps Jews didn't care about pigs, an unclean animal, being drowned. And perhaps they didn't see an ethical question as to the pigs' owners losing their investment since they were foreigners anyway. Or perhaps, it was Peter seeing a ruckus being raised, demons called out, and pigs stampeded into the sea. When he preached it with the connections, Mark wrote it down. I'm just not sure. But it's a tale worth telling.

Preaching Possibilities

I just can't come up with a connection between the lessons today. However, each one has a great message and will easily stand alone.

A. If you must use them all, one could talk about "Today's Lessons for Today's Christians."
   1. God speaks to us even in sheer silence, from the Old Testament Reading.
   2. We are all one equal family of God's children, from the New Testament Reading.
   3. Our God is one of power and compassion, from the Gospel for the day.
B. If we use the Galatians account alone, we can preach with power:
   1. The role of the law for us.
   2. The justification we have through faith.
   3. The membership in God's family of all the baptized.
   4. The unity and equality of us in Christ.
   5. The privilege of being an heir in the kingdom of God.

Possible Outline Of Sermon Moves

A. Begin by telling the story of Jesus' healing the Gerasene Demoniac.
B. Tell the questions you wonder about in the story:
   1. Would Prozac cure this person today?
   2. What are the demons we fight today in our culture?
   3. Why would Jesus treat those pig farmers so badly?
   4. Why would the people want Jesus, who had such needed healing power, to leave their country?
   5. Why did Jesus tell the cured demoniac to tell of the healing, when so many times he told people to remain quiet about it?
C. Offer what you think this story meant to early Christians.
   1. Jesus has compassion for all sorts of people.
   2. Jesus has power over demons.
   3. Jesus was modeling a ministry for those who followed him.
D. Move to what it means to us today.
   1. Unclean spirits and demons still want to possess us.
   2. Jesus sets a model for our attitude of compassion toward the emotionally distressed.
   3. We have a shalom to offer those here today who are emotionally distressed.
E. Examine a possible flip side to the story. Perhaps most of the healing came as the man told how much God had done for him (v. 39). Imagine what the man did upon arrival back home at peace and clothed. Perhaps he started a support group for the addicted ... and so on.

Prayer For The day

Drive out of us, too, O God, those demons that want to possess us and make us addicted, greedy, mean-spirited, and unsettled. Show us the way to tell all we can about what wonderful things God has done for us. And in response to your gift of peace, show us the way to share this Good News with many. In Christ's name. Amen.

Possible Stories And Metaphors

A truck driver going through a town on the truck route stopped at each stop street, got out, banged on the side of the truck with a ball bat, got back in, and drove on. When asked why this strange procedure, he explained: "I have a two-ton truck and four tons of canaries aboard, and I have to keep two tons in the air all the time."

We, too, are overloaded and instead of facing the reality, we rearrange the load (Frank Harrington).

In an Iowa snowstorm the willow trees in back of our home bent over from the weight. The sun came out and melted off the load and the pliable trees straightened up again. Storms come, the Son melts away the heavy load, and we straighten up again.

A news item in *U.S. News and World Report*: the weight of heavy snow has exploded some 1,500 of the mines placed along East Germany's border with West Germany (February 15, 1982).

Many under the weight of their daily life are about to explode. Or is this God's way of saying "No" to maiming other human beings?

The late Katherine Brownfield, who sent me humor, sent me this one. A man frequently prayed this in prayer meeting: "O God, clean out the cobwebs from my mind." One night, a woman followed the man in prayer and prayed thus: "O God, don't clean out the cobwebs. Kill the spider!"

We often fail to get to the source of our problem and only consider the symptoms.

Proper 8, Pentecost 6, Ordinary Time 13

Revised Common	2 Kings 2:1-2, 6-14	**Galatians 5:1, 13-25**	Luke 9:51-62
Roman Catholic	1 Kings 19:16, 19-21	**Galatians 5:1, 13-18**	Luke 9:51-62
Episcopal	1 Kings 19:15-16, 19-21	**Galatians 5:1, 13-25**	Luke 9:51-62

Seasonal Theme   Jesus' acts of compassion and teaching ministry.

Theme For The Day   Handing on the discipleship of kingdom work. We love self, each other, and neighbors.

Old Testament Lesson   2 Kings 2:1-2, 6-14   *Elijah Ascends*

Elijah is making his last visit to the prophetic colleagues. Elijah and Elisha returned to the Jordan River above Jericho where there was no food. This parting of the water is a great story for the telling (Exodus 14:21 and Joshua 3:13). Others were not able to follow them across. The mantel is similar to Moses' rod.

In verse 9, the "double share" was the portion of the oldest son (Deuteronomy 21:17). Elisha wanted to be given along with his position the miraculous power which Elijah possessed.

Elijah ascended in a storm, like Yahweh had descended. See Exodus 1:4 and Job 38:1. This event probably took place about B.C. 851 after the death of King Ahaziah.

This is a story primarily about prophetic succession. The ministry of God will continue through one prophet passing on and another immediately coming on the scene.

Notice, like in the transfiguration, the one who witnesses such an event is changed by the vision of heavenly power (Matthew 17:1-9).

I believe we have just four such going into heaven in our Bible: Moses, Elijah, Enoch, and Jesus.

New Testament Lesson   Galatians 5:1, 13-25   *Christian Freedom*

The freedom mentioned in verse 1 could be the freedom from having to please everyone else, or from doing what others impose on us that we should be or do. Freedom is a gift for being in community and for serving others in love (vv. 13, 14). So Paul is really saying that we should just live by the Spirit and this will guide us as we live together in a community of faith.

The New Interpreter's Bible puts it this way: "A Church guided by Paul's hopeful word would cultivate a community of flexibility and freedom, living with openness toward the unpredictable liberating movement of God's spirit. It is a radical and inspiring vision."

Then these seem to be an implied contract between works of the flesh (which is much more than sexual misconduct) and the fruit of the Spirit.

Works of the Flesh	Fruit of the Spirit
fornication	love
impurity	joy
licentiousness	peace
idolatry	patience
sorcery	kindness
enmities	generosity
strife	faithfulness
jealousy	gentleness
anger	self-control
quarrels	(see v. 25)
dissensions	
factions	

envy

drunkenness, carousing   (see v. 24)

So, Paul, if we practice these fruits of and live in the Spirit, are you saying we don't need any rules and regulations against the working of the flesh? I think so.

The Gospel   Luke 9:51-62   *Spurned In Samaria*

Jesus and his disciples here began their journey to Jerusalem. Discipleship and opposition seem to be the general themes of this portion of Luke. He holds it together with the story of Jesus and his disciples on a journey toward Jerusalem and the cross. Verses 51 and 56 show the enmity between Samaritans and Jews. The text also shows how Jesus taught (modeled) the way disciples should deal with human opposition. He took the opposition without trying to get even. James and John just weren't there yet! Jesus had a bigger mission on his agenda — to go to the cross and work forgiveness for sins and salvation.

Verses 57 to 62 are examples for us of providing excuses for not going all the way in our discipleship. Perhaps he meant that the spiritually dead can bury the dead — the proclaiming of the kingdom to the living is more important.

For this preacher there is a strong condemnation of halfway discipleship. And even more so a sad description of missed opportunities. Here Jesus says is a call to complete full commitment. In any cause that's when it's fun to belong, when we become fully committed without any feeble reservations. Those who had reservations and excuses are never heard of again. Those who committed and followed will be remembered for ever in human history.

Preaching Possibilities

A. I believe that the Old Testament passage (2 Kings 2:1-2, 6-14) and the Gospel from Luke will go together nicely as we talk about discipleship and commitment to a cause and leader: Elisha to Elijah and James and John to Jesus as they go to Jerusalem. There is also a common thread of a journey: Elisha and Elijah going to Bethel and Jesus and disciples going to Jerusalem.

There is another element here. In both stories we have the element of the leader, i.e., Elijah and Jesus, passing on the kingdom work to their disciples. Oh, one more thing, a little later both will ascend and return to God.

B. The New Testament Lesson can stand on its own or support the Old Testament and Gospel texts. It is rich and full of what it means to love Christian freedom. The outline of moves is obvious:

1. Christ sets us free — no slavery (v. 1).
2. We are free to love one another and neighbor and self (vv. 8, 9) — no hate.
3. When we live by the Spirit, we need not give in to flesh, but we ought to know fruits of the Spirit (vv. 16, 22) — no flesh.

Possible Outline Of Sermon Moves

We'll use the Old Testament and Gospel stories.

Title: A Discipleship Journey

A. Begin by telling in your own words the story of Elijah and Elisha going across the Jordan to Bethel.

B. Continue by telling a similar story in your own words — of Jesus and the disciples going toward Jerusalem.

C. Move to what these two discipleship journeys have to teach us today:

1. God hands the task of kingdom work on from one disciple to another:

    a. Elijah to Elisha
    b. Jesus to James and John

2. Kingdom work is not revenge but love of self, each other, and neighbor. Paul adds some additional advice in the Galatians account.

3. Our discipleship is not based on the law but on the good news of freedom. We are free *from* the flesh and *for* works of the Spirit.

D. Move to sharing about your congregation and how the above ought to shape its ministry.
   1. In Christian education we hand the ministry on to the next generation.
   2. In our social ministry we love our neighbor, even those who reject us.
   3. We must present our faith as freeing up people to reach their created potential rather than adding even more burden to their lives.

E. Frame by returning to the two stories you began with.

F. Conclude by telling in your own words the ascensions of both Elijah and Jesus.

Prayer For The Day

Dear God, help us to receive the kingdom work you would give us from those who have gone before us, and show us the way to prepare the next generation to continue the discipleship entrusted to us. When we are tempted to get revenge, teach us to love and to celebrate our freedom in the Christ in whose name we pray. Amen.

Possible Metaphors And Stories

Aung San Sun Kyi, elected president of Myanmar (Burma) who was under house arrest for many months and is winner of the Nobel Peace Prize, writes in her book, *Letters from Burma*, that "*metta* means loving kindness and *thissa* means the truth ... and what we have seen ... proved that love and truth can move people more strongly than any form of coercion." And she is a devout Buddhist!

On the freeways of California they speak of the "rubberneck effect." It means the slowdown of traffic because of drivers gawking at an accident or a car pulled over by the state patrol.

Could we live out our discipleship in a way which would slow down the world as they observed our priorities and deeds?

I wonder if there was a rubberneck effect when the Good Samaritan helped the man in the roadside ditch?

There is a light on each table at Bishop's Cafeteria in Des Moines. A sign says, "For further service push button." When the waiters see the light on, they come to help. Would that we could see the lights burning for those in our community who need service. It's a light calling for our practice of discipleship.

We had three beautiful oak trees in our backyard. But when the house was built, the contractor put fill dirt around them and ran a heavy bulldozer over the ground over them. They began to die. We had to trim out the dead wood, drill holes toward the roots, insert fertilizers, and dig out the fill dirt around them to allow them to breathe. God furnished the rain that summer — beautiful leaves and health returned.

Christian education calls for the same drastic action with the roots of our members. Disciples need to be fed and trimmed and nurtured like those trees. And some had their lives packed down hard from being run over and over.

Proper 9, Pentecost 7, Ordinary Time 14

Revised Common	2 Kings 5:1-14	Galatians 6:(1-6) 7-16	Luke 10:1-11, 16-20
Roman Catholic	Isaiah 66:10-14	Galatians 6:14-18	Luke 10:1-2, 17-20
Episcopal	Isaiah 66:10-16	Galatians 6:(1-10) 14-18	Luke 10:1-12, 16-20

Seasonal Theme   Jesus' acts of compassion and teaching ministry.

Theme For The Day   The sending out of the seventy as witnesses to the Gospel, and our being sent as well.

Old Testament Lesson   2 Kings 5:1-14   *Naaman Cured In The Jordan*

Naaman is a soldier in Damascus and well connected with an unnamed king of Syria. Naaman was a leper, which means he had some sort of skin disease. A slave girl tells Naaman's wife that the prophet Elisha can cure him. So Naaman traveled to Samaria with many gifts. He brought with him an order from his master to heal him. Elisha heard of the impossible demand and sent a note saying to come to him. But when the powerful Naaman arrived, Elisha simply told him by a message to go bathe seven times in the Jordan (v. 10). Naaman was upset, for his rivers (Abanan and Pharpar) are finer than the muddy Jordan. However, he did it and he was cured! Perhaps Elisha's written message for Naaman to go wash in the Jordan was the first written prescription for the treatment of a disciple! I wonder if his trip was covered by his health insurance!

New Testament Lesson   Galatians 6:(1-6) 7-16   *Practical Advice*

Paul is giving these Christians some very practical advice.

1. If we allow our lower nature to rule us, there will be consequences in the end (I'm not sure I agree!). This must be proclaimed in tandem with the fact that God can and does forgive our sins. Still the consequences of our sins remain with us. We must remember we ought not to trade on the forgiveness of God.
2. Then comes the admonition not to get tired of doing good (v. 9). We should continue to work for the good of all, especially those within the family of faith (v. 10b).

In verse 11 we have the large letters. This might mean it's most important, Paul is suffering from poor eyesight, or he just had trouble using a pen. Verse 15 is a great text to proclaim that nothing we can do wins our salvation. In verse 14 he points them to the cross where God's love is best given. Just trust in that and don't get so concerned about things like circumcision.

The Gospel   Luke 10:1-11, 16-20   *The Mission Of The Seventy*

The number 70 here simply is a symbolic number representing the helpers of Jesus (see Numbers 11:16, 17, 24, and 25). The passage tells us that it is very risky to reject God's invitation; to hear God's invitation is a big responsibility; we disciples who are also sent out ought to concentrate on our mission; we must not do our ministry for what we can get out of it; there is plenty to do; and, the one I find most difficult to follow in my culture, *we are to travel light* (vv. 4-8).

Then comes the admonition we preachers often skip over or rationalize away: "... cure the sick" (v. 9). Verses 17 and 20 describe the return of these helpers of Jesus. They returned with joy. Why? Because witnessing to the gospel most affects the ones who do the witnessing. They had gone out, hearts in their throats, afraid, but they still tried. And in the doing of the witnessing there was great unexpected joy. In response to verse 20, William Barclay writes: "It will always remain true that a person's greatest glory is not what he has done but what God has done for him ... It is pride which bars from heaven; it is humility which is the passport to the presence of God."

Preaching Possibilities

A. The three readings for today do have at least one connection: healings. The 2 Kings account tells of Naaman being healed by Elisha's prescription; the Galatians reading mentions " ... a new creation ..." in verse 15; and the Gospel tells us disciples to go out and "... cure the sick who are there" (Luke 10:9).

B. We might also name this Sunday "The Sunday of Holy Advice" and proclaim the following:
   1. From 2 Kings: An immersion in humility could cure a lot of us.
   2. From Galatians: Don't give in to compassion fatigue. Don't boast of anything but the cross of Christ.
   3. From Luke: Travel light, cure the sick, witness to the Gospel, and return in joy.
   If you want, each of the three readings will also stand alone.

C. There is Naaman's dunk in the Jordan, which lends itself to a narrative sermon.

D. There is Paul's large letters, which can be a strong extended metaphor sermon on "Doing what is right."
   1. We will reap what we sow.
   2. We must not get tired in doing good.
   3. We must work for all, especially the family of faith.
   4. We must refrain from boasting except for the cross.
   5. We must become a new creation.
   6. Peace and mercy are ours.

E. I'll go with the Gospel again today. The sending out of the seventy is so powerful if we can convince our hearers that we are also sent out with similar instructions and similar equipment.

Possible Outline Of Sermon Moves

Title: Our Mission, Too

A. Begin by setting the stage for this sending out by telling what the "After this ..." was in verse 1. Jesus was transfigured, healed some folks, and foretold his death. The disciples had an argument about who was the greatest, and a village refused to accept him.

B. Move to telling who the seventy were then — and that they are us now.

C. Move to the instructions Jesus gave them and gives us:
   1. Get going on your way (v. 3)
   2. Travel light (v. 4)
   3. Bring peace (v. 5)
   4. Refrain from trying to better your situation (v. 7)
   5. Cure the sick (v. 9)
   6. Keep focused on your task and proclaim the nearness of the kingdom (v. 1)
   7. Return in joy (v. 17)
   8. Your names are known in heaven (v. 20)

D. Move to how you believe this could be carried out in your congregation if everyone did their best. Issue the challenge to do it and promise you will, too.

E. Close with a story from Possible Metaphors And Stories below.

Prayer For The Day

God of the fruitful harvest, send us out, too, that others might share with us the joy of being your workers and disciples. Help us to practice your advice of traveling light, bringing peace, refraining from bettering our positions, curing the sick, keeping focused, and returning with great joy next worship day, when we come together again in this holy house as your faithful disciples you have sent out. In Christ's name. Amen.

Possible Metaphors And Stories

William Barclay tells of Sir James Simpson, who discovered chloroform. When asked, "What do you regard as your greatest discovery?" He replied, "My greatest discovery was when I discovered Jesus Christ as my Savior." Even the greatest person, in the presence of God, can only say:

"Nothing in my hand I bring,
Simply to the cross I cling;
Naked, came to thee for dress;
Helpless, look to thee for grace;
Foul, I to the fountain fly;
Wash me, Savior, or I die."

In the musical *Evita*, Eva Peron said of herself: "I am content to be the woman who brought the people to Juan Peron."

I am content to be known as one who brought the people to Jesus.

In Shakespeare's play *Antony and Cleopatra*, the messenger tells Antony, "The nature of bad news infects the teller."

And so, too, of the Good News. Reason enough to preach! In order that the preacher might more strongly believe and the witness be effective.

Dick at Our Primary Purpose, an AA treatment center: "I don't lecture; I just tell them how it was with me being drug-dependent." They understood and wanted that same help. Dick said to them, "I don't have to be alone anymore."

So it is with Christians' interpersonal witness: we don't lecture. We just tell them about our relationship with God. And the more we witness, the more we own the gospel, and we don't have to be alone anymore either.

Heads Up Note

The next four Sundays the Second Lesson is from the book of Colossians, one taking up where the last part left off, or continues. If you like to do sermon series, here is an excellent opportunity. Consider the following:

About 60 A. D. Paul wrote to the Christians in Colossia from his prison in Rome a very special letter to tell them that in Jesus we have a wonderful fullness and completeness for our lives here. He also gave them some very practical rules for holy living that we can take to heart as well. We'll be looking at this short letter of Paul's the next four Sundays.

Living A Life In The Christ

A four-part sermon series based on Saint Paul's letter to the Colossians.

A. Proper 10, Pentecost 8, Ordinary Time 15, Colossians 1:1-14
    Lives Worthy Of The Lord
    1. Life in the Spirit (v. 8).
    2. Filled with the knowledge of God's will (v. 9).
    3. Spiritual wisdom and understanding (v. 9b).
    4. Bearing fruit in every good work (v. 10).
    5. Enduring with patience (v. 11b).
    6. Giving thanks to God (v. 12).

B. Proper 11, Pentecost 9, Ordinary Time 16, Colossians 1:15-28
   The Supremacy Of Christ
   1. He is the image of God (v. 15).
   2. He is the head of the church (v. 18).
   3. He has reconciled us to God (v. 22).
   4. He is the hope we have (v. 25b).
   5. He gives us the richness of his glory (v. 27b).
   6. It is this Christ we proclaim to others (v. 28).

C. Proper 12, Pentecost 10, Ordinary Time 17, Colossians 2:6-15 (16-19)
   The Fullness Of Life In Christ
   1. We are rooted and built up in him (v. 7).
   2. In him the fullness of deity lives (v. 9).
   3. We are buried and raised in him in baptism (v. 12).
   4. When we were dead in sin, God made us alive with forgiveness (v. 13b).
   5. He triumphed over sin and evil (v. 15).
   6. (Optional) The whole body grows with nourishment from God (v. 19).

D. Proper 13, Pentecost 11, Ordinary Time 18, Colossians 3:1-11
   The New Life Lived Out In The Word In The Christ
   1. Set your minds on things spiritual (v. 2).
   2. Get rid of earthly stuff (vv. 5, 8).
   3. Clothe yourself with a new self (vv. 9, 10).
   4. In Christ all are equal and without prejudice (v. 11).
   5. Review the series over the last four weeks.

We live lives worthy of the Lord, giving supremacy to the Christ, experiencing a fullness of life and living it out in the world.

Proper 10, Pentecost 8, Ordinary Time 15

Revised Common	Amos 7:7-17	Colossians 1:1-14	Luke 10:25-37
Roman Catholic	Deuteronomy 30:10-14	Colossians 1:15-20	Luke 10:25-37
Episcopal	Deuteronomy 30:9-14	Colossians 1:1-14	Luke 10:25-37

Seasonal Theme   Jesus' acts of compassion and teaching ministry.

Theme For The Day   Identifying our neighbors who are in the side ditches of our community and need our help.

Old Testament Lesson   Amos 7:7-17   *Amos Prophesies*

This is a third vision of Amos following a locust plague (7:1-3) and a supernatural fire (7:4-6) and now the plumb line (7:7-9). This was a cord with a weight at the end, which showed that the wall (Israel) was leaning so much it would surely fall. The divine patience had run out. This royal dynasty would die.

In verses 10-17, Amos is condemned by Amaziah the priest at Bethel. (There are always those, who when the powerful are confronted, will sidle up to them for their favor and tell them what they want to hear.) Shame on you, Amaziah! Amos is asked to hear a call to a new parish where he will no longer threaten these religious with the brutal truth.

Amos' reply makes this book consequential. He declares he is not one of those prophets organized to profit from the temple vocation. Amos just tells of God's inescapable call. He was a shepherd and a worker who punctured the unripe fruit of the sycamore-fig tree so it would become edible.

He scarcely has refused to be still or recant, when he again predicts disaster for the people and their land and that they will be scattered into exile.

New Testament Lesson   Colossians 1:1-14   *Paul's Thankfulness For Faith*

We have the beginning of this short letter by Paul, written while in prison in Rome, to the Colossians in order to refute a heresy circulating there. It trumpets the complete adequacy of Christ over the emptiness of human philosophy. Paul begins by complimenting these Christians on their faithfulness and their love for each other (v. 4). We have here the essence of the Christian life. This is a double loyalty — to Christ and to people. There is not only right thinking but also loving action. These are the twin piers of our life in Christ.

Then comes that which is so beautiful in verse 9. Paul is praying for them. He prays for their patience, strength, and joy. According to Paul's Greek, the patience is a conquering patience and a patience with people. Then comes joy. It is a joy that no circumstance and no person can take away from us. It is not so tough to be joyful when things are going well, but here is a joy regardless of our worldly situation. It is a joy that is *not* the absence of trouble but *is* the presence of God.

The Gospel   Luke 10:25-37   *The Parable Of The Good Samaritan*

It is such a familiar passage, perhaps we can just list some information not so commonly understood.

If the priest had helped and touched the man, he would have his turn of duty in the Temple canceled. Bandits often used decoys on this dangerous road, so the Levite was very cautious. "Samaritan" was often used to describe a person who broke the ceremonial laws (see John 8:48). This Samaritan seemed to have good credit with the innkeeper!

The lawyer probably wore a phylactery around his wrist that would have the law on it from Deuteronomy 6:4-9 and 11:13-20. So Jesus was telling the lawyer to answer his own question by reading what he had strapped to his wrist. Leviticus 18:19 would have been there added by the scribes.

William Barclay adds a comment which rings true for me after many years in the ministry. "It is no new experience to find the orthodox more interested in dogmas than in help and to find the person the orthodox despise to be the person who loves his/her fellow humans. In the end we will be judged not by the creed we hold but by the life we live!"

The Jews had defined love of neighbor to be love of their fellow Jews. This story blows that idea to pieces.

Preaching Possibilities

A. I have previously recommended a series on Colossians. Please see the "heads up" suggestions just before this section on Proper 10, Pentecost 8, Ordinary Time 15. While it is a bit of a stretch, one can connect the three readings by talking of what is "out of plumb" in Israel in the Amos passage, the admonition of Paul in Colossians not to weary in doing good, and Jesus' parable which defines neighbor and calls for acts of compassion for those in need.

B. I have dealt with this parable in *The Parables Of Jesus And Their Flip Side* in the chapter titled "Safer Roads And Real Life" (CSS Publishing Company, 2001).

C. The Old Testament Lesson has a lot to say to us. And it offers a great metaphor — the plumb line. Be sure to see the first metaphor listed below in Possible Metaphors And Stories. How do we measure our practice of discipleship today? And how far out of plumb is the Christian Church and our congregation in following God as God's servants? You might consider hanging a plumb line in your sanctuary and listing below it the elements that indicate on plumb and out of plumb. On plumb: love of Christ and others! But out of plumb: hating others, unwillingness to share, refusal to witness, causing dissension in the church, unkindness, and so on.

Possible Outline Of Sermon Moves

A. Retell the parable in your own words and in the context of your community "A bishop was on his way to preach in St. John's church, when he came across an African family with a flat tire along the side of Route 101," and so on.

B. Ask the congregation to imagine which of the characters in the story they are most like: the Samaritan, the Levite, the innkeeper, the beaten in the ditch.

C. Tell your listeners what you learn from the parable:
1. We ought be willing to help any one in need like:
   a. Prisoners in jail;
   b. Victims of child abuse;
   c. Those infected with AIDS;
   d. Mentally challenged on our streets;
   e. Refugees around this war-torn world;
   f. The hungry; and
   g. Those of different sexual preference.
2. We must help even those who bring the situation upon themselves.
3. Our help ought to go beyond duty. We ought to give our own physical help.

D. Move to the action beyond immediate help. We ought to work to make the roads safe so this won't continue to happen (the flip side of the parable).

E. List out some areas in your community where the congregation could do good and perhaps make a difference.

F. Return to the parable in your context and retell it this time with proper action on behalf of the modern day priest, Levite, and Samaritan.

Prayer For The Day

Help us, O God, to see those beaten and suffering in our ditches here in (*your city*). Show us the proper response to their pain and move us to act as well as pray and feel pity. And let us begin right here in our congregation where there are many who seek loving comfort and support. In the name of Jesus. Amen.

Possible Metaphors And Stories

When you visit the large Roman Catholic Cathedral off the central plaza in Mexico City you will see a long plumb line hanging from its ceiling and extending to the floor in the center of the sanctuary. It measures how far off center the building has moved during and after a recent and large earthquake. Amos recommended the measure long ago, and we still have need of it.

In a graduation ceremony of a Bible school under a colorful large tent, a little boy got lost from his father and began to cry. One of the many graduates up front heard the cry and got up and came back the aisle to retrieve her young son in distress. Without seeing, she knew the cry and took action to comfort. No one else in that large crowd moved, but she did. It all took place in Kathmandu, Nepal, and I was so moved by the attentive compassion. Jesus once told a parable of a Samaritan who heard the cry for help when no one else did, too.

It is in seeking the lost that we realize the full joy of being the found.

"When we don't speak for ourselves, someone else will speak for us," said Jill June of Planned Parenthood of Iowa. She added, "When we don't act, others will act for us." Perhaps this is what church mothers and fathers meant by sins of omission.

Proper 11, Pentecost 9, Ordinary Time 16

Revised Common	**Amos 8:1-12**	**Colossians 1:15-28**	**Luke 10:38-42**
Roman Catholic	**Genesis 18:1-10**	**Colossians 1:24-28**	**Luke 10:38-42**
Episcopal	**Genesis 18:1-10a (10b-14)**	**Colossians 1:21-29**	**Luke 10:38-42**

Seasonal Theme   Jesus' acts of compassion and teaching ministry.

Theme For The Day   Acceptance of each other with different temperaments and making time for Jesus in our lives.

Old Testament Lesson   Amos 8:1-12   *A Fourth Vision*

Amos' fourth vision is a basket of summer fruit (v. 1). Instead of the end of the harvest, Amos says, this is the end of Israel. Last week's announcement of the exhausted patience of God with the plumb line vision has resulted in doom. Then in verses 4-14 we have Amos announcing the elements of judgment day. In verses 4-6 he tells of the ways merchants exploit the people. They come right from religious ceremonies and do their cheating with undersized measures and overweight shekels to balance the customer's silver. In verse 8 we have the threat or prediction of earthquake.

Verses 10 to 14 have the language of mourning — except for baldness in verse 10b! Then comes mourning for an only son and famine. See Deuteronomy 14:1.

One might put together the four visions of Amos and preach a prophetic sermon for our day.
1. First vision: Locust plague   7:1-3 God's warning
2. Second vision: Supernatural Fire   7:4-6 Amos says, "Cease"
3. Third vision: The plumb line   7:7-9 Israel, God's wall is out of whack
4. Fourth vision: A basket of summer fruit   8:1-3 The exhausted patience of God results in a sentence of doom

New Testament Lesson   Colossians 1:15-28   *Christ, The Head Of The Body*

This passage was probably a hymn (vv. 15-20) in which the author wanted to make the point that baptism into Christ means freedom from any other rulers in the universe and participation in Christ's kingdom. Christ's image is expansive:
1. He is God's image (v. 15).
2. All things were created through him (v. 16).
3. He holds all things together (v. 17).
4. He is the head of the church, his body (v. 18).
5. God's fullness is in him (v. 19).
6. Through him God reconciled all things (v. 20).
7. The renewal of life's wholeness and wholesomeness empower us to stand before God as shameless! (vv. 21-22).
8. The inclusiveness of our God's atoning work is claimed (v. 23). Then comes joy. This is characteristically Pauline. See Romans 5:3-11.
9. Preachers are given a marvelous task to do: proclaim Christ so that all our hearers might mature in their faith (v. 28).

The Gospel   Luke 10:38-42   *Mary And Martha Visited*

In just a few words Luke records this clash of personalities. It took place in Bethany in the home Jesus often visited when having business in Jerusalem or when he just wanted some peace and quiet. These two sisters were of very different temperaments. They both loved Jesus and both tried to demonstrate their love for him but in different ways. Mary, the quiet type, simply sat at his feet and listened (v.

39). Martha, one of those dynamos of action, wanted to put on a feast, and she felt she needed Mary's help to do so.

I don't think we ought be judgmental about either of the sisters. They loved Jesus in the way they knew best. Martha just didn't understand that at that time in Jesus' life he most needed quiet and understanding. And Martha also made the mistake of criticizing her sister for not helping in her perceived busyness.

The story pleads for understanding of each other's temperament and for not allowing the busyness of our religious practice to crowd out or spoil the actual presence of Christ with us.

I wonder if Dr. Luke put this story here right after the one about being neighbor to illustrate that we can also love in different ways: by sitting quietly, listening and learning, or by using our God-given abilities to help by serving. It will preach.

Preaching Possibilities

As is almost always the case when the texts in the readings are read "in continuum," they just don't connect together at all, and I believe it is a mistake to try. However, today we have three really strong readings any one of which will provide for good preaching.

A. The Amos prophecy, if not yet dealt with, can be a solid sermon using the four visions as suggested above. The theme can be "The Patience of God." The plumb-line provides for a visual aid in the sermon. Or we can use it for a children's sermon on this day.

B. For the Second Reading, I have already suggested a series of moves in the optional series on the book of Colossians and called it "The Supremacy of Christ." It's a chance to do a teaching sermon about who Jesus is (vv. 15-18) and what he has done for us (vv. 22, 25b, and 27b). Then a good conclusion is to tell your listeners that this information is for us to tell others (v. 28). The frame of the sermon could be: Jesus shows us what God is like and he is the head of the church. He makes things okay between us and God, and gives us our hope and his glory. All this we ought to share with others. And in the sharing of it, we will own it even better.

Possible Outline Of Sermon Moves

Let's go with the Gospel for today and do a sermon based on how people listen to preaching.*

A. *Build a fire:* Tell of a time when you got all wrapped up in the preparation for an event and then really missed the richness of the event itself.

B. *The bridge:* Now go to the Mary/Martha story and show how Martha did the same thing. Then bridge to the fact that many of us are Marthas and we need to slow down and set priorities.

C. *The point:* We must respect each other's temperaments and we must consider giving our presence as well as the products of our busyness to Christ and others.

D. *An example:* Would be the fact that our spouse and/or children need quality time with us. Another, would be the danger of getting so busy with church work we miss out on the presence of Christ in our daily lives.

E. *Your witness:* Confess how in your life and ministry busyness crowds out the teaching and the presence of Jesus, the Christ.

F. *So what:* Give some concrete examples of how you will try to make changes in your lifestyle so you can, like Mary, sit at Jesus' feet and listen.

   1. A regular time each day for prayer and meditation.
   2. The setting of priorities which put devotion and learning in the first place.
   3. The acceptance of people of other temperaments as also serving, in their way, the Christ.

G. *Frame:* Return to your fire and the description of a time when you were too busy with the details. You might read again the Gospel as a conclusion.

Prayer For The Day

Help us, dear God, not to miss Jesus' presence and teaching because we are so busy. Give us the way to a more peaceful and sane lifestyle and also an accepting attitude toward those unlike us in temperament and in daily priorities. And come into our homes this week with your understanding peace. In the name of Jesus, the one who visited Mary and Martha's home, we ask it. Amen.

Possible Metaphors And Stories

When a little, parentless Batak girl, now fourteen, found out I was returning to the guesthouse in Penatang-Siantar, Sumatra, she planted a "welcome garden" near the front door. Then she patiently watered and waited for my arrival.

The just-ready-to-bloom flowers were beautiful, most of all because of her preparation and anticipation of my return. Santi did what she knew best to express her love and welcome. It was touching.

On Samosir Island at Lake Toba, Sumatra, there is a sign in Indonesian over a restaurant door which reads: "Sederhana." It means a modest restaurant, not complicated. It's what Jesus was asking Martha for in Bethany that day he visited her home.

According to Peter Jennings on *ABC News*, television has what they call "appointment shows," which means people arrange their lives so they don't miss them. An example would be *60 Minutes* on Sunday evening. Jesus had come to Mary and Martha's home, and it should have been an "appointment" visit for the sisters. Mary understood that.

Allen So, a young Chinese Christian mother on my *Friends in Christ* e-mail newsletter wrote the following greeting to the other global students: "I would like to pray to God to help everyone of us really come out from the world of things and go into Jesus."

---

*For an explanation of this homiletical technique, see my book, *The Preacher's Edge*, (Lima, Ohio: CSS Publishing Company, 1996).

Proper 12, Pentecost 10, Ordinary Time 17

Revised Common	Hosea 1:2-10	Colossians 2:6-15 (16-19)	Luke 11:1-13
Roman Catholic	Genesis 18:20-32	Colossians 2:12-14	Luke 11:1-13
Episcopal	Genesis 18:20-33	Colossians 2:6-15	Luke 11:1-13

Seasonal Theme   Jesus' acts of compassion and teaching ministry.

Theme For The Day   We have a holy parent who wants to hear our prayers and to answer them.

Old Testament Lesson   Hosea 1:2-10   *The Family Of Hosea*

We move today from the last two Sundays' readings from Amos to this Sunday and the next reading from Hosea, who prophesized soon after the ministry of Amos. Hosea identified the unnamed enemy in Amos as Assyria. His book is first in that portion of the Bible called the Minor Prophets.

In this portion of the book, Hosea's family life serves as a metaphor to describe God's message for the people. Hosea wants to say that Israel commits great harlotry by forsaking the Lord, so he uses his marriage to an unfaithful wife named Gomer. Her name literally means "perfection." She was one of the holy cult women, which to Hosea was no more than common prostitution. The names of their three children are parodies on names of Baal cult children.

"Jezreel" announces the end of the dynasty.

"Not pitied" announces God will not forgive Israel for it's unfaithfulness. God's patience has run out.

"Not my people" announces that the covenant between God and the people is broken. That which goes all the way back to the days of Abraham is finished!

New Testament Lesson   Colossians 2:6-15 (16-19)   *The Fullness Of Life In Christ*

This reading is full of allusions to the heresy Paul is writing to correct and which threatened to pollute the Colossian church. Evidently, the false teachers were teaching that the Christ is not enough. One needs other divine and angelic powers in addition to Jesus. They were advocating for the worship of angels (v. 18), astrology (v. 8), philosophy (v. 8), circumcision (v. 11), ascetic rules (v. 16). In verses 13-15 Paul uses a series of vivid pictures to demonstrate what God has done for us.

1.   When dead, God made us alive (v. 13).
2.   God erased the demands made against us (v. 14).
3.   God nailed our indictment to the cross (v. 14b).
4.   God made the authorities powerless (v. 15).

So Christ is all that is needed. Sin is forgiven and evil conquered. So the admonishment of verses 6 and 7 holds. Continue to live your lives in Christ, remaining faithful and abounding in thankfulness.

The Gospel   Luke 11:1-13   *Jesus Teaches About Prayer*

A few things to notice about Luke's record of Jesus' teaching a prayer formula for disciples. We start by calling God "father." A father can be approached by his children and delights to provide for them. Before asking anything for ourselves, we reverence God. All life is covered, such as present needs, past sins, and future trials.

Notice, too, it ends without "... the kingdom, the power, and the glory," which was first a choir response and which later got incorporated into the spoken corpus of the prayer. In verses 5-13 we have a parable about going to a neighbor for bread. It gives us encouragement to ask in prayer with the confidence God will answer. This is a parable of contrast. Jesus is saying if this irritated neighbor would give bread for a late arriving guest of his neighbor, think *how much more* God will give it. Barclay writes: "... we are not wringing gifts from an unwilling God, but that we are going to one who knows our needs better than we know them ourselves and whose heart towards us is the heart of generous love."

And God always answers our prayers; however, the answer given is not always what we wanted or expected. So go right on asking, searching, and knocking.

Preaching Possibilities

A. The three readings could connect this way: "Three pictures of God."
   1. Hosea says God's patience has run out.
   2. Paul says God has forgiven our sins.
   3. Luke says pray, and God is like a father who wants to provide.
B. The Hosea account lends itself to narrative preaching as we tell the story of Hosea marrying a prostitute and bringing three children into the world, each one's name communicating truths about God to the people. The fact the wife is a prostitute will get and hold attention and keep the message close to the ground. The three children's names will make an easy outline of truths by using their names. (See my explanation in the comments on the reading.)
C. If you are following my earlier recommendation to preach a series on the Colossians texts in continuum reading that I have provided, a suggested outline of moves for today is listed there.
D. The Gospel has two definite parts: the disciple's prayer and the parable of asking late at night for bread from a neighbor. Both are about prayer, but I would select one or the other and try to focus on it.

   Because there are many model sermons on the Lord's prayer, I'll go with the parable in this lectionary workbook.

Possible Outline Of Sermon Moves

Title: Asking For Bread

A. Begin by running the story. Retell verses 5-8 in your own words. Give some background on how they would all be sleeping together on the floor and the father would be reticent to disturb the whole family.
B. Tell of a time when you were wakened in the middle of the night and you really didn't want to get up.
C. Move to what Jesus is trying to teach disciples like us by telling this parable:
   1. While it's not always what we want, God does answer prayers.
   2. If this man would answer, think how much more it is so that God will answer!
   3. There is a holy hospitality here on the flip side of the story we Christians ought to consider following as well.
D. Move to verse 9. Pick up your Bible and read the verse slowly and deliberately as a great promise from God to all your hearers today.
E. An optional move would be to address the subject of how family members ought to treat each other who have such a loving and gracious God as theirs.
F. Or move to consider when and how you and your congregation are tempted to say with the bothered neighbor late at night, "Do not bother me ..." (v. 7b).
G. Close with a story from Possible Metaphors And Stories below.

Prayer For The Day

Teach us disciples to pray also, dear God, and give us the reassurance that you always answer. Please help us to open the door when we are asking for help and not to be upset at the inconvenience of it all. Thanks for being the kind of Holy Parent who is always ready to listen and to provide. In Jesus' name. Amen.

Possible Metaphors And Stories

New Christians are so often my best teachers of theology. One such person in Kathmandu, Nepal, told us so simply, "To pray for a blessing is to throw oneself into the stream of God's will." It changed my view of prayer forever!

The late Katherine Brownfield, who sent me humor, sent me this gem: A little boy was asked in Bible school to memorize the Lord's Prayer. Sitting on the floor in the living room, head bowed and chubby hands folded, he reverently said: "Our Father, who are in heaven, how did you know my name?"

God knows us by name, each one, as God knows every sparrow which falls from the heavens.

Peter Narum told me about a flood. It was up to the first floor the first day and a boat came and offered to remove the homeowner from the home. The answer was: "No, I trust God."

The second day, water was up to the second floor and a boat came and offered to help. Same response: "No, I trust God."

The third day, the man was on the roof and the water was still rising. A helicopter came to help. "No, I trust God."

In heaven now, the man said to God, "I trusted you; why didn't you help?"

God answered, "I tried; I sent two boats and a helicopter."

God often sends answers to our prayers through others.

In the television special, *September Gun*, Ben Sunday, a gunfighter, tells a nun, "The secret of good baked beans is to be hungry as hell," and "When you shoot, pray; when they shoot, duck."

There are times to pray and times to act. A combination of both is probably the best: action and prayer.

Proper 13, Pentecost 11, Ordinary Time 18

Revised Common	Hosea 11:1-11	Colossians 3:1-11	Luke 12:13-21
Roman Catholic	Ecclesiastes 1:2; 2:21-23	Colossians 3:1-5, 9-11	Luke 12:13-21
Episcopal	Ecclesiastes 1:12-14; 2:(1-7, 11) 18-23	Colossians 3:(5-11) 12-17	Luke 12:13-21

Seasonal Theme   Jesus' acts of compassion and teaching ministry.

Theme For The Day   Our need to resist greed and to practice a lifestyle of Christian stewardship.

Old Testament Lesson   Hosea 11:1-11   *Like A Loving Father*

A great passage begins about the depth and the nature of God's love. A father-son love is used in this passage to illustrate God's love for us. Even though Israel was like a son to God and God continually called the son, the son gave in to the attraction of Baal worship. Verses 3 and 4 contain the fatherly patience and care for his son. In verses 5 and 7 the son matures as Israel but refuses to return to his parent — so stern discipline is applied.

Verses 8 and 9 have the climax of the passage. Like a loving parent, instead of punishing Israel like those cities such as Sodom and Gomorrah which were destroyed (Deuteronomy 29:23), the father's compassion grows warm and tender. Here is redemptive love rather than human vengeance. This parent will not come in wrath (v. 9b) but in love.

So God the father of Israel will return his son from Egyptian-Assyrian domination to their homes again. So God causes good to come out of what we humans would consider evil (v. 11).

The passage is rich with metaphors, including the major one of God being the father and loving God's son, Israel.

New Testament Lesson   Colossians 3:1-11   *New Life In Christ*

The first part of this reading is the reading for Easter, series A. I have previously suggested you do a sermon series on these Second Lessons from Colossians and given an outline of sermon moves for this reading in the "heads up" note on page 145. Let's take it in outline form:

1. In baptism we die and rise again. So there ought be a new life after baptism because now our thoughts are set on heavenly things. We have a new set of values (vv. 1-4).
2. A great name for Jesus Christ: your (or our) life (v. 4). See Philippians 1:21.
3. The ethical section of the letter begins. We must kill our evil practices (see Romans 8:13). So a radical shift of our values must take place (vv. 5-9a).
4. The baptism practice of removing the old garments and putting on a new white robe afterward (vv. 9, 10).
5. To become a Christian is to remove the barriers which divide us humans. Racism, sexism, nationalism, ageism, classism, all this stuff is gone. Christ is in all of us and we are all united in Christ (v. 11). A great verse!

The Gospel   Luke 12:13-21   *The Parable Of The Rich Fool*

Today we have a parable of Jesus which is easily told in either contemporary context or in Palestinian context as Jesus told it. It's a warning about greed and life's abundance of possessions. In a culture where many display bumper stickers reading, "The one with the most toys wins," it is for us and for now.

It was a common custom to ask rabbis to settle disputes about money, thus the question in verse 13. Jesus used the occasion to teach his disciples about stewardship of possessions and to give a specific warning of how the desire to acquire possessions and keep them was not the good life. This will be a hard sell in the U.S.!

William Barclay tells us two things about this farmer whose land produced so abundantly.

1. He never saw beyond himself. This is the opposite of the disciple's life and Christian values. It is in giving away that we experience unexpected joy. Barclay continues with, "The Romans had a proverb which said that possessions were like sea water; the more a person drank the thirstier that person became."
2. The second thing about this rich farmer is that he never saw beyond this world. All his plans were done on the basis of life here and now. The person who lives like this his/her whole life is in for a cruel shock.

Preaching Possibilities

A. Under the theme of "three things you can be certain of about the Christian life" we can connect all three of these readings together.
   1. Hosea — God loves us like a loving parent loves his/her child.
   2. Colossians — Life in Christ after baptism is a whole new ball game.
   3. Luke — the great joy of life for Christians is in the practice of holistic stewardship.
B. Of the three readings I like so much the Hosea metaphor of God loving like a parent one's child. It will extend all the way through using the Second Reading and the parable in Luke as examples. Any parent preaching on this Old Testament passage will have plenty of examples from his or her own family life growing up and, if permissible from one's children, from their own parenting. As far as sermon preparation and delivery, "It's a piece of cake."
C. Please see page 145 for an outline of sermon moves if you preach on Colossians alone. It is also a rich text.
D. However, because I believe we neglect the subject of Christian financial stewardship except when we are in our annual drive for pledges, I'll go with the Gospel.

Possible Outline Of Sermon Moves

A. Introduction: Jesus told his disciples a story which really speaks to me and I think ought to you also. The story has to do with greed, a self-centered collection of possessions, and Christian financial stewardship. I'll read it from Luke's account and then imagine how it might go if it were told today in our community.
B. Read the parable from a visible Bible. (So people can see where it's coming from.)
C. Retell the parable in your context: "The owner of a bread store had a marvelous increase in sales, so he decided to double the size of his store...."
D. Tell what you see right away in this story.
   1. Life's satisfaction is not really in acquiring many possessions. Greed is a big part of our human nature. Relate an example from below.
   2. It is in giving away we know the joy of discipleship. Relate an example from below.
   3. Our best priorities come from seeing beyond this world. Our planning ought always to consider that we live here for a short time and the rest in eternity. Relate an example.
E. Confess to your congregation how hard it is for you to follow this parable's advice in your own life.
F. List some steps you believe all should take because of today's Gospel: tithe, share, travel light.
G. Frame your sermon by repeating in reverse order your main points and then refer to your contemporary telling of the parable, giving it a different ending.

Prayer For The Day

Dear Holy Parent who loves and forgives us like a loving Father with his children, teach us to share and to be good stewards of the abundance you shower down upon us. Help us to fight off the greed, which continually wants more and more and resists our giving away that which could bring real joy. And please help us to know when we have enough. In Jesus' name. Amen.

Possible Metaphors And Stories

In Hong Kong, there is an advertisement for Swiss watches, which is a good example of Christian stewardship. The picture is a father hugging his son with the caption: "You never actually own a Patek Philippe watch, you merely look after it for the next generation."

An article in *USA Today*: "McThief Probe"

"A customer at the Euclid, Ohio, McDonald's drive-up window was mistakenly handed the day's cash receipts. The company sometimes conceals the 'take' for the day in one of their regular paper bags to foil thieves. The person receiving the bag of money may not have committed any crime according to the authorities."

God drops undeserved gifts on us, too.

Douglas John Hall writes regarding stewardship: "Stewardship does not describe any one dimension of the Christian life, it describes the whole posture called Christian. The stewardship of all believers — stewardship is the church's mission."

Life on the farm always had unwritten rules I observed and followed, and I assumed everyone did. Whenever our neighbor, Grace Miller, baked, she would send over a pie for us. I always had the task of returning the pie pan to the Millers. My mother always filled it with something like cookies when she sent it back — never an empty pan. And when my father borrowed a tool like a mower, we always cleaned and oiled it before I drove the Model A Ford we used for a truck to tow it back.

That's the way it ought to be in our practice of stewardship. We return a little of all which has been given us.

Proper 14, Pentecost 12, Ordinary Time 19

Revised Common	Isaiah 1:1, 10-20	Hebrews 11:1-3, 8-16	Luke 12:32-40
Roman Catholic	Wisdom 18:6-9	Hebrews 11:1-2, 8-19	Luke 12:32-48
Episcopal	Genesis 15:1-6	Hebrews 11:1-3 (4-7) 8-16	Luke 12:32-40

Seasonal Theme   Jesus' acts of compassion and teaching ministry.

Theme For The Day   The faith of our mothers and fathers as a teaching example for us.

Old Testament Lesson   Isaiah 1:1, 10-20   *Rebuke And Promise*

This Sunday and next our Old Testament Lesson is from the book of Isaiah, the greatest of the writing prophets. From Isaiah we get a more complete view of God's judgment and salvation. In today's reading there is both scolding and promise characteristic of his writing.

Verses 10-17 are strong rebukes of the people. They are as evil as Sodom and Gomorrah (v. 10). Isaiah says they should hear God's word and the teachings (Torah). Ritual just doesn't count any more because of their unfaithfulness. Jeremiah made the same claim (Jeremiah 7:21-26). They have so much blood on their hands, God refuses to listen to their prayers. Most importantly they are to stop their evil, do the good, work for justice, aid those oppressed, and protect the orphan and widow (v. 17).

Then comes a promise of forgiveness in verses 18-20. Even though we are still sinners, our God is willing to forgive, anyhow! This wonderful promise makes the earlier scolding bearable.

New Testament Lesson   Hebrews 11:1-3, 8-16   *God's Pilgrims*

The next four Sundays we will read from the book of Hebrews for our New Testament Reading.

The following may be used in the worship bulletin today: "The theme of this book is that Jesus the Christ is all we need in revelation and as a mediator of God's grace. Jesus, the Christ, is superior over everything. Today's reading is about the significance of faith. The first part tells us how important faith is and the second part gives examples like Abraham, Isaac, and Jacob."

The hope and faith described in verses 1-3 anticipate the future confidant of God's care for us. The writer, whoever he was, wants us to be certain this is God's world; and even when it doesn't appear so, somehow God continues to rule it.

Verses 8-16 give Abraham as the great example of confident faith. We could say about his faith:

1. It was a risk-taking faith. To live the Christian life is to be willing to take risks and live an adventure.
2. It was a faith which saw the bigger picture. He saw beyond the world and daily life here. He had a vision that made all the work and struggle possible.
3. It was a patient faith. To wait, when it seems nothing is taking place, takes faith. He did not give up nor lower the goals and expectations. Some definitions of words used in 13-16.

Strangers — *xenoi* — can mean a refuge.

Foreigners — *parepidemos* — staying temporarily and having their permanent home somewhere else. (See Ecclesiastics 29:22-28.) We Christians are always on the way as a pilgrim of eternity.

The Gospel   Luke 12:32-40   *Be Like Watchful Slaves*

Only in Luke do we have this beautiful imagery of disciples as God's sheep. But it is common in the Old Testament: Psalms 80:1, 95:7, 100:3; Isaiah 40:11; Jeremiah 23:1-4; Ezekiel 34. The metaphor pictures disciples as willing to accept God's authority and rule. I like verse 34 a lot and have learned its importance over many years of trying to be one of Jesus' disciples. First, we ought to learn what is our treasure, then our heart will follow.

Verses 35-40 refer to the second coming of Jesus the Christ and to the time God calls us into eternity. The point is to be ready for either at any time. And the servant is praised who is ready.

Notice how it begins by describing a person dressed for action. Verses 39 and 40 make the point again. This time it is from the Q source (Matthew 24:43-51). If the homeowner knew the time a thief was coming, he or she could be ready to protect the home. So be ready for the coming of Jesus anytime.

Preaching Possibilities

A. I will use all three readings today, as they have a delightful common theme.
B. However, each one will easily stand alone as well.
   1. The idea of one's sin and God's forgiveness in the Isaiah passage will preach well.
   2. And for a textual sermon, try using verse 34 of Luke 12. Locating our treasure is crucial to our own lives as disciples and stewards and it is so important in our parenting.
   3. Also the Hebrews account gives us an opportunity to preach about faith. See the three truths about faith listed under the New Testament heading. One could begin by telling about Abraham and his willingness to trust God, go to a time when you had a hard time trusting God, and then back up to verses 1-3, telling your hearers what that means to us today.
   4. Verses 13b and 14 of the Hebrews reading are rich and ready for textual preaching. We are pilgrims on our way to eternity and that has radical implications for our lifestyle here.
      a. We need not accumulate much here.
      b. We must learn to travel light.
      c. Our ultimate loyalty is to the Christ of eternity.
      d. Others must be told of these great pilgrim truths.
   5. Verses 35-40 of Hebrews are yet another opportunity to preach on the second coming of Christ. Your hearers might want to hear the various interpretations of that belief.
      a. One day Jesus will return in the same manner as he departed at the Ascension.
      b. When we die, Jesus comes to take us home to eternity.
      c. And the one most radical which I like: Jesus already came again in the Easter resurrection and Pentecost and is here. Let's stop standing around waiting and celebrate his presence with us here and now.

Possible Outline Of Sermon Moves

A. Introduction: Ask what the hearer's favorite Bible verse is and then tell of your memory work as a child learning the verses or how one became most important to you.
B. Explain that all the readings today are about great faith and that the church forefathers and mothers selected them to be read as some of the most important passages of scripture.
C. Theme: three readings about faith.
   1. Isaiah's faith was that God promises forgiveness even when, and for, those who are unfaithful.
   2. The author of Hebrew's faith was confirmed in the great patriarch Abraham, who was a pilgrim like we are.
   3. Luke's faith was that we are like a flock Jesus the Good Shepherd cares for. We are to be ready for Jesus' coming anytime.
D. Move to a story about faith below.
E. Tell of your own faith and how it fluctuates strong and weak and what you need to do to nurture it by your spiritual life practices.
F. Move to another metaphor from the section below.
G. Sing a verse or two about faith from your hymnal.
H. Frame your sermon by reminding them of the faith of Luke, the author of Hebrews, and Isaiah.

Prayer For The Day

God of our homeland and giver by the Holy Spirit of our faith, show us the way to be confident in our hope and beliefs. Grant that we are always ready for your return and help us celebrate your real presence with us in the meantime. In Jesus' name. Amen.

Possible Metaphors And Stories

Robert Louis Stevenson said: "It is better to travel hopefully than to arrive." These saints of the past lived alertly in hope and expectation.

"Sometimes you have to leap and build wings on the way down." I heard it said in a restaurant in Mesa, Arizona. But it ought to be whispered daily to us who are timid in faith.

In southern Egypt the temples are built on the east side of the Nile, where the sun comes up. On the west side of the Nile, where the sun sets, are the tombs. Where are we building our faith temples?

The newscaster recently told of an owner of a jewelry store putting a bag of diamonds worth $175,000 on top of his car and driving off to the airport. They have not been found yet. It's so easy to lose our treasure and sometimes not even know it for a while.

In Shakespeare's *King John* we hear the words: "Welcome home again discarded faith," and in *Much Ado About Nothing*, "He wears his faith but as a fashion of his hat."

Proper 15, Pentecost 13, Ordinary Time 20

Revised Common	Isaiah 5:1-7	**Hebrews 11:29—12:22**	**Luke 12:49-56**
Roman Catholic	**Jeremiah 38:4-6, 8-10**	**Hebrews 12:1-4**	**Luke 12:49-53**
Episcopal	**Jeremiah 23:23-29**	**Hebrews 12:1-7 (8-10) 11-14**	**Luke 12:49-56**

Seasonal Theme   Jesus' acts of compassion and teaching ministry.

Theme For The Day   The judgment and divine love of God for us very important sinners.

Old Testament Lesson   Isaiah 5:1-7   *Isaiah's Awful Love Song*

This is not a happy song and has been connected to two additional passages: verses 8-23 and verses 24-30. This song is probably based on a love song where the vineyard is the bride (Song of Solomon 8:11-12). The vineyard was well tended but produced putrid fruit — literally "stinking things." So the vineyard is judged and destroyed. It is Judah that is the vineyard. God has cared for them; however, the result was not justice but bloodshed. We find the same imagery in Psalm 80:14-15. Perhaps Hosea knew the analogy (Hosea 2:3-6). It is also later in Ezekiel 19:10-14; Jesus used it in Mark 12:1-9.

New Testament Lesson   Hebrews 11:29—12:22   *The Meaning Of Faith*

We continue in Hebrews with examples of great faith. Verse 29 is the example of crossing the sea of reeds (Exodus 14:21-29). The fall of Jericho under Joshua's leadership (Joshua 6:1-21) continues the examples. Then comes Rahab, the prostitute who is praised! This is astounding that she would be listed as one of the heroes/heroines. However in James 2:25, 26 she is also made an example of faith by good works. Then follows a list of the faithful and other trials and triumphs. The heroes seem to increase to a large crowd and come much nearer to the writer's own time. Endurance under persecution is the main focus. There is a sense of building climax to 12:1. In 1-2 the writer uses the image of a racer, determined and stripped down for this last running. Jesus has arrived at the goal ahead of us and it is on him we fix our eyes. He is the one who is the best example of all of faith. "... has taken his seat ..." is a quotation of Psalm 110:4.

The Gospel   Luke 12:49-56   *Interpreting The Time*

These verses are in poetic form. Jesus uses the image of fire to represent judgment. Compare this passage with Luke 9:54. The peace which Jesus brings is not the quiet of apathy but the serenity of devoted discipleship. Verses 54-56 simply say we ought to be able to interpret the signs of the time just like we can tell the weather. What we need to read the signs is not a special cleverness but just an insight which self-disregard brings into being. We have to say about the passage that the essence of Christianity is that loyalty to Christ has to be stronger than any other loyalty here on earth. I won't take it any further than that. It is a distasteful passage to me which wreaks of too much vengeance and judgment.

Preaching Possibilities ·
A. It's not the best set of readings I would choose. The Isaiah and Luke readings will connect for a sermon about the judgment of God.
B. Or one could preach on faithfulness and judgment using the Old Testament and Gospel as examples of impending judgment and the New Testament Reading as an example of faithfulness.
   1. Isaiah saw the situation as God giving the people everything they needed, and they responded by being unfaithful.
   2. Jesus told the people that loyalty to him would cause divisions even within families. He said they ought to be able to see the wrongness of their times and know the impending result.

162

3. The writer of Hebrews tells of genuine faithfulness and gives many examples. We are urged to endure even under persecution, keep our eye on the goal, and press on.

Possible Outline Of Sermon Moves

A. Begin by reviewing what Isaiah said in last week's reading. The people have blood on their hands but God will forgive.

B. Move to this week's reading. Isaiah likens the peoples' behavior to a vineyard which has good soil and good care, but it produces awful fruit in spite of all its nurture. Because of this lack of good fruit, the vineyard will be destroyed.

C. Move to our time and fruit. We have been given many blessings and God's undeserved grace and forgiveness. But we have also produced some awful fruit: racism, sexism, ageism, nationalism, terrorism, bigotry, greed, revenge, and so on.

D. Speak of the terrible effects on the one who has the above as well as the one who is the victim of it. Really punch this idea home!

E. Move to address the good and bad fruits a congregation can have and its effects on its members and on the community.

F. Make your own witness by stating this has not been your favorite sermon to preach, as it is much too grim and judgmental and pictures God as vindictive rather than the God you know as full of grace and forgiveness.

G. Close with a story which illustrates the above and thank God for the Holy Spirit's help getting you through a tough Sunday of textual preaching.

Prayer For The Day

We thank you, dear Holy Parent, for providing us with so much which ought to produce a lot of good works out of us. Be patient with us when we so often fail to respond in the right way to all your loving kindnesses, and remove from us those things hurtful to others and disappointing to you. In Christ's name. Amen.

Possible Metaphors And Stories

The conductor of a community orchestra was upset because of poor attendance of musicians at the rehearsals. So he publicly thanked the one member who had not missed a rehearsal. The response was, "It's the least I could do since I won't be at the concert tonight."

Others' responses can be very disappointing but we must not judge them for it. Only God knows all their circumstances.

March 9, 1909, the city water tank in Des Moines collapsed and nearly washed away First Lutheran Church. After rebuilding, there was a foreclosure on their church during the Depression and the congregation bought it back at a reduced price. It's now debt free. Our baptismal water could have the power to move churches. Jesus has bought us back with a big price. We are debt free. All is forgiven.

Andy Rooney on *60 Minutes* claimed no one is to blame for anything in our country.

"... the good boy got in bad company; it was the pusher's fault not the drug taker; the person was legally insane at the time of the crime." He ended by saying, "Don't blame me for what I just said. The devil made me do it." Christians can own their behavior and seek forgiveness but often still have to pay the price of it.

The grass in the yard is all brown now for lack of rain, but weeds are thriving in the cracks in the concrete. Interesting how the good often seems to wilt away in very favorable places and the unwanted seems to thrive where we don't want it to survive.

Heads Up Alert On Jeremiah

Perhaps you would like to include in your worship bulletin the following: For the next six weeks we will be reading from the book of Jeremiah for the Old Testament Lesson. In the *New Revised Standard Version* of the Bible we read: "Jeremiah was always conscious of his call from the Lord to be a prophet, and as such proclaimed words that were spoken first by God and were therefore certain of fulfillment. Judgment is one of his all-pervasive themes. He was careful to point out, however, that repentance, if sincere, would postpone the inevitable. Jeremiah conceived of God as the Creator of all that exists, and as the all-powerful and everywhere present Lord. At the same time he emphasized that God was very much concerned about individual people who were accountable to God."

Proper 16, Pentecost 14, Ordinary Time 21

Revised Common	Jeremiah 1:4-10	Hebrews 12:18-29	Luke 13:10-17
Roman Catholic	Isaiah 66:18-21	Hebrews 12:5-7, 11-13	Luke 13:22-30
Episcopal	Isaiah 28:14-22	Hebrews 12:18-19, 22-29	Luke 13:22-30

Seasonal Theme   Jesus' acts of compassion and teaching ministry.

Theme For The Day   The practice of mercy over rules and regulations; compassion for people over organization.

Old Testament Lesson   Jeremiah 1:4-10   *The Call*

In the beginning of this book we have the call of God to Jeremiah to be a prophet. He feels from the very beginning God wants him to be a prophet. He is young (probably fourteen or fifteen), but is certain he can do it because of the help from God he will receive. Yahweh has put the powerful words in this tough and determined young man.

What Jeremiah speaks is what happens! If it is doom on the nations — that's what happens. If it is peace, peace will follow. He will be able to be the prophet to the nation right there in Jerusalem. And his words will affect the fate of many nearby and far off.

New Testament Lesson   Hebrews 12:18-29   *A New Relationship With God*

This reading is a contrast between the law giving on Mount Sinai and the new covenant of which Jesus is the mediator. See Deuteronomy 4:11 and 19:12-13. In the Sinai law giving, we read of the inapproachability of God — they met death if they dared try. There is also the sheer majesty and the real terror of God. But to the Christian there is a new covenant, and we see the contrast beginning with verse 22 in a new relationship with God. In this new covenant we can expect the new Jerusalem and a new creation. Our lives are re-created and made new. And there are angels and a joyful assembly.

There is also God's elected people. Two words are used here, the word for the firstborn who receives the inheritance and registry among the loyal citizens of the kingdom. Then the writer assures us that it was Jesus who made this new relationship possible. Verse 24 contrasts the blood of Jesus and the blood of Abel (Genesis 4:10). Abel's blood called for vengeance, where Jesus' blood opened the way to reconciliation.

Verses 25-29 are not easy. Moses gave us the oracles but Jesus' words were God's voice. The Old Testament and covenant were not the full revelation. That came in the New Testament (covenant). When the day comes when the earth will end, everything will be shaken *except* our relationship with God, which cannot be shaken. We can remain true to God, and our relationship with God will remain solid. But to be untrue runs the high risk of fire and destruction.

The Gospel   Luke 13:10-17   *Healing On The Wrong Day*

The Jews should have been thrilled Jesus healed one of their own people. Instead, they are critical of his doing it on the sabbath. You would expect great celebrations, for the woman had been bent over and suffered eighteen years! Of all days, the sabbath ought be a day of healing and compassion. Besides, Jesus pointed out that those critical of him break the no work law when they water their donkey on the sabbath. This is the last time we read of Jesus being in a synagogue. Perhaps he gave up on the religious and after this went in the streets and on the hillsides. The president of the synagogue represents many in our day who love systems and rules and constitutions more than people. In discipleship the person always comes before the rules. Much of the trouble in churches comes from arguing over legalistic details of procedures. We must always love God and people more than systems.

Heal the woman, Jesus; she has suffered long enough. Then amend the rules to accommodate this act of compassion!

Preaching Possibilities

A. The Old Testament Jeremiah account of the call will stand alone and provide an opportunity to deal with the subject of "call" for your hearers. Notice Jeremiah was young, he was a layperson, and he had a specific ministry to carry out because of God's call on his life. In other words, there was a commission along with the call. He was to be global and bold in carrying out that commission.

B. The New Testament Reading contrasting the old and the new covenants will connect with the Gospel story of healing and the controversy it brought in church! The old covenant based on law rebelled against healing on the sabbath. The new covenant put compassion above rules of the law. The connection is there but it is not as obvious or strong as I would like.

C. I'll go with the healing miracle in the Gospel.

Possible Outline Of Sermon Moves

For a treatment of this miracle, see "Mercy On The Wrong Day" in my book, *The Miracles Of Jesus And Their Flip Side* (CSS Publishing Company, 2000).

For our outline today, let's use Eugene Lowry's "sequence of a sermon" from his book *The Homiletical Plot.**

1. *Oops!* It should have been a grand day in the synagogue when all the faithful gathered for worship. Instead, everyone was upset, ashamed, and bewildered. Read the miracle account here: Luke 13:10-17.

2. *Ugh!* So in a place of praise of God and love for each other, they were hurling accusations and insults because there were some who put rules and ceremony above compassion and mercy. Tell how easy it is to become a slave of religious rubrics and laws failing to have compassion.

3. *Aha!* But Jesus demonstrated a different way. He put people and their needs *first* before the religious rules and constitutions. Contrast the president's mode of behavior with that of Jesus the Christ.

4. *Whee!* The good news is that God loves us and is willing to free us from the religious rules and demands which can oppress us and keep us from loving others. Especially this is true of those who are not lovable or will never appreciate our mercy.

5. *Yeah!* If we will put people first and their needs for love and compassion, it will change the soul and personality of our congregation. And it will give us unexpected joy in a different practice of our faith and ministry in daily life.

6. Tell a story here of compassion from Possible Metaphors And Stories below.

Prayer For The Day

Help us to be people of compassion, O God, and show us the way in our congregation and our worship gatherings to show mercy above the constrictions of liturgy and rubrics. Remove legalism and desire for power to control, so we can be tenderhearted, loving people, together and individually. Straighten our backs, too, when they become all bent out of shape with infractions of the strict rules. In Jesus' name. Amen.

Possible Metaphors And Stories

It was at the Special Olympics in Hong Kong and reported in the *South China Morning Post* where I read it. Eleven of the physically-challenged lined up for the 100-meter dash. The gun went off to start the race. Almost immediately one fell down and skinned his knee. The others stopped running and went back offering to kiss the knee and make it better while helping him to his feet. Then, hand in hand, they all walked the rest of the way and across the finish line together. The crowd in the stands stood and applauded for a good five minutes. The judge pronounced all eleven first place winners. The crowd roared its approval again. Compassion, how sweet it is.

166

East Indians have a word *Bade Dilwala*. *Bade* means huge, *dil* means heart and *wala* means a person. So this phrase means one with a huge, loving heart. A good description of how we ought to be as disciples of Jesus.

A bumper sticker at Mercy Hospital said, "Take me to Mercy." In the Christ, God's mercy has come to us!

Rolly Martinson tells the story of a boy who would not stop clicking his heels each time he stood up in church. His father finally pushed him down with his hand on his head. The boy said, "You may have shoved me to where I'm sitting down on the outside; but I am still standing up on the inside." Perhaps how the outside looks doesn't tell what the inside image is.

───────────

*The sequence of a sermon, according to Eugene Lowry in *The Homiletical Plot*, may be drawn like this:

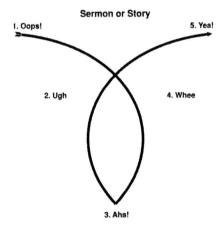

1. Upsetting the equilibrium.
2. Analyzing the discrepancy.
3. Disclosing the clue & resolution.
4. Experiencing the Gospel.
5. Anticipating the consequences.

Proper 17, Pentecost 15, Ordinary Time 22

Revised Common	Jeremiah 2:4-13	Hebrews 13:1-8, 15-16	Luke 14:1, 7-14
Roman Catholic	Sirach 3:17-20, 28-29	Hebrews 12:18-19, 22-24	Luke 14:1, 7-14
Episcopal	Ecclesiasticus 10:(7-10) 12-18	Hebrews 13:1-8	Luke 14:1, 7-14

Seasonal Theme Jesus' acts of compassion and teaching ministry.

Theme For The Day Christian disciple way of life which includes humility, hospitality, and charity.

Old Testament Lesson   Jeremiah 2:4-13   *For No Reason Yahweh Deserted*

Verse 2:4 is an introduction to the coming section. The question is asked: What did God do to deserve abandonment by the people to pursue worthless things?

Then in 5-13 Jeremiah makes his point like one would in a law court. The defendant is challenged to explain why he deserted Yahweh for other gods — in certainty that there is no good reason. See Psalm 115:8. The priest and people are oblivious to their history. The rulers here rebelled against Yahweh's guidance. And worst of all, Baal is used to prophesy instead of Yahweh. The heavens should be shocked about the people changing their loyalty from Yahweh to other gods and forsaking Yahweh. Verse 13 is really powerful because this is a city where water is at a premium and cisterns are by far the major water source.

New Testament Lesson   Hebrews 13:1-8, 15-16   *Living The Christian Life*

After a strong warning, now the author gives some general advice for Christian living:
1. Let brotherly love continue.
2. Show hospitality (see Philemon 22).
3. Entertain angels (Genesis 18 as Sarah and Abraham did).
4. Remember those in prison and those being tortured.
5. Hold marriage in honor.
6. Keep free from love of money (see Psalm 118:6).
7. Remember their leaders of the past who brought them the Gospel.
8. Jesus remains the same today as he was yesterday.

Verses 15 and 16 continue the list:
1. Continue to offer praise of God (see Leviticus 7:12).
2. Do good and share what you have — expressions of Christian love.
3. Sacrifices are pleasing to God.

It is a great list for Christian living; but it will need distillation to preach well. Perhaps we could say: Love each other, have sympathy for those in trouble, be content with what you have and be willing to share it, and continue to worship God with praise.

The Gospel   Luke 14:1, 7-14   *Humility And Hospitality*

Jesus, the law breaker who often healed on the sabbath, was being watched closely because this meant he worked on the sabbath, which was against the Jewish law. Verses 7 to 11 really are talking about humility, an important characteristic of the Christian life, and, I would say, of truly great people. There is a promise of practical life here: Those who exalt themselves will be humbled. Try that idea on with our current pop culture advice to promote one's self, get what's coming to you, and demand your rights.

The second position is as simple: Do charity not for what you will get out of it or what we would call the pay back. Just do it. This asks us to examine the motives behind our good works. It also claims we will be rewarded for this kind of giving that does not plan for any return. Barclay says that there are many reasons one gives:

1. Out of a sense of duty;
2. Out of self-interests;
3. In order to feel superior;
4. Because we cannot help but give;
5. and I would add, in order to be loved.

The only real Christian giving is uncontrollable love. However, for whatever reason, poor or honorable, that which is given can be used by God and God's disciples to great good!

Preaching Possibilities

A. I think there is not a common theme connecting the three readings together; but I believe we can put the New Testament Reading and the Gospel together to gain some practical guidance for Christian living. The list above under New Testament Lesson can be further distilled to make our outline using both New Testament and Gospel.

B. If we want to use the Old Testament Jeremiah lesson, while not so obvious, it can stand alone.
1. God has cared for us over the years as well.
2. We also can drift away and seek after other gods.
3. Our nation has also drifted away and deserted the God who has blessed us with so much.
    The "other gods" might be sexual excitement, wealth addiction, hedonistic pleasure, power over others, love of things, and so on.

C. Then, do you think we could use verse 13 and talk about the stewardship of natural resources?

Possible Outline Of Sermon Moves

Title: Humility, Hospitality, and Charity: it's a Christian lifestyle

A. Begin by putting Luke 14:8-10 into a contemporary setting. "It was a large banquet with the governor as speaker. Everyone tried to get the seats close to the speaker's podium...."

B. Read verses 8-10.

C. Tell what truths you think Jesus was trying to communicate:
1. True greatness is in being humble. We need not be the best or have the biggest, and so on.
2. The Christian disciple does not seek honor or reward or greatness.
3. Often when we aren't expecting it or trying for it we are rewarded anyway (read v. 11).

D. Move to verses 12-13 and put them in contemporary context. "A couple decided to give a dinner party at their local restaurant...."

E. Read verses 12-13, holding the Bible in your hands.

F. Tell what truths Jesus was teaching here:
1. Don't do kindnesses in order to be repaid for it.
2. Do loving acts not for those who will repay you but for people who probably never will appreciate it.

G. Move to read verse 14. Tell how verses 11 and 14 connect together and recommend a lifestyle of humility, hospitality, and charity.

H. Tell a story to illustrate this teaching.

I. Plan out loud where you will sit and who you will invite to your next banquet.

Prayer For The Day

Help us, O God, to be your humble servants who are always hospitable and full of charity for others. Teach us to love the unlovely whom you love and to give generously without thought of credit or being rewarded for it. In Jesus' name. Amen.

Possible Metaphors And Stories

In Shakespeare's *Romeo and Juliet*, Juliet says to Romeo, "The more love I give to thee, the more I have." There it is again — we give it away and it most affects us.

It was a long breakfast line at the pastors' retreat. Some came to the "traveler" toaster and took their slices of toast without putting in new bread. Soon there were no slices and all had to wait.

Stewardship is providing for those who will come after you. Upon taking your toast, you place new slices in the toaster for those farther back in line.

There is an unwritten code of the Bataks of Sumatra that dictates right and wrong behavior. It's called the *adat*. It governs their ethics, morals, and social protocol. It is a very strong force in the life of Batak Christians as well. Often the *bius* will interpret just what the *adat* is in a particular situation and will mete out the proper punishment if the rules are not obeyed. The young often learn the *adat* not by reading it in a book, but rather, seeing it practiced by others who follow it.

We Christians have an *adat* also. It is learned by how we live out our lives of discipleship consistent with Christ's interpretation of God's commands. We must always ask how well we are passing on our *adat* to the next generation and to new Christians of any age.

I now have a pill box with compartments for each day of the week to make sure I get the correct medications and remember to take them each day.

In our religious lives we need to have certain things regularly in order to stay spiritually healthy: prayer, forgiveness of others, thankfulness to God, witness to others, humility, hospitality, and charity.

Proper 18, Pentecost 16, Ordinary Time 23

Revised Common	Jeremiah 18:1-11	Philemon 1-21	Luke 14:25-33
Roman Catholic	Wisdom 9:13-18	Philemon 9-10, 12-17	Luke 14:25-33
Episcopal	Deuteronomy 30:15-20	Philemon 1-20	Luke 14:25-33

Seasonal Theme   Jesus' acts of compassion and teaching ministry.

Theme For The Day   The radical nature of following Jesus as disciples and our ever-present help along the way.

Old Testament Lesson   Jeremiah 18:1-11   *The Potter And The Clay*

Jeremiah gives us another metaphor for God and Israel. After seeing the local potter making a pot out of a spoiled one, he says God can do the same to Israel. God has the power to smash it on the potter's wheel and start over or to keep it if it amends its ways. If Israel will not remain faithful, God will bring about the collapse of the nation. One wishes Jeremiah would have added the words, "In order to reshape her," but he does not. It's a rich metaphor but a rather unforgiving message typical of those Jeremiah can utter. Better watch out, Jeremiah; Israel is bound to get resentful and hateful toward any prophet who sounds such an unpleasant message.

New Testament Lesson   Philemon 1-21   *A Slave Now Brother*

The brief letter of Philemon is a letter of Paul's to an owner of a slave, Onesimus, who had taken from him and then run away. Paul wrote this letter pleading for Philemon to welcome his runaway slave back as a Christian brother. Paul appeals on several levels:

1. Onesimus is his son (v. 10).
2. He will be useful to Philemon again if he returns (v. 11).
3. He has served Paul in Philemon's place (v. 13).
4. If he returns he will remain forever (v. 15).
5. He is now a brother in Christ (v. 16).
6. If Paul is his partner he should receive Onesimus back (v. 17).
7. Paul will pay anything Onesimus owes Philemon (v. 18).
8. Paul is confident Philemon will do even more than what he asks of him (v. 21).

Paul knew well the art of persuasion! In addition to all the above logic, he begins with abundant flattery (vv. 4-17).

The Gospel   Luke 14:25-33   *The Cost Of Discipleship*

Jesus was now heading toward Jerusalem and the cross. Those who followed thought they were headed toward an empire and ruling power. So he was quite frank to say that following him means giving up all and having to love the Christ above all else. This calls for a love that is willing to sacrifice everything for the Christ we follow.

This passage helps us understand the problem Jesus faced and we face as well. We have many who follow Jesus but only a few disciples. And then there are those who are loyal to the church as an organization, but not loyal to the Christ as our Savior.

The tower was one of those stone structures along the edge of a vineyard from which they watched for thieves or birds, and so on.

So this passage says we are not to take discipleship lightly but count the cost like one does before starting to build a structure or the military does before they enter upon a battle.

Then comes the big one! Verse 33 tells us being a disciple means traveling light and giving up our passion to acquire and then protect possessions. It sounds impossible! But Jesus also promises he will help us carry out these costly requirements of discipleship.

Preaching Possibilities

A. It's a stretch but we could put the three readings together under the theme of Discipleship.
    1. Jeremiah tells us God can so mold us into new shapes and beings.
    2. Paul tells us a disciple is a radically new person who can even receive back a runaway slave who has stolen from him.
    3. Jesus teaches that to be his follower and disciple means a radical new way of life with a new set of priorities:
        a. We love him more than anyone else.
        b. We give up our passion for possessions.
        c. We carry a cross like Jesus did.
        It will preach and we can add some good illustrations to the above as windows to the truths we are proclaiming.
B. The three readings will also stand on their own today.
    1. Jeremiah teaches about reshaping us and the creator's power and willingness to start over with us.
    2. Philemon teaches us a beautiful lesson about the radical nature of disciple love.
    3. Luke records Jesus' own words about how radical and costly discipleship really is. I'll go with the latter since it is called for in all three categories of lessons for today.

Possible Outline Of Sermon Moves

A. Begin by telling the entrance and membership requirements you must meet in order to belong to a couple of organizations you belong to. Perhaps Kiwanis or Rotary or Soroptimist or ...
B. Move to the requirements to belong to your congregation.
C. Tell your hearers what Jesus told them was required to be one of his disciples.
    1. Love him more than family or anyone else
    2. Carry a cross like he will do
    3. Carefully count the cost before joining
    4. Give up all our possessions
D. Explain that there is a difference between being a church member and being a disciple of Christ. Use several of the examples below which illustrate the high cost some are paying now for their discipleship.
E. Move to the *so what?* What are the possible steps the hearers can take because of these things we learned today?
    1. Reformat the "Inquirers class" for new members.
    2. Examine what kind of, how many, and how essential are the possessions we have and the ones we want.
    3. Begin to tithe our income and time for our discipleship.
    4. Consider more information to our young confirmands about what it really means to be a disciple.
F. Frame by reviewing your moves in reverse order and close with another story.

Prayer For The Day

We want to follow you, Jesus. Help us to practice radical discipleship in our lives. Show us the way to teach each other and invite others into your discipleship. Give us a sanity in the way we deal with our addiction to wealth and things. We know we can't do it alone — be our help along the way. In Jesus' name. Amen.

Possible Metaphors And Stories

I was in Kathmandu recently and learned of the bombing of our little Lutheran flat church by the Maoists. It's not easy being a disciple in Nepal!

After Easter when the Christians wanted a large sign in front of their worship space to say: "Hallelujah Christ is risen," each one of the worshipers brought one letter to the service so no one would be caught with the entire sign. When they all got there and the sign was in place, it spelled out: "He Is Risen, Hallelujah." He was risen indeed!

In interviewing Hong Kong Christians about how they were preparing for the Chinese takeover in July 1997, I heard some inspirational answers. Their solution was to learn all the Bible they can in case they don't have access any longer, to learn how to minister to each other in case there are no pastors, and to learn how to witness to the gospel so that the faith might live on. Oh, that we in the United States might sense that same urgency in the practice of our faith.

Our granddaughter, Hannah Marie, came for a visit. When I got into the hot tub after her and commented, "Ouch, Hannah, this is really hot," she replied, "It's all right, Grandpa; it gets used to you." Perhaps we try to adjust too much to the world rather than live out our discipleship and let the world adjust to us (or not).

Heads Up Notice

For the next seven Sundays our Second Lesson will come from Paul's letter to Timothy. The letters were written by Timothy's spiritual father, Paul, when he was on his fourth missionary journey and had left young Timothy to care for the congregation at Ephesus. The letters are ones of instruction and encouragement for ministry. Second Timothy was written when Paul was again in prison and Paul was asking for Timothy to join him. He also was concerned about the churches and wanted Timothy to champion the gospel even if it meant he would have to suffer for it. Also through Timothy, Paul wanted to write to the Ephesian congregations.

Proper 19, Pentecost 17, Ordinary Time 24

Revised Common	Jeremiah 4:11-12, 22-28	1 Timothy 1:12-17	Luke 15:1-10
Roman Catholic	Exodus 32:7-11, 13-14	1 Timothy 1:12-17	Luke 15:1-32
Episcopal	Exodus 32:1, 7-14	1 Timothy 1:12-17	Luke 15:1-10

Seasonal Theme   Jesus' acts of compassion and his teaching ministry.

Theme For The Day   Wonderful pictures of a God who delights in our prayers and the return of sinners.

Old Testament Lesson   Jeremiah 4:11-12, 22-28   *God's Judgment*

Verses 11 and 12 describe the impending disaster as being like the hot wind from the desert (*sirocco*) which will be too strong to help with the winnowing or cleaning out of the city. It is only destructive in its violence.

Verses 22-28 describe Yahweh looking down on the land after the disaster. Nature has become an instrument of punishment of Israel. God states its end but he just could not do otherwise but destroy. Verse 27 is the author's comment and I am glad for it. God's judgments are never altogether bad. God brings something worthwhile out of this chaos ... "I will not make a full end."

New Testament Lesson   1 Timothy 1:12-17   *Gratitude For Mercy*

The argument of Paul is this: If Christ could change the likes of Paul whose sins were great, he can change any of us. There just isn't any limit to his transforming power. This man who was such a persecutor and man of violence is now counted an apostle and faithful!

Verse 14 lays it all to God's grace to cause the conversion. Verse 15 occurs four other places in the Pastoral Epistles and nowhere else in the New Testament. In it we have the basic facts of the Christian faith. Paul never left the idea that Christian salvation was for sinners. Here also is a mark of sincere humility. He calls himself the "foremost" sinner.

Verse 16 also points to the mercy of God and the patience of God.

Verse 17 is a typical Pauline doxology. In it is a wonderful all-absorbing adoration and majesty of God. Romans 1:23 gives us a parallel Pauline saying using the word immortal. The *only* God comes from an emphatic expression of Jewish monotheism.

The Gospel   Luke 15:1-10   *The Parables Of The Lost*

It would be a severe shock to the Pharisees and scribes to see Jesus eating with those they called sinners and even with tax collectors! They took satisfaction in the obliteration of a sinner and not in his/her salvation and acceptance. So Jesus told the parable of the lost sheep and of the shepherd's joy.

A shepherd who was personally responsible for his sheep had a tough time keeping track of them, as they ate of the scarce pasture and strayed in all directions. Let's not make too much of the shepherd leaving his 99. Often the flocks were combined in a communal flock and/or fold and there would be others to watch them while the shepherd tried to track the lost one. And, of course, when the shepherd returned with the lost, there would be great joy in the fold.

This is a picture Jesus painted of God. God is as happy about finding one lost sinner as that shepherd is in finding the lost sheep. So we learn that God is like this — full of joy when a lost one finds his/her way home.

The second parable of the lost being found is in verses 8-10. This coin was worth something. Because the Palestinian house was dark, she would need to provide some candle light for the search. She probably lived on the edge of poverty and thus the find was significant.

This coin may have come from her headdress, which marked her as a married woman — it was like a wedding ring in our culture.

Jesus said that God is like this. There is great joy when one sinner is found and returns. No Pharisee had ever pictured God that way! Our joy is to know that God is one of seeking love. We could name it theologically the "divine initiative." The joy is like a woman near starvation finding her lost money or a woman long married finding her lost wedding ring.

Preaching Possibilities

A. One could use all these readings under the theme of three pictures of God.
1. Jeremiah pictures a God who judges the people and must punish them, like the hot wind that comes out of the desert.
2. Paul pictures God to Timothy and the Ephesian congregation as one who is full of mercy and a God who wants very much to save sinners using a lot of patience.
3. Jesus pictures God as having great joy over even one sinner being found and returning home.
B. We can also put the Second Lesson and the two parables in Luke together and talk about how different our view of God is than the view of the scribes and Pharisees. Paul and Jesus both teach that God wants most for all of us to be saved and "found."
C. For a treatment of Luke 15:1-10 see my work titled "The Never Lost Ninety-Nine" in *The Parables Of Jesus And Their Flip Side* (CSS Publishing Company, 2001). The "flip-side" in this story is about those who were never lost at all. We who are securely inside the fold (church) are to support our shepherd's attempts to find the lost. Also don't neglect to say that it is in the seeking the lost that we realize the full joy of being the found.

Possible Outline Of Sermon Moves

Because all three pericopes call for the same readings from Timothy and Luke this Sunday, I'll go with them today.

Title: Delightful Pictures Of God

A. Begin by describing your own pictures of God when you were a young child. (Mine was a grandpa and Santa Claus combination.)
B. Move to calling attention to the fact we have two delightful pictures of God in the Timothy letter and two in Luke reporting of two parables which Jesus told about lost sheep and a lost coin.
C. Talk about Paul's letter to his spiritual son, Timothy, and how he pictured God as:
1. God who is patient and full of grace and mercy.
2. One who wanted *everyone* to be saved.
D. Move to the Luke account and tell how Jesus pictured God as:
1. filled with joy when the lost are returned and
2. a God whose angels celebrate with all heaven when repentance takes place.
E. Move to your own witness as to what all this meant to you. Begin with, "If all this is a good picture of God, then this means to me that we should ..." Some examples:
1. Be aggressive in our outreach.
2. Be intentional in our in-reach to the inactive.
3. Be happy when those of any category return or come for the first time.
4. Pray for the wisdom to do the above wisely.
F. Tell a story of lost and found and the joy afterwards.
G. Frame your sermon by reviewing the four teachings in reverse order from the two readings.

Prayer For The Day

Help us to know the joy of being the found as we also seek out the lost as part of our discipleship. Move us to including everyone in our invitation to come to you again or for the first time. We pray you will also bless us with a sense of your joy whenever the lost are found. In the name of the greatest finder of all, Jesus the Christ. Amen.

Possible Metaphors And Stories

We who live in California know the desert hot air which is like Jeremiah's. We call them the Santa Ana winds and they are devastating to our countryside. It happens when the wind, instead of blowing its usual cooling direction of west to east off the Pacific Ocean, reverses itself and blows over the dry hot desert out toward the ocean, east to west. Quickly it brings oppressive heat and extremely low humidity to dry out everything to make conditions ripe for a horrid firestorm. It's like Jeremiah's *sirocco*.

At the Dallas/Fort Worth airport, I saw a bag falling off the baggage cart on the way to an airplane. A supervisor finally came out, placed a red tag on it, and took it to the conveyor loading a plane for the same destination. We were lost and we have been found by the Christ who puts us on our way to our correct destination again.

I saw an old man in the hot parking lot of the hospital. He had lost his car while visiting his wife. I drove him all around the lot but he did not recognize it. When I looked at his ticket, I discovered he was in the wrong lot. We went to the other side of the hospital and there it was. He probably had come out of a different door than he had entered.

There are so many lost in the heat, frustration, and confusion of our lives. We must invite them to come over to the other side.

My outboard boat motor, which had been stolen, was repurchased in a sting operation by the police and I now have it back. My motor has now been twice purchased. So, too, me. Once purchased through my baptism and again on the cross.

January 21, 1991: Helicopters and fighter planes left the security of their airbases to fly into enemy territory in order to rescue just one downed pilot. It's like the story Jesus told of a shepherd who left the field to rescue just one lost sheep.

Proper 20, Pentecost 18, Ordinary Time 25

Revised Common	Jeremiah 8:18—9:1	1 Timothy 2:1-7	Luke 16:1-13
Roman Catholic	Amos 8:4-7	1 Timothy 2:1-8	Luke 16:1-13
Episcopal	Amos 8:4-7 (8-12)	1 Timothy 2:1-8	Luke 16:1-13

Seasonal Theme   Jesus' acts of compassion and teaching ministry.

Theme For The Day   God would have us pray for all people and wants all to be saved. So God paid a big price for us.

Old Testament Lesson   Jeremiah 8:18—9:1   *A Balm From Gilead*

Jeremiah is sorry for the suffering of Israel. He can just hear the people asking, "Where is God? Why doesn't God help us?" In this case in verse 19 the king mentioned is not the Davidic king but is Yahweh. And God's reply is simply to ask, "Why do the people provoke me with this disloyalty?" Add to their misery the fact that harvest season is past and they don't have any food for the year ahead.

This is an often sung and quoted verse about the balm of Gilead (v. 22). East of Jordan is Gilead where a gum was produced from its trees. It was often used as a salve for wounds. Israel is wounded but there is no use calling for all Gilead's healing balm — it will not cure this wound. Such a sad song, Jeremiah.

New Testament Lesson   1 Timothy 2:1-7   *Instructions For Public Prayer*

Also a reading for the day of Thanksgiving, this scripture, which was written while Paul is on his fourth missionary journey, is Paul's instruction to his young spiritual son concerning prayer. Perhaps the writer is quoting from a prayer. Verse 2 is also from a prayer.

If we compare these verses with Paul's picture of the strenuous Christian life in 2 Corinthians 6:3-10, it raises serious doubts of Paul as the author of Timothy. Notice that we are to pray "for everyone." It is tempting to pray just for our own narrow needs and community. To pray for everyone widens the vision of the one who prays. And we ought to pray for those in ruling positions that we might have a quiet and tranquil life.

Verse 4 has been controversial over the years. There is an implied universalism. It speaks of God's salvation offered to all. God wants to save all.

Most scholars treat verse 5 as a quotation. Also in this verse is something exclusively Christian: Christ as mediator. Then comes the atonement in verse 6. The word *ransom* comes from Jesus' words (Mark 10:45). So Christ is presented as an exchange price in the place of all.

Verse 7 has Paul claiming he was appointed by God to be a herald preacher (see 2 Timothy 1:11). Perhaps this is included to motivate Timothy to defend Paul's true apostleship to some at Ephesus who denied it. "Faith and truth" embrace both the spirit of the author and the content of his message.

The Gospel   Luke 16:1-13   *The Parable Of The Dishonest Manager*

There is lots of irony in this parable and we must keep that in mind as we try to understand it. This story seems to be the exact reverse of the rich man in 12:16-21. Jesus often commended astuteness like this. Examples would be the publicans and harlots who go into the kingdom of God ahead of the Pharisees who are so cautious (Matthew 21:31) or the woman in Mark 7:24-30.

God loves to forgive and is ready to do so; but that involves our forgiving others, too.

I'll admit I find it difficult to preach on this parable. The commending of this steward who was carrying out embezzlement and the rascal debtors who joined him in his dishonesty are hard for me to endorse. Perhaps we could draw the conclusion that we Christians ought to put as much energy on the things that obtain the spiritual as we do on the things which have to do with money and comfort.

Verses 10 and 11 say that our carrying out of a small responsibility is proof of our fitness to doing the greater thing. Verse 13 gives us the teaching that serving God is not part time. We either belong to God or we don't, just like a slave back then either belonged to his/her master or he/she didn't. Herein lies the weakness of our discipleship. We try to do it half-heartily and that's a miserable way to live and practice the faith. It's all or nothing here, folks!

Preaching Possibilities

A. We could use all three lessons today and talk about "God's judgment: three different views."
   1. Jeremiah's view is that God will punish like the hot desert winds of Palestine.
   2. Paul's view is that God has mercy and most wants to forgive.
   3. Jesus' parable says we ought to put as much energy in our spiritual work as we do in gaining worldly wealth.
   4. Luke's view is that it's all or nothing. Either we are Christian and loyal to him or we aren't.
B. The parable in Luke will stand alone. But I think it can easily be misunderstood or wrongly interpreted, so I'll leave it alone.
C. Verses 12 and 13 of Luke 16 are rich and full of meaning and can stand alone, in my view, for a powerful sermon on life's priorities.
D. But I'll go with Timothy's letter from Paul today.

Possible Outline Of Sermon Moves

A. Introduction: Tell of someone who is very special to you and how you would like to share with them that which you have learned over the years.
B. Move to today's New Testament Lesson which is a letter to young Timothy whom he considered like a son.
C. Move to the advice Paul gave Timothy.
   1. Pray for everyone, including those in high position, and do it that all might live in quiet and peace because of their leadership (vv. 1, 2).
   2. Remember that God wants everyone to be saved and know the truth. Our attitude and ministry must always be inclusive and not exclusive (v. 4).
   3. Jesus Christ became a human and served as a mediator and ransom for humankind (vv. 5, 6). This means we have a direct connection to the divine and we have had a big price already paid for our sins.
   4. Paul was appointed to preach these truths not only to the Jews but also out to the Gentiles.
D. Try placing a summary prayer after each of the four moves above. Perhaps someone of the opposite sex of you, and in a contrasting voice, could offer the prayers throughout the sermon.
E. Move to the *so what?* Answer what you and your congregation should do in response to the above truths:
   1. If you don't have a congregational prayer band/chain and prayer ministry, get one started.
   2. Go out intentionally and invite people of other colors to join you in your discipleship.
   3. Celebrate in praise the high price God has paid for you. You are loved and very valuable.
   4. Consider to whom God has appointed you to go in order to preach the good news.
F. Have a final prayer offered which sums up those things we have learned about ourselves and our God today.

Prayer For The Day

We thank you, dear Holy Parent, that you have made us heralds of the gospel. Keep us mindful here of the great price Christ paid as a ransom for our sins and we pray his mediation will continue for us in heaven. We rejoice that we have you as our God who would have all be forgiven and saved. In Jesus' name. Amen.

Possible Metaphors And Stories

, Lyndon Johnson, President of the United States, asked Bill Moyers to offer prayer at the White House (Moyers was a former Baptist minister). He started very softly, so LBJ said, "Speak up, Bill." Moyers replied without ever looking up: "I wasn't speaking to you, Mr. President." Our prayers often are spoken for other people to hear rather than God.

Just north of our church was Bethel Mission, a homeless shelter for "knights of the road." I was walking up there to hand out some hats on a cold January day when I saw two men, one black, the other white, helping a Native American enter through the mission door. All had been drinking. The Native American had a black garbage bag with all his possessions over his shoulder. He was new to the mission. The others were old-timers.

Why can't we do this same kind of welcoming of brothers and sisters well-dressed and sober?

During Nikita Khrushchev's visit to the U.S. he bought material for a new suit. When he got home he was told there was not enough cloth to make the suit. When Khrushchev protested, the tailor told him: "... but you are not as big a man in the U.S. as in Russia." Our greatness is of little consequence as we move to other surroundings, but being purchased with the blood of Christ makes us precious wherever we are.

Note: The above three stories can fit after each of the first three moves in the suggested Possible Outline Of Sermon Moves.

Proper 21, Pentecost 19, Ordinary Time 26

Revised Common	**Jeremiah 32:1-3a, 6-15**	**1 Timothy 6:6-19**	**Luke 16:19-31**
Roman Catholic	**Amos 6:1, 4-7**	**1 Timothy 6:11-16**	**Luke 16:19-31**
Episcopal	**Amos 6:1-7**	**1 Timothy 6:11-19**	**Luke 16:19-31**

Seasonal Theme   Jesus' acts of compassion and his teaching ministry.

Theme For The Day   The evils of all-pervasive love of money and greed and the need for hearts of compassion and love of the unlovely.

Old Testament Lesson   Jeremiah 32:1-3a, 6-15   *Jeremiah Buys A Field*

Jeremiah has been arrested and confined in prison and then transferred to the court of the guard in the king's palace. A person, when selling his land, always had to offer it first to members of the family who had "... right of redemption" (v. 7b). This was a "buyer's market" since the city is under siege. Jeremiah buys the land in spite of the future being very insecure. Then in verse 15, Jeremiah reveals that this purchase is symbolic and foretells that Israel will one day be restored. It is a message of hope after one of doom by Jerusalem. After Jerusalem fell, this became an all important hope by which the people lived.

New Testament Lesson   1 Timothy 6:6-19   *Warning Against Materialism*

This passage about love seems more stoic than Christian. The positive nice thoughts are godliness, contentment, righteousness, faith, love, endurance, gentleness, eternal life, called, good confession, blessed, mortality, unapproachable light, honor, eternal dominion, good works, and generous share.

In verses 11-16 we have an excerpt from a baptismal address. The reference to a confession points us in that direction. Verse 12 is inspired by 1 Corinthians 9:25-26. Opposition to the Roman cult of the emperor is written as God-inspired in verse 15.

Verses 17-19 are another warning against materialism. Verse 18 echoes Romans 12:13-16. So Paul advises his young son in the ministry to practice godliness and be content with what he has. He further says to be aware of the love of money. And the things he should do are to be righteous, godly, full of faith, loving, and gentle. And again, he reminds Timothy to be rich in good deeds rather than wealth. It's chock full of good advice of what to beware of and what to work for. And it will surely preach.

The Gospel   Luke 16:19-31   *The Rich Man And Lazarus*

A very well written parable, no word is wasted and it is nearly impossible to miss the point Jesus was trying to make. The rich man is usually called Dives, which is the Latin for "rich." This guy was really rich! His clothing was very expensive. He feasted in luxury *each day* — eating exotic and costly food. So here is real self-indulgence. In those days people ate with their hands and wiped them with chunks of bread which were thrown away. Lazarus was waiting for this discarded bread.

Lazarus means "God is my help." He was so weak he couldn't scare off the dogs who bothered him. So here we have abject poverty and extreme wealth.

The point here is not that Lazarus was cruel to Dives; it was simply that he never noticed him! He must have been one of those humans whose heart just can't move to pity at all.

The part about refusing to warn the brothers (vv. 27-31) is tough to understand. Still, it's true, if all these years they never noticed those in need, they probably won't notice even if someone returns from the dead (read Jesus' resurrection).

Barclay writes, "It is a terrible warning to remember that the sin of Dives was, not that he did wrong things, but that he did nothing."

Preaching Possibilities

A. For my treatment of the Gospel parable see "Dog-Licked Sores And Linen Underwear" in *The Parables Of Jesus And Their Flip Side* (CSS Publishing Company, 2001).

   Paul's advice about wealth addiction and Jesus' parable about Dives and Lazarus go together nicely today. I doubt we can add anything from Jeremiah this time. The parable and Paul's advice can easily stand alone as well.

   If we need to proclaim hope when all seems lost, it is certainly there in the Jeremiah account.

B. The Second Reading makes a nice outline on the Christian lifestyle: The list is long on what we should try to accomplish and how we should try to be. The list is also full of warnings against materialism. We could title our sermon: "The Love Of Money Or The Love Of God" or "The Choice Is For Greed Or Righteousness."

   I'll go with the parable illustrated and supported by Paul's words to Timothy.

Possible Outline Of Sermon Moves

A. Begin by sharing a time when "panhandlers" on the street really bugged you and you acted as if you did not see them.

B. Introduce the Dives and Lazarus story by telling it in your own words in either the context of that day or now where your people live, work, and play.

C. Move to describe the two characters in the story:
   1. Dives, filthy rich who lived in his own decadent world not even noticing the poor at his gate.
   2. Lazarus, so poor and weak he couldn't lift his hands to shoo away the dogs.

D. Move to tell the people what was Dives' sin. He did nothing; he didn't even notice!

E. Move to Paul and quote 1 Timothy 6:6-10.

F. Move further to see how easy it is for us to overlook the poor at our gate. For we are the rich in this global village!

G. Quote verses 17-19 from Timothy and then give your own willingness to live differently because of today's lessons.

H. Frame your sermon by retelling the parable in your own context: "A beggar sat by the church door on weekdays." Then state how you would like the parable to end: And Jesus warned the brothers shortly after Easter and that opened up a whole new lifestyle for them. And, how the poor enjoyed it around their houses!

Prayer For The Day

Dear Lord, open our eyes and hearts to see and then respond to the needs of the poor in our communities and around the world. Give to us tender hearts that feel the pain and suffering of others. And teach us how to guard against the all-pervasive addiction to wealth in order that, contrary to our human nature, we will become people of compassion and sharing. In Jesus' name. Amen.

Possible Metaphors And Stories

During one of my visits with our foster daughter, now living in Montevideo, Uruguay, she wanted to show me the cathedral where the Pope had recently visited and celebrated mass. When we got to the massive main doors, there was a homeless woman lying there in rags throwing up. Our daughter, Beatriz, bent over to see if she could help. Her husband, Antonio, said the woman was there every day and that we should step over her and go in to see the fabulous church. Beatriz refused and stated: "First we help this woman; then we'll see the beauty of the cathedral."

The big fire at Thousand Oaks, California, was started by a homeless man trying to keep warm. Many million-dollar homes burned to the ground. Perhaps they failed to take in the man.

We pay a price whenever we ignore the poor and homeless. Eventually it comes back to our own lives and homes.

Carol left for church in a hurry. Our pet cat was on the roof of the station wagon. It dug its claws in and tried to hang on but the faster the car went, the more the cat slid to the rear. At the bottom of Hanley Hill we all could see the cat's tail showing in the rear window of the wagon.

Our frantic lifestyle is similar. We try to hang on as we go faster and faster, losing ground all the time. There is a better way.

Two hunters were road hunting for deer in a pick-up in South Dakota. One was watching left, the other, right. With a sudden bang they had hit a buck standing in the middle of the road neither had seen.

There is so much we can miss that is right in front of us if we'll just take notice.

At Drake University, Allen Boesak of South Africa said, "I'm here because some of us believe there is another America ... one which cares about our struggle."

Can we move above self-interest and greed?

Proper 22, Pentecost 20, Ordinary Time 27

Revised Common	Lamentations 1:1-6	2 Timothy 1:1-14	Luke 17:5-10
Roman Catholic	Habakkuk 1:2-3; 2:2-4	2 Timothy 1:6-8, 13-14	Luke 17:5-9
Episcopal	Habakkuk 1:1-6 (7-11) 12-13; 2:1-4	2 Timothy 1:(1-5) 6-14	Luke 17:5-10

Seasonal Theme   Jesus' acts of compassion and teaching ministry.

Theme For The Day   The Christian life of discipleship and sincere faith in Jesus Christ.

Old Testament Lesson   Lamentations 1:1-6   *A Funeral Dirge*

Written by Jeremiah, Lamentations is the only Old Testament book that is made up solely of laments (bemoans). These were written to express the feelings of the people after their city was destroyed and the Temple burned to the ground.

This passage needs little interpretation. Jerusalem has been captured and sacked, the Temple had been burned. The people have been taken into captivity. Jerusalem is pictured as a widow without anyone to be with her while she grieves over the loss. Chapter 1 has this emphasis of uncomforted aloneness. In verses 5-7, this funeral dirge centers on enemies and then moves to a righteous God who is punishing the people for their transgressions. Verse 6 refers to Jerusalem's rulers. It's a sad song, Jeremiah.

New Testament Lesson   2 Timothy 1:1-14   *Encouragement From Experience*

Donald Guthrie of the London Bible College in *The Pastoral Epistles* gives a helpful outline for this portion of 2 Timothy.
1.   Salutation (vv. 1-2);
2.   Thanksgiving (vv. 3-5);
3.   Encouragement from experience (vv. 6-10):
    a.   The gift of God (vv. 6-10);
    b.   The testimony of Paul (vv. 11-12); and
    c.   The charge to Timothy (vv. 13-14).

In the salutation Paul claims his apostle status and also reflects his deep conviction that his life here has a divine purpose. The "... in Christ Jesus" is consistent with Paul's letters of being in Christ. See Galatians 2:20. Paul always reflected his Jewishness in insisting that worship, morality, and service go together — so we have verse 3. The tears in verse 4 probably are Timothy's upon last leaving Paul.

In verse 5, the thought of Timothy's sincere faith causes Paul to remember his mother's and grandmother's faith as well. The fact Timothy's father is not mentioned probably means his Greek father (Acts 14:1) was not a Christian. We do know Timothy benefited from a devout home life seen to by Lois and Eunice.

As we read verses 6-14, we get the impression that Tim's character needs some strengthening of backbone. In verse 7 we have a ready made three-point outline for preaching: God gives a spirit of:
1.   power,
2.   love, and
3.   self-discipline.

Perhaps this is the gift of God Paul mentions in verse 6.

There is an interesting new word in Greek in verse 8. *Sunkakopathio* means to take one's share of ill-treatment (see also 2:3). Here it is translated as "... suffering for the gospel." In verse 11 we have another threefold formula — Paul is for the Gospel to be a herald, an apostle, and a teacher.

183

These verses tell us that faith is a very strong force in the world. If we approach that which to the world seems impossible with strong faith, it becomes possible. Let's remember all the fantastic accomplishments achieved in our history because someone had faith they could be done. We also have God's power built into our faith and so have an extraordinary helper in the "impossible" task.

Verses 7 to 10 relate to our New Testament Reading 2 Timothy 1:7 and say we can't put God in our debt. We will never have a claim on God. That which we have done is only what we should have done *anyway*. We must remember that discipleship is a full commitment and is never just partial. And what we then receive from God is not what we have earned but a gift our graceful God gives.

Frankly, if I ever write a piece on "Parables I don't like," this will be one of them. I don't like the treatment of the master to the slave who worked all day. And I believe the answer to verse 9 is a "yes"! It seems to me cruel to force the slave to do more after a hard day's work. I don't like the idea of slave and master either.

Preaching Possibilities

A. As indicated above we can make a direct connection between verses 7-10 in the Gospel and Timothy 1:7. It's all about the false idea that we can make it so that God owes us. While not an easy theme, it could be developed.

B. Certainly verse 5 in the Gospel has possibilities of a topical sermon on discipleship and faith. It must reflect what some of our hearers are asking for also, "increase in faith." What are the ways we can deepen our faith?
    1. Learning how to pray well;
    2. Being with others of faith;
    3. Sharing our faith with others;
    4. Developing a loyalty to Christ as well as Church; and
    5. When we do increase it, we will have great power to do great things on God's behalf. We are shy about this one!

C. Perhaps the Lamentations passage could produce a sermon on the idea of mourning and its value. Or we might approach it from the view of why God allows such things to happen to God's people. If so, we will need to distinguish between what God *allows* and what God *causes* to happen.

D. There might also be a possible way to use all three readings by uniting them around the title: "Sad, in Prison, and Lacking Faith." Jeremiah is grieving, Paul is in prison, and the disciples were asking to have their faith increased.

Possible Outline Of Sermon Moves

A. Consider trying a letter sermon today. Take the message Paul is writing to young Timothy and put it in an e-mail format which most would recognize and make it in contemporary language and context. It might be read by you from a laptop computer in the pulpit or write it in "Snail Mail" format on stationery placed in an envelope which you can open and read from the pulpit.

B. It might begin like this: "Dear Tim, I have written to you there at Ephesus previously while I was in prison. Don't forget my advice to remember that if Christ can change the likes of me, he can change anyone (Proper 19). God wants to save everyone (Proper 20). Watch out for the dangers of materialism (Proper 21). In this letter I want to be sure to say to you to be strong in your faith like your mother and grandmother...."

C. Some continuing paragraphs for the letter could be about:
    1. Jesus gives us a promise of real life (v. 1);
    2. We are called to a sincere faith (v. 5);
    3. God has given you the spirit of power, love, and self-discipline (v. 7);
    4. You are called to a holy calling (v. 9);

5. Keep your standards of teaching high (v. 13); and
6. You have treasures; guard them carefully (v. 14).

D. In Christ's Love, Paul the Apostle, Rome, Italy.
E. Be sure to place the stationery in the envelope and seal it in front of the congregation. Or, in case of the e-mail, tell the hearers to use spell-check and then "send."

Prayer For The Day

Holy God, we rejoice today in the memory and advice of Saint Paul to Timothy on how to live the Christian life. Help us to increase our faith, watch out for materialism, and realize the potential of our call to discipleship by you. We need your spirit to aid us in being loving and self-disciplined disciples. In your name. Amen.

Possible Metaphors And Stories

The Indonesians have a saying about corruption: "As long as the hen eats the corn, we still can catch it."

Betsy Stark, ABC's financial reporter on Peter Jennings' *Nightly News*, called April "confessional season" for corporations. They are "confessing" that their earnings will not be as great as they had said they would. This affects the stock market negatively.

At a PLTS chapel service, Christine Sinnott talked of an eagle stirring up its nest. I went outside and saw four eagles soaring over Tilden Park Hills in an updraft. What if when we walked outside church we always saw it happening?

There used to be a commercial for Honda lawnmowers which tells of a test each of their mowers meet: "the Clara Johnson test." It must start on the first pull by Clara. What test do we insist on in our lives? The Christian lifestyle, the discipleship test, the "if Jesus were watching test"?

Proper 23, Pentecost 21, Ordinary Time 28

Revised Common	Jeremiah 29:1, 4-7	2 Timothy 2:8-15	Luke 17:11-19
Roman Catholic	2 Kings 5:14-17	2 Timothy 2:8-13	Luke 17:11-19
Episcopal	Ruth 1:(1-7) 8-9a	2 Timothy 2:(3-7) 8-15	Luke 17:11-19

Seasonal Theme   Jesus' acts of compassion and teaching ministry.

Theme For The Day   Our fellowship of thanksgiving for God's abundant blessings.

Old Testament Lesson   Jeremiah 29:1, 4-7   *A Message To Those In Exile*

Zedekiah is going to send an envoy to Babylon so Jeremiah asks them to carry a letter to all the Jews now in exile there. He tells the exiles to go right on and build a life for themselves there, for they will be there for a long time. He says to be good citizens there as they will benefit from it. I wonder if the advice of verse 6 might have another motive — to increase the number of Jews so that they would become more and more powerful, perhaps even enough to eventually overthrow. Just a suspicious thought.

New Testament Lesson   2 Timothy 2:8-15   *God's Approval*

For Paul, the most prominent Christian truth is the resurrection of Christ. So this is "his" Gospel. It's what he is suffering for and what he is enduring so that the elect will know this good news.

Verses 11-13 are part of a Christian hymn Paul is quoting. It says that even if we are facing hardship now we have great things to anticipate. So Paul is saying his suffering is all worthwhile.

Paul then gives Timothy advice for dealing with false teachers. Right beliefs are called for. We who teach must never forget our responsibility to those who listen. Verse 15 calls for a value of self-discipline and being a living example of the truth with God's blessing. (See Ephesians 1:13 and Colossians 1:5.) Its an interesting piece of advice to try to do our ministry always asking if God would approve and even be pleased.

The Gospel   Luke 17:11-19   *Jesus Cleanses Ten Lepers*

Luke uses this story to illustrate that outcasts like these Samaritan lepers are more ready to accept Jesus' ministry than his own, the Jews. It might be based on Luke 5:12-16. Instead of crying, "Unclean," these call for mercy. Sending them to their priest is a kind of test to establish that they really have the disease. The Samaritan who returns to give thanks is an example for Israel (Luke 4:27). He also serves as an example of thankfulness to God. Could it be that the other nine just did their thanking God in their synagogue that day?

Notice Jesus says that it is faith which does the miracle of healing. I wonder what all never takes place in our lives and churches because we just don't have the faith that it will?

This text is often used for a day of thanksgiving in our American churches.

Preaching Possibilities

A. It's a stretch but we could use all three readings by going with the theme of: "Reaction to hard times."
   1. Jeremiah's reaction was to go on with life and make the best of it.
   2. Paul's advice was to figure it was all worthwhile if it brought others to Christ. And to be sure we kept living a faithful example for others.
   3. The Samaritan's way was to approach Jesus for mercy and when it was given, to express thanks.
B. The Jeremiah text is difficult to use on its own but could be referred to in preaching on either the New Testament Reading or the Gospel.
C. Paul's advice will do well for a sermon on "This is my Gospel" based on verse 2:8. It is an opportunity to give your own witness to the faith. The hymn "This is my story, this is my song ..." could be used.

1. Begin by telling the background of Paul writing to Timothy and move to Paul's situation when he was writing this letter. Then move to what is Paul's "Gospel" as he calls it in verse 8.
2. Now make our own witness:
   a. The good news for me is ...
   b. The way that affects my life is ...
   c. What I pray for this congregation is ...
   d. The hope I have in our future together is ...
3. Close by using verses 11-13. See if you can put it to a plainsong chant. Or use a verse from a hymn you can sing from your hymnal.

Possible Outline Of Sermon Moves

For a treatment of this particular miracle of healing see "One Out Of Ten Isn't All That Bad" in *The Miracles Of Jesus And Their Flip Side* (CSS Publishing Company, 2000).

Let's use my formula for presenting the miracles in narrative form.

A. *Tell the story in your own words.* You can do it in your own context or back then in Jesus' day. "Ten patients came into the local trauma center at the same time to seek relief from their auto accident ..."
B. *Tell what it teaches us about God.* God will hear us and help if we believe ...
C. *Explain what it reveals about us.* We often forget to give thanks for many ways God blesses us and for the daily miracles of healing to our bodies.
D. *Prayerfully discover why the author wanted this preserved.* Luke was a doctor with great interest in healing. He also wanted to make the point that outcasts like this Samaritan leper were more ready to receive Jesus' ministry than his own people, the Jews.
E. *Look for a fresh flip side focus.* We often keep our distance from Jesus and we do have a ministry of healing to carry out in our ministries.
F. *Answer the so what?* Let's intentionally invite to our congregation the contemporary outcasts and lepers of our day. Let's begin a ministry of healing and let's develop more ways of thanking God for all our blessings.
G. *Frame by returning to the first few sentences.* Return to your narrative of ten appearing in the trauma center and have them all go to church the next Sunday and join in singing "Now Thank We All Our God."

Prayer For The Day

Give us thankful hearts, O God, and move us often to speak our appreciation for all you do for us. Show us the way to include all sorts and kinds of people into our fellowship. And here at worship, let the praise be loud and glorious and the thanksgiving sincere. In Jesus the Christ's name. Amen.

Possible Metaphors And Stories

Tom Brokaw, on the Thanksgiving evening news, said, "When we sing the dirges, we must also sing the anthem." He went on to say we must recognize not only the miseries of life but also the joys. So it is being a sinner and living in an imperfect world.

"All the races of men have sprung from the same blood and thus have the same bloodline ... as I in my age am a drop of the great river, a member of the church, so am I a brother of the fathers who came before me and the children who come after me" (Wilhelm Loehe).

I purchased three goldfish for our fountain. When I let them out, two swam in a tight little circle as if still in the plastic bag. One really went for it and swam all around from side to side. Sometimes we remain confined by our own lack of risk-taking.

I saw a sign hanging from a crane which said simply: "My Linda's O.K." What marvelous things we have to celebrate!

Proper 24, Pentecost 22, Ordinary Time 29

Revised Common	**Jeremiah 31:27-34**	**2 Timothy 3:14—4:5**	**Luke 18:1-8**
Roman Catholic	**Exodus 17:8-13**	**2 Timothy 3:14—4:2**	**Luke 18:1-8**
Episcopal	**Genesis 32:2-8, 22-30**	**2 Timothy 3:14—4:5**	**Luke 18:1-8a**

Seasonal Theme   Jesus' acts of compassion and his teaching ministry.

Theme For The Day   The lamentations of Jeremiah and his promise of a new covenant which Jesus did bring to fruition.

Old Testament Lesson   Jeremiah 31:27-34   *Sour Grapes And A New Covenant*

We finish up today with our Old Testament Readings in Jeremiah. Phew! It has been nine weeks of Old Testament moaning, lamenting, and grim prophecy. The verses 31-34 are also read for Reformation Sunday for the Lutherans.

Verses 27-28 picture Yahweh as a farmer and his planting seed, Israel, which he will nurture carefully. Verses 29-30 are a strong statement on the importance of the individual — each will be responsible for one's own sins (see Ezekiel 18).

Verses 31-34 are about a new covenant. This is quite different from Jeremiah's negative teaching. And what is important is inner conviction. This way the broken covenant between Yahweh and Israel will somehow be restored. Ezekiel states a similar idea in Ezekiel 36:24-28.

Jesus used the phrase "a new covenant" at the Last Supper. Our Bible is now organized, as a result, into the Old and New Testaments. This is Jeremiah at his prophetic best "... God forgives and holds their sins against them no more" (v. 34). See Numbers 11:26-29 and Joel 2:28-29.

New Testament Lesson   2 Timothy 3:14—4:5   *Paul's Charge To Timothy*

In Paul's instruction to his young spiritual son he wrote both positively and negatively:

Do
1. Continue in what you have learned (v. 14).
2. Proclaim the message (v. 2).
3. Be persistent, convince, rebuke, encourage with patience (v. 2).
4. Be sober, endure suffering (v. 5).
5. Carry out your ministry fully (v. 5).

Don't
1. Go to teachers to suit your own desires (v. 3).
2. Turn away from listening to the truth (v. 4).
3. Wander away to myths (v. 4).

We have an interesting use of scripture in verses 16 and 17: it is useful for teaching, for correction, for proof, and for training in righteousness — so that we can be proficient and equipped to do good works. The person Paul had in mind was for church leaders. Verse 16 here is very similar to Romans 15:4.

Verse 4:1 is from an early baptismal creed. Verse 4:3 is intriguing to me. "Itching ears" may mean hearers who heard only superficially, like the tickling of their eardrum but penetrating no further. The literal translation is "having the hearing tickled." Sounds to me like that person who hears to be entertained and not challenged or confronted.

Just a brief thought about Paul advising Timothy to "... be an evangelist." I think a big part of this good advice is the effect witnessing and inviting on behalf of the gospel has on the one who does the witnessing. So Paul, knowing this great truth, wanted Timothy to have even stronger ownership of the gospel by communicating it to others. Yes, indeed!

The Gospel   Luke 18:1-8   *The Widow And The Judge*

There must have been a connection for Luke with this parable and the passage before it on the prayer of the disciples, "Thy kingdom come," which is a persistent one. Verse 1 tells us what it is about: the need to pray and not give up.

These judges were nicknamed "robber judges." Unless you could bribe them, you would never get your case settled.

The story is simple enough. The widow was so persistent she finally won out and the judge issued a verdict. In verse 5 the Greek for "wear me out" is literally "give me a black eye"! Perhaps he feared physical violence from her as well as exhaustion!

The point is easy. If a rascal of a judge will grant this persistent woman her request, think how much more God, a loving parent, will grant our persistent requests.

Somehow I just don't like the idea of comparing God with a rascal judge who had to be bribed. I realize Jesus was saying the "how much more" but it doesn't seem like one of the most meaningful parables.

Preaching Possibilities
A. Because today will be the last use of Jeremiah, there is a wonderful opportunity to sum up his message ending with the second part of today's reading which promises a new covenant. I don't see a good way to connect any of the readings with each other.
B. The Second Reading from Timothy is rich with Christian conduct, which one could announce is "for a Pastor Timothy." Then use the idea that we are all called to be ministers in our daily lives and thus it applies to all God's people. There is also an opportunity for some good humor in telling about the "itching ear" in the Second Reading and the judge's black eye in the Gospel.

I'll go with Jeremiah and at the end mention "... his chosen ones" from the parable in Luke. Those who now have the new covenant are promised a God who will hear us.

Possible Outline Of Sermon Moves
A. Introduction: We have been reading from the book of Jeremiah the last eight or nine weeks and have heard him give a stern warning to the people for their unfaithfulness.
  1. They have deserted Yahweh for no good reason (Proper 17).
  2. The people are like clay in the potter's hands (Proper 18).
  3. God's judgment is coming like the hot wind of the desert and it will be devastating (Proper 19).
  4. Gilead's balm will not even help (Proper 20).
  5. Israel will someday be redeemed like the field Jeremiah purchased (Proper 21).
  6. Israel will be like a widow without anyone to comfort her in her loss (Proper 22).
  7. The people might as well go on with their lives in exile; it's going to be a while (Proper 23).
  8. And today's reading, Proper 24. Each person will be responsible for one's own sins ... so far.
B. Move to the second part of today's reading. It's the promise of the new covenant.
C. Read verses 31-33.
D. Define our two covenants or Testaments:

Old	New
Keep the law	Accept God's grace through faith
Be circumcised	Be baptized
Have a clean record	Have faith
The Ten Commandments	The Savior Christ

E. What was Jeremiah promising? That even though we have sinned and not remained faithful, God will work out a new agreement with us and it will be put in our hearts.
F. Move to announcing that all this came true in Jesus. We have a meal of celebration in observance of this new covenant. We have a section of the Bible telling us about his new covenant.

G. Move to the parable in the Gospel and how it tells us that when we new-covenant people ask God in prayer, we will be heard.

H. Move to a farewell to Jeremiah. So today we say farewell to this sad prophet and his warnings and lamentations and say hello to the Christ whom he promised in the new covenant.

Prayer For The Day

We give you thanks, dear God, for the prophets of old like Jeremiah who warned the people of the result of their unfaithfulness but also foretold the coming of a new covenant we know now to be made possible by Jesus on the cross and out of the grave for us. Thank you also for always listening to our prayers. In Christ's name. Amen.

Possible Metaphors And Stories

A female patient in the hospital said to me after a radical breast removal for cancer: "I prayed to God not to let this happen to me — but he (*sic*) didn't hear me." Because God doesn't answer our prayer requests doesn't mean God doesn't hear them.

In an historical museum along the Mississippi River in Iowa, there is a sign at the helm of an old riverboat which reads: "In a storm pray toward heaven, but row toward shore." There are times to pray and times to act on the prayer and actually become the way God answers it.

"In every age the church with the Holy Scriptures at its sides has had some witnesses to the truth and clarity of the Word of God who are more deserving of our trust than anyone who wears a cross and fine purple but contradicts the words of Scriptures" (Wilhelm Loehe).

Boris, preaching his "Senior Sermon" in the Lutheran Seminary chapel in Hong Kong, began by saying: "Where there is hope, there is religion, but, where there is religion there isn't always hope." Finally, Jeremiah got to hope and it's a new covenant.

Proper 25, Pentecost 23, Ordinary Time 30

Revised Common	Joel 2:23-32	2 Timothy 4:6-8, 16-18	Luke 18:9-14
Roman Catholic	Sirach 35:12-14, 16-19	2 Timothy 4:6-8, 16-18	Luke 18:9-14
Episcopal	Jeremiah 4:(1-6) 7-10, 19-22	2 Timothy 4:6-8, 16-18	Luke 18:9-14

Seasonal Theme   Jesus' acts of compassion and teaching ministry.

Theme For The Day   Saint Paul's legacy and farewell which calls for keeping the faith and finishing the race.

Old Testament Lesson   Joel 2:23-32   *The Blessings Of God*

The passage begins with a glorious promise of early and late rain and the blessing derived from it. Verses 24-27 list out some of the blessings when the land has ample rain, contrasted with locust and drought. We are told that Israel can count on Yahweh's action toward her. Verses 28-32 continue the blessings of God with the pouring out of the spirit upon the people — there is a new power for them. The spirit will bless everyone. Moses had asked for it (Numbers 11:29). We have the signs in verses 30 and 31 of the day of Yahweh. To "call upon the name of the Lord" (v. 32) is to serve him in the temple liturgy.

According to Charles F. Kraft in *The Interpreter's One Volume Commentary on the Bible*: "Acts 2:17-21, the Pentecost speech of Peter, verses 28-32 are quotes as found in the LXX. The events of Pentecost were seen as part of the pattern proclaimed by the prophet." Verse 28 gives us the outpouring afterward. Romans 10:13 also quotes verse 32a.

New Testament Lesson   2 Timothy 4:6-8, 16-18   *Paul's Finish*

This is the last New Testament Reading from Timothy for this church year. We have had seven in a row. And this one is definitely a closing one. Paul says he has given his all like a sacrifice poured out (see Philippians 2:17) and he has now come to the end. He is confident of his place in heaven. He regrets that all deserted him when he needed them — but Jesus stood by him and he was able to proclaim the gospel to the Gentiles. Not bad for a rabid converted Jew who at one time was out to persecute the early Christians!

The word for "departure" is rich (*analusis*). It is for a soldier taking down his tent or the loosing of a boat from its moorings. Perhaps to young Timothy it seemed Paul was coming to his end. But Paul saw it as being released from all those things which held him back here on earth (see also Philippians 1:23).

The tense of verse 16 suggests that this was a defense which was preliminary and that it was successful. Still, it's sad that this great missionary who had given his all had no one there to speak on his behalf. "Out of the mouth of the lion" is a common metaphor for escaping some severe danger. It's doubtful the lion referred to the emperor or the amphitheater.

For preaching, the three assertions will do powerfully: 1) fought the good fight; 2) finished the race; and 3) kept the faith. The results are a crown of righteousness.

The Gospel   Luke 18:9-14   *The Pharisee And Tax Collector*

So much here in these few sentences! This Pharisee was a very good member of the church. There are a number of good things about him: he fasted, he tithed, he prayed, he was in church. But his attitude was pride in all these things. He prayed to himself rather than to God.

But it was the one who admitted to God his/her sins whose prayers God heard. This teaches us several things about prayer:

1. In comparing ourselves, the comparison should be with Jesus' example and not with other sinners.
2. We can't pray well with hate in our hearts for other people. We do not place ourselves above others when we pray.

3. Pride can block the acceptance by God of our prayers. True discipleship ought to have a realistic humility.

This Pharisee may not have been there to pray at all but rather to show off to others how great a Jew he was. Still, where is a better place for a fellow like that to be than in the church?

Preaching Possibilities

A. If you have not addressed the spiritual discipline of prayer recently, the Gospel parable teaches it well. The above three lessons in the Gospel for today will work. I don't think the three readings are selected to go together on any common sermon theme.

B. The Old Testament Reading from Joel will preach about God's promises and the outpouring of God's spirit. The early and late rain for a country suffering from severe drought and plagues of locust is strong imagery. It's a good time to talk about natural disasters, what insurance companies call "acts of God," and why God *allows* or *causes* them to take place.

C. But because the farewell of Paul to Timothy is our last reading from Timothy, and because there are such rich phrases employed by Paul, I'll go with the Second Reading.

Possible Outline Of Sermon Moves

A. Begin by telling your hearers this is the seventh reading from Timothy. And that the Timothy books are two very special letters in which Paul is writing to his spiritual son. So far we have heard Paul say to young Timothy:
1. Don't drift away to false teachers and continue to be persistent in your witnesses (Proper 24).
2. Even when facing hardships we can anticipate great things ahead (Proper 23).
3. Live up to your mother and grandmother's strong faith (Proper 22).
4. Be careful about materialism and be content with what you have (Proper 21).
5. Pray for everyone in an inclusive manner (Proper 20).
6. There are no limits to God's transforming power (Proper 19).

B. Move to Paul's farewell words to Timothy, and read verses 6-8.

C. Call attention to the three assertions of Paul in verse 7.
1. "Fought the good fight." The Greek here is for a military victory or first place in an athletic event.
2. "Finished the race." Here we have the idea of not winning the race, but finishing it. This is endurance in Christian life and service.
3. "Kept the faith." There have been various interpretations of this often quoted phrase. It could be keeping the rules of a race or a military man's oath of fidelity (Calvin) or continuing to guard the deposit like a steward. One commentary regards it as simply a business formula for keeping an appointment.

D. Relate an example which puts Paul's message into your context. See below.

E. Consider the flip side of the above three assertions.
1. Gave up and surrendered to enemies;
2. Only ran part of the way and dropped out; and
3. Drifted away from the faith.

F. Look for a familiar hymn verse for the three assertions and have the congregation sing between each assertion above (or could be sung as a solo by one of the congregation).
1. Could be "Onward Christian Solders,"
2. Could be "Lead on O King Eternal," and
3. Could be "Faith of our Fathers."

G. One more move can be for you to say what this means to you and your congregation.
1. There are times when we would remain quiet rather than "fight" for our Christianity.
2. There are times in our Christian discipleship when we want to quit part way through.

3. There are many times when we are tempted to compromise our faith to be loved by everyone or to take part fully in our consumerism culture.

H. Frame your sermon by returning to the fact that it's Paul's farewell and it's our own farewell to the books of Timothy.

Prayer For The Day

We need your help, O God, to remain faithful and diligent in our discipleship. We rejoice you have given us faithful models like Timothy and Saint Paul. Help us to be models of discipleship for others who know us as well. And, dear God, teach us to pray in the right way. In Christ's name. Amen.

Possible Metaphors And Stories

A little Asian girl twiddling her thumbs was observed at the Washington, D.C., airport. She was sitting next to her father, twiddling her thumbs at the same speed as he. He would slow up; she would slow up. He would move them rapidly and so would she. He never noticed.

Little people watch us and often copy our actions. It's a big responsibility to be an adult whom children watch.

In an NBC special on *The Life of Florence Nightingale,* a war between Russia and England in 1853 was depicted. Nightingale felt "called by God" to go to Turkey to help care for the soldiers as a nurse. "You will be going to a country in the worst of circumstances." Florence replied, "No, the worst of circumstances for Christians is to do nothing."

Richard Mills, whom she loved, wrote to her as she was about to leave: "Florence, hold your head high — few of us can ever say, 'I made a difference' — you are one of those few."

In 1991 *Newsweek* did a story on economic hard times. The following were three responses in the letters to the editor:

"It takes an enormous amount of gall for the administration to try to solve the problems of others when our own country is going down the drain."

"What next — serfs and peasants?"

"Hard times," wrote one, "free us to discover what we truly value in life."

Going through white water rapids is quite an experience! When we went through the roughest one of all, part way through, we lost our rudder and then our guide fell in. Some fell into the center of the rubber raft and some fell out into the river. Finally came the calm water and I thought we had made it, only to discover all were gone. I was on the raft alone! The guide and all the passengers had been dumped. I think we often experience that kind of disaster in the wake of our hollow victories.

Heads Up Alert

The next three Sundays we will read from 2 Thessalonians. It's a good chance to preach a three-sermon series on this wonderful little book.

Consider these themes: *Vital signs and commands.*

A. Proper 26 — 2 Thessalonians 1:1-4, 11-12 — three vital signs of a Christian Church:
1. a strong faith,
2. love for one another, and
3. steadfastness under suffering.

B. Proper 27 — 2 Thessalonians 2:1-5, 13-17 — three vital signs of a Christian disciple of Jesus:
1. chosen by God,
2. sanctified by the Spirit, and
3. having the glory of Jesus Christ.

C. Proper 28 — 2 Thessalonians 3:6-13 — three commands to follow:
1. Keep away from lazy believers.
2. Imitate Saint Paul in discipleship.
3. Do your work quietly and don't be weary in well doing.

Consider placing something like this in next week's bulletin:

The next three weeks we'll be reading from 1 Thessalonians for our Second Reading. Paul founded this church and had to leave after a very short ministry. In first Thessalonians he writes to them about the second coming of Christ and in this second letter he deals with the subject of "last things." Our pastor will begin today a series of three sermons based on the Second Readings from Thessalonians. The titles will be: (list)

Proper 26, Pentecost 24, Ordinary Time 31

Revised Common	Habakkuk 1:1-4; 2:1-4	2 Thessalonians 1:1-4, 11-12	Luke 19:1-10
Roman Catholic	Wisdom 11:22—12:22	2 Thessalonians 1:11—2:2	Luke 19:1-10
Episcopal	Isaiah 1:10-20	2 Thessalonians 1:1-5 (6-10) 11-12	Luke 19:1-10

Seasonal Theme   Jesus' acts of compassion and teaching ministry.

Theme For The Day   Jesus came to seek out the lost of every generation and place. A big change is called for when and if we take him home with us.

Old Testament Lesson   Habakkuk 1:1-4; 2:1-4   *Complaint And Reply*

In this reading we have the prophet complaining to God that he has complained to God about the official corruption in the country and Yahweh has failed to answer him. Justice is no longer applied and when this happens there is strife and contention.

Yahweh's answer to Habakkuk's complaint is in verses 2:1-4, assuring him that soon God's vision will come. These assuring words are followed by the certainty that the unrighteous person's wealth and power will not be stable and that the righteous person's will be maintained.

The New Testament ringing endorsement of this idea is to be found in Romans 1:17, Galatians 3:11, and Hebrews 10:38-39. Martin Luther was deeply influenced by these passages and they became the lynch pin of the Protestant Reformation.

If you wanted to deal with the theological question of how God may use evil nations' armies to bring punishment on a transgressing nation, it is included in verses 1:5-7. I won't go there!

New Testament Lesson   2 Thessalonians 1:1-4, 11-12   *Christ's Glory*

As we move toward the close of the liturgical church year, we turn to this letter to the church of Thessalonica which deals with last things. In the first passage we have Paul identifying three elements of an active and live church:

1. a strong faith,
2. love for one another, and
3. steadfastness under persecutions.

In this latter we have our old friend of a Greek word: *hipomone,* which is a victorious endurance not a passive one.

Then Paul moves to the thought in verse 11 that God will empower us in our call and that Christ's glory might be in us, which is quite a responsibility. Still, we have God's grace, which makes it all possible. It's a nice idea that when Christ comes he will be glorified in his saints and admired by believers. Like old professors or pastors take glory in their former students, so Christ takes glory in us. Can it be so?

The Gospel   Luke 19:1-10   *Shorty In The Sycamore Tree*

Of this story, E. J. Tinsley in his commentary on Luke writes, "This whole incident, found only in Luke, turns out to be a reproduction in miniature of the meaning of the mission of Jesus, and it seems that Jesus himself saw it that way ... The whole incident is a pointer to the coming, in the Son of Man, of salvation to the house of Israel — Zacchaeus is a son of Abraham."

There is a marvelous self-giving of Zacchaeus like it ought be so of all disciples and followers of Jesus. This was a man probably hated by most. Perhaps he was wealthy but lonely, so he was trying for God's love. He would not give up easily, so ran ahead and climbed this tree. When Jesus received him, he made some drastic changes in his lifestyle. He gave half of his possessions to the poor (v. 8)! We often soft-pedal the need to make major changes in our lives upon becoming one of Jesus' disciples.

The story comes to a close with verse 10, which says Jesus came to seek the lost. The lost here, according to Barclay, means not doomed to hell, but being in the wrong place. A person is lost when he/she has wandered from God and he/she is found when he/she again takes his/her place in God's household. And to seek the lost is to discover the joy again of being the found.

Preaching Possibilities

A. One could connect the three readings with a general theme of strong faith, but it's a far stretch.
   1. The Old Testament Habakkuk — a strong faith that God will eventually hear and act.
   2. The New Testament Reading in 2 Thessalonians — a strong faith that is a vital sign of a vital congregation.
   3. The Gospel Reading — a strong faith which overcame obstacles to seeing and inviting Jesus into Shorty's home.

B. The Second Reading is rich with indications of a vital congregation for which Paul commends the Thessalonians. See the comments in the Gospel section. Also see my suggestions for a series based on this reading and the two following Sundays.

C. Of course Zacchaeus up a tree is a nice story about overcoming obstacles to be a disciple, about Jesus' mission to come to sinners and the "lost," and about the radical nature of lifestyle changes indicated when we invite Jesus into our lives.

Possible Outline Of Sermon Moves

A. Retell the story in a modern setting like — Jesus came to (*your town*) and the mayor gave a parade. An IRS man no one liked couldn't see ...

B. Move to describe how hated this tax man was and why (because of the abuse of those who collected taxes for Rome).

C. Move to telling your hearers what the story says to you.
   1. We can often overcome barriers if we persist.
   2. Jesus came to the lost and sinners like us.
   3. When we invite Jesus into our homes, it calls for radical lifestyle changes.
   4. We must love the unlovely because Jesus loves them.

D. Move to ask your hearers to identify which person they are in the story.
   1. A member of the crowd who hated and grumbled.
   2. A short man up a tree who was lonely and was seeking Jesus.
   3. Jesus who was seeking the lost and lonely.

E. Frame your sermon by returning to the opening story and give it a different ending. "So the community, including the mayor, declared it a special holiday because another home was specially blessed with Christ's presence."

Prayer For The Day

Dear God, make us glad people whenever another one is found by Jesus and takes him home with him. Remove from us the crowd's tendency to grumble; rather, help us to celebrate God's love wherever and with whomever it is manifested in our own community. And show us the lonely of our day and places that we might serve as the instruments through which God loves them. In Jesus' name who wants to come to our house, too. Amen.

Possible Metaphors And Stories

A while back there were a number of letters to the editor of *The Lutheran* magazine about how to usher people in and out of church. Finally a letter came like this: "Usher them in, usher them out; I say lock the doors and see if they can live with each other!" Good point. Can we realize in the church the brotherhood and sisterhood we are always talking about?

Pastor David Rowe points out: "There is an old African proverb which says it doesn't matter whether the elephants are fighting or making love, the flowers still get trampled." While we discuss, debate, deliberate, let's look around and see the people who are being hurt.

A little boy in Northern Ireland was riding a bicycle and singing: "The Protestants got all the housing." A priest stopped and asked him to sing something different, like "Jesus was born in a stable." So the little boy rode away singing: "Jesus was born in a stable, because the Protestants got all the housing."

What songs do we sing and what is the symbolism of them for others who hear them?

Proper 27, Pentecost 25, Ordinary Time 32

Revised Common	Haggai 1:15b—2:9	2 Thessalonians 2:1-5, 13-17	Luke 20:27-38
Roman Catholic	2 Maccabees 7:1-2, 9-14	2 Thessalonians 2:16—3:5	Luke 20:27-38
Episcopal	Job 19:23-27a	2 Thessalonians 2:13—3:5	Luke 20:27 (28-33) 34-38

Seasonal Theme   Jesus' acts of compassion and teaching ministry.

Theme For The Day   We need not fear our death, as God has worked it all out for us to be secure in his eternal heaven.

Old Testament Lesson   Haggai 1:15b—2:9   *The Future Glory Of The Temple*

Haggai was a prophet who pressed the people to rebuild the Temple in Jerusalem. He preached the results of disobedience and the blessings of obedience. If the people give their loyalty to God and God's Temple, blessings will be the result.

There were a few who knew Solomon's Temple before it was destroyed. Haggai at nearly eighty years of age could remember its splendor and wanted it rebuilt again even more glorious (v. 9). The people are reminded of the covenant with Israel in verse 5 when they came out of Egypt.

In verse 9 the word *prosperity* can also be translated "peace," so we need not limit it to great wealth. The shaking in verses 6 and 7 is used other places to describe God's judgment in political turmoil. See Judges 5:4-5, Nahum 1:2-5, and Hebrews 12:25-29.

Verse 5b seems to me to be central in this passage for preaching: God is with us, so we need not be afraid. May it still be so!

New Testament Lesson   2 Thessalonians 2:1-5, 13-17   *The Overcoming Of Evil*

In the first part of this very difficult passage we have Paul writing his belief that there would be a final battle in which that power which is opposed to God would be destroyed. All this would take place after a growing rebellion against God. Even though this seems difficult to interpret to our people now, there are some things we are taught.

1.   There is an organized power which opposes God in this world.
2.   Still, somehow God is in control.
3.   God will ultimately win out.

We have in verses 13-17 then a kind of summary of our life in Christ. We are chosen by God; our call brings with it a task; God and godly people help us with our responsibilities as one of the called; and we are thus set apart for God here and saved for eternity. What we may have to suffer here is small potatoes compared with eternity planned for us.

Verse 17 seems to conclude this passage with a benediction you might use this Sunday in place of your customary one.

The Gospel   Luke 20:27-38   *About The Resurrection*

The Pharisees believed in the resurrection and the Sadducees did not. The Pharisees believed in fate and the Sadducees in free-will. So the question was supposed to make resurrection of the body look silly. Jesus' answer will serve us well in many realms of our beliefs about God. We cannot think of eternity in the terms of this age and earth. Jesus took his answer a step further and pointed out that God was the God of Abraham, Isaac, and Jacob (Exodus 3:1-6). God would not be a God of the dead. Jesus uses here an argument all could understand in language which all could comprehend as well.

Luke's source here is Mark 12:18-27. This account comes from what was called "levirate marriage" which is described in Deuteronomy 25:5-10 and was meant to keep the family alive by having sons. If a man died without having any sons, his wife was expected to marry her husband's brother. Any sons produced by that marriage were considered to be sons of the first husband.

Preaching Possibilities

A. We could use all three readings to address what we Christians believe about "last things."
   1. Jesus teaches in the Gospel for today that eternity will not be like it is here on earth.
   2. Paul teaches in the Second Reading that evil must be defeated and God will ultimately win out.
   3. Haggai tells us that whatever comes, we ought not be afraid because God is with us.
B. If you want to deal with the devil and the presence of evil in our world this Sunday, you can do it using the Second Reading. See the three truths listed in the comments on the scripture and also the Possible Metaphors And Stories.
C. The Old Testament is a lovely story of an old man who still remembers the glory of Solomon's Temple and is urging the people to rebuild. We could talk about the importance of God's house in our community as a place of remembering all God has done for us, a place where we are the body of the alive Christ in the world, and a place of Good News and God's presence through God's sacraments.

Possible Outline Of Sermon Moves

Let's deal with eschatology today without using the word or words so few know!

A. Begin by stating your first ideas about what happens to us when we die.
B. Move to the question asked by the Sadducees of Jesus.
C. Explain why they asked such a question and the idea of levirate marriage in the Jewish law of that day.
D. Move to what we Christians believe about eternal life:
   1. Jesus has prepared a place for us there.
   2. It is a very different existence than on earth.
   3. We have a resurrection of our spiritual bodies like Jesus had a resurrection as the first example.
   4. We gain eternal life with God only by God's grace through our Holy Spirit-aided faith.
E. Move to what we ought do about this:
   1. Plan our funeral as a witness to what we believe.
   2. Do stewardship estate planning now for after we have died.
   3. Relax and not worry about our eternity. Jesus paid our admission fee on the cross and has promised to escort us there so we are ready anytime it comes.
F. Frame by returning to how your early idea of heaven and eternity has changed.

Prayer For The Day

Be with us, O God, when we die and take us to the place you have prepared for your disciples. Give us the confidence of your love that we need not fear our death or grieve the death of our baptized loved ones. And help us always to celebrate the presence of your spirit with us to overcome the power of evil which is always after us. In Jesus Christ's name. Amen.

Possible Metaphors And Stories

I preached in Wozi, Liberia, one night through an interpreter into the Loma language. Wozi is in the center of animism. They had laid a vine around the entire village to keep me out. During my preaching the "Lion" came to town to try to scare my young listeners away from hearing the gospel. They also played drums and danced outside the building to drown out the gospel proclamation. But through all the fear and superstition we were heard, and the Holy Spirit moved some to believe. What noise competes with the gospel where you live and worship?

At the airport, there was a limo driver holding up a sign: "Katz." Others recognized family members right away. They hugged and kissed and some even brought flowers to welcome them home. When we come home to God, we will be known. And the family of God will recognize us and welcome us there.

Tom Skinner at an Evangelical Outreach conference told us: "God's intention is that the church shall establish itself in an alien territory so people can see what heaven is like. We pray it in the Lord's Prayer. It's like when the English came to Africa and Africans could see what living in England is like." So each day let us live that others might glimpse into a vision of heaven.

I watched them say good-bye for the last time. They were two old evangelists way up in the bush in Liberia, Africa, where I had transported Old Man Mopolu to see Mama "Gannah" (Amanda Gardner). She wagged her finger in his face and said, "Now, ol' man, don't you give up on this God business. And when we get to heaven all the people goin' to be there to greet us and give us a big hand clap." Might the same be said of all of us.

Proper 28, Pentecost 26, Ordinary Time 33

Revised Common	Isaiah 65:17-25	2 Thessalonians 3:6-13	Luke 21:5-19
Roman Catholic	Malachi 3:19-20	2 Thessalonians 3:7-12	Luke 21:5-19
Episcopal	Malachi 3:13—4:2a, 5-6	2 Thessalonians 3:6-13	Luke 21:5-19

Seasonal Theme   Jesus' acts of compassion and teaching ministry.

Theme For The Day   The prophecy and promise of Jesus about discipleship and last things.

Old Testament Lesson   Isaiah 65:17-25   *The New Creation*

The promise of Isaiah is a new creation where and when the past transgressions will be set aside and a new created order called into being. No longer are laments necessary; but, rather, rejoicing. The new creation will include long life, no crying or suffering, no early death of children, and no more having their homes or crops taken away from them. And their children will have much better lives in which God will delight. God will hear their prayers almost before they speak them. Peace shall be in Jerusalem. The serpent is a symbol of evil which will be kept restrained.

The promise is that God not only loves us, but that God takes delight in us (v. 18).

New Testament Lesson   2 Thessalonians 3:6-13   *Until That Day*

In this congregation Paul had to deal with the wrong idea about the second coming of the Christ. Some thought because it was so soon they might as well quit work and wait for the time. So they were what Paul wrote in the Greek, "truant" from their work. Paul advised them to get back to work and he made the assertion that they should follow his example. All his ministry he continued to make his tents and earn his own financial support. He also quoted a saying probably common in the workshops of his day (v. 10b). Notice the admonition is for those who are "unwilling" to work. This is far different from those who just can't find work. The "unwilling" says to me that person who had work available but refused to do it.

The Gospel   Luke 21:5-19   *Promise Of Things To Come*

There are several different concepts which makes this a tough chapter to interpret:
1. the coming suffering for being a Christian,
2. the fall of Jerusalem,
3. the second coming of Christ, and
4. the day of the Lord.

Someone was commenting on the beauty of the Temple and that triggered Jesus to prophesy. Jesus says it will all come down. Notice the frankness of his saying that if they followed him there would be rough times ahead. Jesus evidently could accurately predict these future outcomes because he could glean them from present signs.

To this he added they would not have to go through their persecution alone and that no matter what came they would be safe (v. 18). Verses 12 and 19 deal with the coming persecution.

Verses 9, 11, 25, and 26 take their images from the Jewish "day of the Lord" which all would recognize. Also Jerusalem did fall to the Romans in A.D. 70.

Preaching Possibilities

All three readings deal with a future which can be anticipated by God's people. I am sure they were chosen by our foremothers and forefathers because of our now being at the end of the liturgical year.
A. The three together might go like this:
   1. The Old Testament — A new day is coming when God will actually "delight" in us.

2. The New Testament — Keep at it in the meantime not taking advantage of your beliefs.

3. The Gospel — You have a lot of suffering ahead but you don't go through it alone.

B. I believe one of the nicest thoughts today is in the Old Testament Lesson, verse 19: God delights in us. To be delighted in is more than a superficial love or respect. To have a God who delights in us means to me:

1. above all other creatures, God delights in us.

2. a God who delights in us is approachable by prayer.

3. a God who has this kind of delight in us will go to the cross for our forgiveness.

4. To be "delighted in" ought to affect our attitude toward God and toward others profoundly.

C. In dealing with the Second Readings, we could use the following warnings: idleness, busy-body-ness, weariness in doing the right thing. They all can be like a poison which can infect and destroy a congregation. Careful, lest the sermon become a moralistic lecture absent of Gospel.

Possible Outline Of Sermon Moves

Title: Understanding The Terms

A. Introduction: Today's Gospel talks about what we Christians believe about last things.

B. Move to defining the terms:

1. "Day of the Lord" which includes the present age and the age to come, (vv. 9, 11, 25, and 26).

2. "The fall of Jerusalem" (vv. 5, 6, 20-24).

3. "The second coming of Christ" (vv. 7, 8, and 9).

4. "Persecution to come" (vv. 12-19).

C. Move to the truths we can learn from this passage (see comments on the scripture).

1. Jesus was always frank about what it meant to be a Christian.

2. As Christians we ought be able to learn from our history.

3. We do not have to suffer for our faith alone.

4. Ultimately we will be safe — not even our hair destroyed!

D. Give your own witness as to what all this means for you and for your congregation. We can keep on even when it's tough being a Christian. We ought to be God's support for each other. We can take risk knowing God protects us. Give an example or story or metaphor from below.

E. Frame your sermon by returning to your opening statement about last things and how confusing it can be.

Prayer For The Day

Spare us, O God, from being morbidly curious about what happens in the "end times." We rejoice that you delight in us as Isaiah claims and that you will see us through even the most difficult times in our discipleship. In our curiosity about your second coming, let us never forget you are already with us here and now. In Christ's name. Amen.

Possible Metaphors And Stories

An advertisement on Hong Kong television for AIG insurance simply states: "The greatest risk is not taking one."

When a knight came to the court of King Arthur, he did not come to spend the rest of his days in knightly feasting and celebration. He came reporting for duty, asking what mission he might be sent on which would be done for Arthur. So, too, our discipleship.

Editor David Miller of *The Lutheran* magazine in a Bible study for returned missionaries: "We are not just loved; we are delighted in by God according to our Bible. I delight in that!"

Reformation Sunday

Lutheran   **Jeremiah 31:31-34**   **Romans 3:19-28**   **John 8:31-36**

Theme For The Day   We are saved by a new covenant of grace and what Jesus did for us on the cross. We continually need reforming.

Old Testament Lesson   Jeremiah 31:31-34   *A New Covenant*

This important teaching of Jeremiah is sometimes called the gospel before the gospel. It is the height of the Old Testament. It is quoted in Hebrews 10:16-17 and is the foundation of the words Jesus spoke at the Last Supper (1 Corinthians 11:25; Luke 22:20). It is responsible for our speaking today of the Old Testament and the New Testament. It's not the giving of a new law but rather a new reason to keep the law. Because we have forgiveness of our sins and relationships with God, we have a different incentive to keep the law.

The Interpreter's Bible says of this passage that there are "... three provisions in the new covenant and these three steps leading to it.

1.   ... a desperate move, for it is the way to the deeper homecoming.
2.   ... a difficult move, which consists in not remembering the former things. And
3.   ... is forgiveness, and behind forgiveness is love" (pp. 1037-1039).

This whole thing seems to me close to Ezekiel's idea of the new heart (Ezekiel 11:9, 18:31, and 36:26).

Verse 33b is the basis of the covenant. Yahweh is Israel's God and Israel is Yahweh's people.

New Testament Lesson   Romans 3:19-28   *Justified By Faith*

This passage complements the Old Testament Lesson as in it we learn of a new covenant. Here we have the conditions of that covenant: All who believe have not their own, but God's righteousness through Jesus Christ; all of us have sinned and are justified by God's grace; Jesus' sacrifice on the cross worked atonement for us; and, the really big one for Reformation Sunday, it is by our faith and not by any works laid out in the law which makes justification possible. This all began with Paul's letter to the Galatians (2:16) and became a fundamental part of Paul's understanding of the Gospel. It is the linchpin of Martin Luther's Reformation theology as well.

The Gospel   John 8:31-36   *True Disciples*

It is only when we set aside all the previous preconceptions — prejudice, our own wants and drives — can we see the whole picture, the real truth. Especially the truth about ourselves. Verse 35 tells us that a son or daughter is always free but a slave cannot get free by him/herself. In verse 36 John uses the Greek *hyios* which he only uses in relation to God for Christ.

In this reading one can detect a debate taking place, with Jesus addressing the two points of the Jew's argument: Freedom and their lineage from Abraham. On the latter Jesus confronts them on the basis of their actions. The question is whether the Jews will accept that they are from the same inheritance as Jesus. Abraham is ancestor of both.

Preaching Possibilities

A. It's a rare Sunday when all three readings so fit together and build on each other. No doubt with Luther's emphasis on "scripture alone" our foremothers and forefathers selected these texts, all three being central to their author's works. If we use all three, an outline could go like this:

   1. Introduction: Perhaps a story from Luther's life and times. Luther's insistence on the authority of the scripture.

2. Move one: Jeremiah tells us of a new covenant. And we really needed one, for we just couldn't keep all the rules so that God would remain our God.

3. Move two: Paul gets to the heart of it as he tells us if we have faith we can have God's righteousness. We all have sinned but we also have forgiveness from a grace-filled God.

4. Move three: John tells us what Jesus taught him. It's that we have a certain freedom and it comes from learning the truth from God. We learn the truth about ourselves, our God, and our ability to save ourselves.

5. Relate what these truths in these three readings mean to you personally and what you think they mean to those who hear your sermon today.

6. Return to your opening story about Luther's life and times and frame your sermon.

Of course any of the three lessons will stand alone.

B. The Jeremiah account can be a sermon on "Our deal with God." Because we have forgiveness and a new relationship with God, we know a different godly love for us.

C. The Romans 3 account begs for a textual sermon on verses 23 and 24 on "Justified by grace through faith in Jesus Christ." You have your three points:

1. Justified, what does it mean?
2. Grace, how do we deserve it?
3. Jesus Christ, how did he do it?

D. The John account also is rich. We have the distinction between slavery to sin and daughter and son-ship of God. We could talk of freedom from what? It could be freedom from sin and freedom to discipleship.

Possible Outline Of Sermon Moves

A. Let's try a letter sermon today. Some suggestions would be: A letter from Katie Luther to son Paul about his dad, a letter from Katie Luther in Torgau to Pastor Buggenhagen at Wittenberg after Luther's death, a letter from Martin to Katie from the city of Worms just after he took his stand, a letter from Martin at the Wartburg during his kidnapping escapade.

B. If it is your first one, you could include the following elements:

1. The salutation and inside address.
2. The reason for the letter is to tell Paul about how his father died at Eisleben.
3. A paragraph about what his father confessed on his death bed: he still believed in faith alone, scripture alone, and the priesthood of all believers.
4. Katie's description of what she believes this means for her son Paul to live out in his own discipleship. He, too, is a priest in God's sight!
5. Some closing comments about Luther's belief on marriage and family and congregation as marital community.
6. A closing expression of endearment for her son.

Prayer For The Day

We celebrate this Reformation Sunday our heritage of living out our discipleship as freed and saved sinners. We pray we might also always be a reforming and reshaping church not resisting but encouraging change and renewal as our reformers of the sixteenth century did as well. In the name of Christ who asked for new wine skins for new wine. Amen.

Possible Metaphors And Stories

Tegucigalpa, Honduras: "A Honduran peasant has been freed after spending nineteen years in prison because penal authorities did not learn that he had been acquitted in 1976." Gusto Adolf Amador, now 57, was charged in 1975 with stealing colored pencils from a marketplace in the capital, but a court acquitted him the following year. The written release order did not arrive at Tegucigalpa central penitentiary, where Amador was held, for the next eighteen years (*San Francisco Examiner*, May 1, 1994).

Even though acquitted, we live as prisoners.

Pastor Helmut Hasse, who just recently retired as parish pastor after thirty years at the city church in Wittenberg, Germany, told of the day the Berlin Wall came down. During the worship service a man sat in the anteroom and listened to the radio for the news. He came out and told Hasse the wall was coming down. The pastor announced the news of new freedom to the filled church. He said they stamped their feet, cried, hugged each other, and sang, "Hallelujah." For a long time there was "no good order" in the sanctuary. Freedom at last.

In little Peace village in Sumatra they will show you a large haviara tree where the "Apostle to the Bataks," Ingwer Ludwig Nommensen, a missionary from the Rhenish Church in Germany, would buy slaves, give them freedom, and bring them into the Christian faith.

The Cathedral of Mexico City has a wire suspended from the ceiling to the floor with a plumb line weight on the end of it to show how far the building has moved and still is moving off center. I wonder if it could measure how much we move off the gospel center?

All Saints' Sunday

Revised Common	Daniel 7:1-3, 15-18	Ephesians 1:11-23	Luke 6:20-31
Roman Catholic	Revelation 7:2-4, 9-14	1 John 3:1-3	Matthew 5:1-12
Episcopal	Ecclesiasticus 44:1-10, 13-14	Revelation 7:2-4, 9-17	Matthew 5:1-12

Theme For The Day   Remembering all the saints of God and the lifestyle Jesus asks us to live in order to be one of his saints and disciples.

Old Testament Lesson   Daniel 7:1-3, 15-18   *Ultimate Victory*
     Daniel writes down those things which happened while Israel was held captive in Babylon. Here we have Daniel's dream of "... four great hearts" representing four empires which tried to rule the world without giving homage to the living God. Verses 15-17 are an interpretation of the dream. Four Kings will attempt this rule but eventually Israel will rule the kingdom. Daniel always ends his prophecies with God triumphing. If the people will just trust in God, in the end they will experience victory. Is Daniel right in this message?

New Testament Lesson   Ephesians 1:11-23   *Sealed With The Holy Spirit*
     Verse 11 is a homiletical gold mine! What have we inherited because of and through Christ? The Jews inherited the privilege of being the first to expect the coming of the Anointed One of God. The Gentiles were sealed with the Holy Spirit. Like a package was sealed in the early days to show from whom it came and that it was intact, the Holy Spirit shows we belong to God. This same spirit shows us God's will and helps us do it. In verse 14 we have the use of the Greek word *arrabon*, which means a down payment to pledge the rest will be paid. So the Holy Spirit is a taste of the joys of heaven. It also guarantees that one day we will have eternal blessedness with God.
     In most of our denominational baptismal liturgies we have the words which are similar to, "Child of God, you have been sealed with the holy spirit...."

The Gospel   Luke 6:20-31   *Beatitudes And Woes*
     These passages are Luke's version of the Beatitudes even though they do differ a good bit from Matthew's version in Matthew 5:3-10. The term "the poor" has an interesting history. Those who were left behind in Jerusalem after its capture in 586 B.C. were referred to as "the poor" because they were destitute and represented defenseless and poor people who remain loyal to God. See Psalm 72:2. The weeping in verse 21 was a lamenting before God over sins. Jesus had a sense from the prophet's fate that his disciples would suffer. He also promised a reward for their faithfulness to those who did not expect a reward. In verse 24 riches are condemned outright. Jesus always advised that wealth would make his discipleship difficult and next to impossible. Luke tells of this teaching in 12:13-21 and 16:29-31 as well.
     The "woes" are doubtful as words of Jesus. They do not agree with the next passage to love one's enemies. But there are valuable warnings here. Complacency and not caring are condemned and we must speak boldly about the dangers of wealth, comfort, good fortune, and fame.
     Then comes this passage on radical love. Jesus is the best model. Another example is Stephen (see Acts 7:60). Plato insists that it is better to suffer an injustice than to do one — this remains the goal of the Christian ethic. Verse 30 is also difficult — in spite of the risk, it is better to err on the side of generosity. Verse 31 is understandable and perhaps the best of the radical Christian love called for in this passage.

Preaching Possibilities
A. No doubt for All Saints' Sunday those who selected these readings for the Sunday we remember those saints of our congregation who have died over the last year and sing that glorious, "For all the

saints ..." wanted us to see the fate of the saints in the Daniel passage. We are to remain faithful to God and the victory will eventually be ours. In the New Testament Reading they wanted us to see what is the inheritance of the saints and the blessedness of being sealed by the Holy Spirit. This is the down payment of God's eternal care. Then in the Gospel we have listed the blessedness of being a Christian disciple — that which our deceased congregational saints knew well. The three will work well together today.

B. I think the Ephesians reading is so rich and can easily stand alone as we address "Our Inheritance" or "The Inheritance of the Saints." We do have to remember that many still think of saints as those special people beatified rather than all the baptized for whom Jesus died on the cross (and made a down payment for our eternal life). As those who are God's people, disciples, we have an inheritance.

1. Live in praise and glory (v. 12);
2. Sealed with the seal of the Holy Spirit (v. 13);
3. Have a guarantee of redemption (v. 14);
4. Loved by God (v. 15);
5. Be given the spirit of wisdom and revelation (v. 17);
6. Know the hope to which we are called (v. 18);
7. Know the riches of our inheritance of the Saints (v. 18);
8. Know the greatness of his power (v. 19); and
9. Be a part of Christ's body which is the church (23).

Possible Outline Of Sermon Moves

Title: The Saints Of God And Their Discipleship

A. Begin by asking the congregation to define in their mind just exactly what a saint is. Then give your definition.
B. Move to naming two or three who are being remembered today in the service and ask what the congregation believes makes them saints. Answer that the price Jesus paid on the cross, and so on.
C. Move to the Luke or Matthew account for today and the Beatitudes by Jesus to the disciples.
D. Explain these are not predictions of how it will be one day but are congratulations on how it is now for the saints of God.
E. Call attention to additions Luke gives:
   1. The rich already have received their comfort (v. 24).
   2. Those who have plenty may not later (v. 25).
   3. The laughing now will cry later (v. 25).
   4. Those who try to please everyone will be in trouble (v. 26).
F. Call attention to the radical love we disciples are to have:
   1. We are to love our enemies and do good to them (v. 27).
   2. We are to bless those who abuse and curse us (v. 28).
   3. We are to turn the other cheek and give to people who have any need (vv. 29, 30).
   4. And we must love as we would like to be loved (v. 31).
G. Sum it up by giving the do's and don'ts in your own words and shorter verbiage than this passage.
H. Use one of the Possible Metaphors And Stories below.

Prayer For The Day

Dear God, we do rejoice and give thanks today for all the saints living now and those who have gone before us which make up such a glorious company of the baptized. As we contemplate those lives lived in our midst today, we pray we might learn from them the do's and don'ts of sainthood and rejoice for your death on the cross for us all. In Jesus' name. Amen.

Possible Metaphors And Stories

In September of 1997 the world lost one of its living saints. The prayer written by Mother Teresa that every Missionary of Charity says before leaving for his or her apostate and also used as the Physician's Prayer in *Shishu Bhavan*, the children's home that Mother Teresa oversaw in Calcutta, follows:

"Dear Lord, the Great Healer, I kneel before you, since every perfect gift must come from you. I pray give skill to my hands, clear vision to my mind, kindness and meekness to my heart. Give me singleness of purpose, strength to lift up a part of the burden of my suffering fellow men, and a true realization of the suffering that is mine. Take from my heart all guile and worldliness that with the simple faith of a child, I may rely on you" (From *A Simple Heart*, by Mother Teresa, published by Ballentine Books, 1995).

Pastor Carlos Schneider told of Ted and Tom, who sat in the balcony at St. John's, Sacramento. Ted has died. Tom sits in the same place and keeps a place open for his deceased brother even when the balcony is crowded ... "the communion of the Saints" lived out by Tom of St. John's, Sacramento.

Some boys in a ski boat needed a tow. I went over and towed them into a nearby marina. They offered to pay. I told them just to purchase a tow rope and carry it in their boat to help others.

We who have been forgiven from the cross ought to forgive others; we who have been so richly blessed ought to bless; we who are so loved, to love ... and so forth.

At the Indonesian Batak celebration, called a "Hula Hula," of pregnancy, birth, marriage, ordinations, or a very special visit, all sit on straw mats on the floor and eat with their fingers and drink. Speeches are made and when the speaker says something especially wise and worthwhile all assembled say in unison, *"Ima tutu,"* which means, "May it be so!"

The Beatitudes in Matthew 5 are the *Ima tutus* of Jesus. Blessed are the poor, those who mourn, who grieve, and so forth. *Ima tutu*. May our ministries make it be so.

Day Of Thanksgiving

Revised Common   Deuteronomy 26:1-11   **Philippians 4:4-9**   John 6:25-35

Theme For The Day   Living and praying thankfully and responding in our giving appropriately to all God has done for us.

Old Testament Lesson   Deuteronomy 26:1-11   *First Fruits And Tithes*

Before the people entered the promised land there needed to be some rules for living established. And now that they finally have arrived there needed to be a regular liturgical expression of their thankfulness for this bountiful land and God's providential care on their freedom from slavery and long journey through the wilderness. So they are to practice first fruit offering. The first portion to be harvested should be offered to the priest at the temple. There follows a list starting with verse 6 of the care God had provided them — the Lord brought them out of Egypt (v. 8) and brought them into the promised land (v. 9).

Verse 11 tells them all the people should hold this celebration of the Lord's bounty.

New Testament Reading   Philippians 4:4-9   *Paul's Urging*

This congregation whom Paul so loved is urged to live lives of rejoicing and thankfulness. They are assured that because the "Lord is near" they need not worry and they should pray prayers of Thanksgiving. Paul then promises them God's peace in verse 7. It is a good antidote for anxiety.

Verse 8 pleads with these Christians to think on the honorable things in life knowing that would profoundly affect their behavior in that direction. Paul also urges imitation of him (see 3:17). Notice in verse 7 it is not the peace of God, but, rather the God of peace which will be with them.

Other prayers of urging to rejoice can be found in 1:18-19; 2:17-18, 28; 3:1; 4:10. Joy is also called for in 1:4, 25; 2:2, 29; and 4:1.

The Gospel   John 6:25-35   *The Bread From Heaven*

In this passage we have Jesus giving the people, even though they don't seem to understand, the meaning of the feeding miracle in 6:1-15. Jesus is speaking on a much deeper level than the folks are understanding him. Some believe, and the more worldly-minded reject, what he is teaching. Massey H. Shepherd, Jr., in *The Interpreter's One Volume Commentary on the Bible* has an interesting comparison: "The dialogue has close parallel with the conversation of the Samaritan woman (ch. 4), the symbol of bread here being comparable to the symbol of water there."

The bread in the miracle of feeding and the manna in the wilderness will disappear whereas God's bread will give eternal life (Deuteronomy 8:3 and Isaiah 55:2-3a). Homiletically this Gospel has advice for us on Thanksgiving. We ought to be thankful not only for the bounty of physical provisions, but especially we have a life in Christ here and right on into eternity.

No doubt the crowd was chasing Jesus because he had fed them plenty of bread and they were looking for more, rather than looking for food which lasts for eternal life. Verse 35 has the phrase, "I am the bread of life," which can also be translated "living bread" and "life giving bread." The gift is not only given by Jesus, but Jesus himself is the gift — and that person who receives it won't hunger any more.

Preaching Possibilities

Each of the three readings has been selected for a thanksgiving theme and thus can stand alone or be used in any combination.

A. The Old Testament — First fruits giving is still appropriate for an expression of our thankfulness to God for all the ways God provides for us.

B. The New Testament — Paul urges his Christians to live lives of thanksgiving; and, when they pray to pray thankfully.

C. The Gospel — Jesus reminds the people of God's provisions for them during their travel in the wilderness and how he gives a much more important spiritual food which leads right on into eternity. We are thankful for this spiritual, as well as the material, blessing.

I'll use all three in my preaching as follows.

Possible Outline Of Sermon Moves

Title: The Thankful Lifestyle

A. Begin by telling of first fruits practices in Liberia, West Africa, as told in Possible Metaphors And Stories below.

B. Move to Deuteronomy calling for such a practice. Tell your people the background of this passage and why they needed some liturgical practices for thanking God and remembering all God had done for them.

C. Move to the Gospel and tell the story of the people chasing Jesus looking for more bread and what he tried to teach them on a spiritual level.

D. Move to the ministry of Paul and how he advised his congregation to live their whole lives thankfully and when they prayed to pray thankfully. And how the unexpected bonus to that is a certain peace no matter the external circumstances.

E. Move to what all this says to you this Thanksgiving.
   1. We ought to make our offerings reflect thankfulness with our tithes.
   2. We ought to see beyond our physical blessings to our spiritual blessings. God with us. Eternal life promised, a fellowship unbreakable. The Good News and sacraments.
   3. We ought to change how we pray. Instead of a "laundry list" of wants, we ought to be listing our thanks for all our gracious God has done and is doing for us.

F. Tell a story from Possible Metaphors And Stories below.

Prayer For The Day

Help us to have thankful hearts today and here, dear Holy Parent, that we might be keenly aware of all you have done and are doing for us. Teach us to pray and live lives which are thankful, too. And move us to respond to all our blessings by giving generously so others would know your good news and your abundant blessings as well. In Jesus, the living bread's name. Amen.

Possible Metaphors And Stories

I preached one Sunday morning at St. Luke's, Phebe, Liberia. An old ordained deacon presided at the service. At the time for the offering, a woman brought forward a pan of peanuts on her head and placed it at the altar. Another brought a bucket of corn. These were the first of their harvest and they were literally offering them to God as their "first fruits offering"; then, the following week they could harvest the rest of the crop for themselves. Here was the biblical "first fruits offering" in practice!

From Robert Fulghum's book, *Uh-Oh*: "A Hudson Bay start meant the frontiersmen always camped the first night a few short miles from the company headquarters. This allowed the gear and supplies to be tried out, so if anything had to be kept behind it was still easy to return. A thoughtful beginning spared the travelers later difficulty."

A prayerful beginning to each day's journey will also make the trip go better equipped all day.

Mark Page, who donated a beautiful electronic organ for our seminary chapel, at its dedication said: "If it were possible for an organ to be happy, this one certainly is."

Happiness is elusive — what brings it to us, and is it important over the long haul?

Carolyn Foelsch Rocco, daughter of the first president of our seminary, left her stole at a restaurant and didn't realize it for quite a while. The restaurant called to tell her. It was a gift. I wonder what gifts I have lost and didn't realize it.

Christt The King
Proper 29, Pentecost 27, Ordinary Time 34

Revised Common	**Jeremiah 23:1-6**	**Colossians 1:11-20**	**Luke 23:33-43**
Roman Catholic	**2 Samuel 5:1-3**	**Colossians 1:12-20**	**Luke 23:35-43**
Episcopal	**Jeremiah 23:1-6**	**Colossians 1:11-20**	**Luke 23:35-43 or**
			Luke 19:29-38

Theme For The Day   Christ is our king and calls us to a loyal citizenship in his kingdom.

Old Testament Lesson   Jeremiah 23:1-6   *An Ideal King*

After a year of reading from the Old Testament prophet and hearing of the exile of the people because of their unfaithfulness, we finish the church year this Christ the King Sunday with Jeremiah's assurance that Israel will be restored and both Judah and Israel will live in safety. He will come from David's lineage.

It's still an undeveloped idea but we can find here a future Messiah promised. So there will be better times under this ideal king. It fits for this last Sunday of our church year.

Verses 1 through 4 assume the Jews as dispersed; they probably were added later. There is a note of getting even with those who have scattered the people into exile. Then in verse 3 we have the gathering out of the foreign lands of the exiles by faithful shepherds back to the promised land. There is in this a picture of a shepherd who has scattered and one who gathers them back into their fold again.

New Testament Lesson   Colossians 1:11-20   *The King's Kingdom*

These two great thoughts catch my imagination. God enables us to share in the inheritance of no less than the saints (v. 12)! The Jews were the chosen ones; but, Paul claims that Jesus opens the door to the Gentiles and to all the people — we have the inheritance, too.

The second great thought is that God has transferred us into God's kingdom. The Greek is *methisteme*. It's the word for transferring all the people and their belongings when they have lost the battle. The people of the defeated country are transferred to the victor's land. So the people of the Southern kingdom were transferred into Babylon. Paul claims we Christians have been transferred into God's own kingdom.

In verses 15 to 20 we learn several things about Jesus.
1.   He is the image of the invisible God (v. 15); he shows us what God is like.
2.   All things were created through him (v. 16b); he is creator.
3.   He is the head of the church (v. 18); he holds us all together.
4.   He is the firstborn from the dead (v. 18b); an example of how it will be for us.
5.   He is the full revelation of God (v. 19); nothing more is needed.

Verse 20 lays it out for us that through the Christ we are reconciled to our God. His sacrifice on the cross made peace for us with God. This reconciliation extends to all creation. It is a redeemed Universe. God's love permeates all creation.

The Gospel   Luke 23:33-43   *The King Of The Jews*

Of course, the reason for choosing this particular passage for this Sunday is the two references to Jesus as king. "King of the Jews" was placed as a sign on the cross at crucifixion and "... remember me when you come into your kingdom," was said by the thief who was on the cross beside Jesus.

Jesus was set between two known criminals in order to humiliate him in front of this crowd and to identify him with thieves. The sign on the cross, "This is the King of the Jews," was on the sign which was a part of the march through the city to the place of crucifixion. It was shown in front of the criminal on his way to execution. Luke mentions it here in verse 38 as part of the mockery that was taking place. Yet in the rest of the Gospel he has often called attention to the fact of the real kingship of Jesus and the salvation he brings. So there is irony here (on this cross Jesus was king indeed!).

In verse 42 the common thief (Demas or Dismas) seems to recognize something the crowd does not see. His penitence seems to enable him to view the possibility of salvation even at this late hour. Verse 43 is a king's assurance, for the word *paradise* means a walled garden into which a Persian king would invite honored guests to walk with him. So at this pleading, Jesus the King grants the penitent thief to walk in the garden of the courts of heaven. We thus see, in his crucifixion between two thieves, Jesus as King.

Preaching Possibilities

A. There are many approaches to this last Sunday in our liturgical church year. We could do a review of the life and teachings and ministry of Jesus as portrayed this year in Luke. It could be written like a letter to Theophilus ending with the facts that there will be another letter coming (Acts) which will further tell of the apostles' ministry and the marvelous beginnings of the early church.
B. Or it could review the main themes of Luke's Gospel.
  1. Jesus loved all sorts of people.
  2. His parables stress the poor and oppressed.
  3. Luke tells of Jesus' relationships to women and their role as disciples.
  4. The theme of joy is all through the book.
  5. Jesus brought hope and joy of salvation to a sinful world.
  6. Luke wrote especially with Gentiles in mind explaining Jewish customs and beginning by tracing Jesus' genealogy clear back to Adam.
C. The New Testament Reading enables us to do a sermon on "The Inheritance of the Kingdom" by defining two things: What do we inherit and what's this kingdom, anyway? Our inheritance is Jesus' atonement on the cross, his resurrection so we might also, and his spirit with us now. The kingdom is where and when the saved try, with the Spirit's help, to live out their lives of discipleship following what Jesus taught, such as the beatitudes and the rest of the Sermon on the Mount.
  I'll go with putting all three of the kingly readings together.

Possible Outline Of Sermon Moves

In the worship bulletin or in your preparation for worship time at the beginning of the service tell your people how this is the last Sunday in the liturgical church year and thus called "Christ the King."
A. Begin the sermon with naming where there are kings yet today. I know of Norway and Nepal and the Kingdom of Brunei. There must be others.
B. Move to explaining that king was a common office in Bible times and that it is a descriptive title which claims one who rules over us.
C. Move to the three readings for this Christ the King Sunday and what they tell us.
  1. Jeremiah prophesied the coming of an ideal king. This is a promise that when this king comes the people will live in peace and safety. This king (Jesus) will be like a faithful shepherd who will gather the scattered sheep into the secure fold again.
  2. Paul writes to the Colossians that God has transferred us into God's kingdom.
  3. Luke wrote to Theophilus the story of the crucifixion of the Christ. He told of a plaque over his head on the cross which read: "This is the King of the Jews." And one of the thieves crucified with him said, "Jesus, remember me when you come into your kingdom."
D. Move to explain what it means to have Jesus as our king and to live in his kingdom.
  1. Our loyalty is first to Jesus, our King, and to his kingdom.
  2. There are many blessings living in the kingdom. They are listed in the Beatitudes in Matthew 5.
  3. The world's priorities are not the same as God's kingdom priorities.
  4. We easily move from citizenship in the kingdom here to the kingdom of Heaven.

E. Move to a Possible Metaphor And Story from below.
F. Move to explaining Luther's view of the two kingdoms (of God and of the world) and how, when we pray, "Your kingdom come," we pray that here on earth it might be like in the kingdom of heaven.*
G. Ask the hearers to pray with you, "Your kingdom come; your will be done on earth as in heaven."

Prayer For The Day

King Jesus, we would be your subjects here at (*your church*) and we would like to make our congregation and ministry more like the heavenly kingdom into which we will transfer one day. Show us the way to faithful discipleship and teach us to live in your secure fold at peace with each other. In Christ the king's name. Amen.

Possible Metaphors And Stories

At the Augustana-Hochshule (Seminary) in Neuendettelsau, Germany, I was told that the facilities now used by that school were a large ammunition factory during the Third Reich, with workers living in what is now the dormitory and officers living in what are now the faculty homes. The Nazis placed it there, close to hospitals and homes for orphans and elderly, in hopes that Americans would not bomb it. Now there is an example of swords into plowshares!

I noticed at Chicago's O'Hare Field that the pilot has two neon lights, orange and red, to line up. When the pilot does that correctly the plane is parked in exactly the right place. I believe it's that way for discipleship. Get stewardship and evangelism in the right proportions in our lifestyles and we are at the right place.

The late Pastor David Ullery told me the story of two Salvation Army women who were at a convention and undressed to go swimming. "That's a strange navel you have," said one to the other. The other responded, "Okay, the next time you carry the flag."

We all carry a flag or flags for cause or causes in our lives. Often second best crowds out the best for Jesus' disciples.

In *The Robe*, Lloyd C. Douglas tells of a slave called Demetrius who on Palm Sunday pushed his way through the rejoicing crowd to get a look at Jesus. He was asked, "See him up close?" Demetrius nodded. "Crazy?" "No." "King?" "No," muttered Demetrius soberly, "not a king." "What is he then?" "I don't know," mumbled Demetrius, "but he is something more important than a king."

In A.D. 156 Polycarp, a Christian martyr, was put to death in Smyrna. The man who wrote the record of it for the centuries boiled it down in a few words: "Statius Quadrates, proconsul," he wrote, "Jesus Christ, king forever." I wonder if he guessed that in this century we should be reading that. Who was Statius Quadrates proconsul? Long since sunk into oblivion. But still above the world's turmoil, the affirmation resounds: "Jesus Christ, King forever!"

---

*See Matthew 13:44-50 for three parables of Jesus which describe "The Kingdom."

U.S. / Canadian Lectionary Comparison

The following index shows the correlation between the Sundays and special days of the church year as they are titled or labeled in the Revised Common Lectionary published by the Consultation On Common Texts and used in the United States (the reference used for this book) and the Sundays and special days of the church year as they are titled or labeled in the Revised Common Lectionary used in Canada.

Revised Common Lectionary	Canadian Revised Common Lectionary
Advent 1	Advent 1
Advent 2	Advent 2
Advent 3	Advent 3
Advent 4	Advent 4
Christmas Eve	Christmas Eve
Nativity Of The Lord / Christmas Day	The Nativity Of Our Lord
Christmas 1	Christmas 1
January 1 / Holy Name of Jesus	January 1 / The Name Of Jesus
Christmas 2	Christmas 2
Epiphany Of The Lord	The Epiphany Of Our Lord
Baptism Of The Lord / Epiphany 1	The Baptism Of Our Lord / Proper 1
Epiphany 2 / Ordinary Time 2	Epiphany 2 / Proper 2
Epiphany 3 / Ordinary Time 3	Epiphany 3 / Proper 3
Epiphany 4 / Ordinary Time 4	Epiphany 4 / Proper 4
Epiphany 5 / Ordinary Time 5	Epiphany 5 / Proper 5
Epiphany 6 / Ordinary Time 6	Epiphany 6 / Proper 6
Epiphany 7 / Ordinary Time 7	Epiphany 7 / Proper 7
Epiphany 8 / Ordinary Time 8	Epiphany 8 / Proper 8
Transfiguration Of The Lord / Last Sunday After Epiphany	The Transfiguration Of Our Lord / Last Sunday After Epiphany
Ash Wednesday	Ash Wednesday
Lent 1	Lent 1
Lent 2	Lent 2
Lent 3	Lent 3
Lent 4	Lent 4
Lent 5	Lent 5
Passion / Palm Sunday (Lent 6)	Passion / Palm Sunday
Holy / Maundy Thursday	Holy / Maundy Thursday
Good Friday	Good Friday
Resurrection Of The Lord / Easter	The Resurrection Of Our Lord
Easter 2	Easter 2
Easter 3	Easter 3
Easter 4	Easter 4
Easter 5	Easter 5
Easter 6	Easter 6
Ascension Of The Lord	The Ascension Of Our Lord
Easter 7	Easter 7
Day Of Pentecost	The Day Of Pentecost
Trinity Sunday	The Holy Trinity
Proper 4 / Pentecost 2 / O T 9*	Proper 9
Proper 5 / Pent 3 / O T 10	Proper 10
Proper 6 / Pent 4 / O T 11	Proper 11
Proper 7 / Pent 5 / O T 12	Proper 12
Proper 8 / Pent 6 / O T 13	Proper 13
Proper 9 / Pent 7 / O T 14	Proper 14

Proper 10 / Pent 8 / O T 15   Proper 15
Proper 11 / Pent 9 / O T 16   Proper 16
Proper 12 / Pent 10 / O T 17   Proper 17
Proper 13 / Pent 11 / O T 18   Proper 18
Proper 14 / Pent 12 / O T 19   Proper 19
Proper 15 / Pent 13 / O T 20   Proper 20
Proper 16 / Pent 14 / O T 21   Proper 21
Proper 17 / Pent 15 / O T 22   Proper 22
Proper 18 / Pent 16 / O T 23   Proper 23
Proper 19 / Pent 17 / O T 24   Proper 24
Proper 20 / Pent 18 / O T 25   Proper 25
Proper 21 / Pent 19 / O T 26   Proper 26
Proper 22 / Pent 20 / O T 27   Proper 27
Proper 23 / Pent 21 / O T 28   Proper 28
Proper 24 / Pent 22 / O T 29   Proper 29
Proper 25 / Pent 23 / O T 30   Proper 30
Proper 26 / Pent 24 / O T 31   Proper 31
Proper 27 / Pent 25 / O T 32   Proper 32
Proper 28 / Pent 26 / O T 33   Proper 33
Christ The King (Proper 29 / O T 34) Proper 34 / Christ The King/
                                         Reign Of Christ

Reformation Day (October 31)   Reformation Day (October 31)
All Saints' Day (November 1 or   All Saints' Day (November 1)
   1st Sunday in November)
Thanksgiving Day   Thanksgiving Day
   (4th Thursday of November)   (2nd Monday of October)

*O T = Ordinary Time